228

Keith Foskett was born in Dorking, Surrey. He has dabbled in various professions including salesman, chef, dustman, financial adviser and decorator.

Once described as an anomaly (it was apparently a compliment), he is partial to a decent bottle of Rioja, a plate of Paella and woolen underwear. He now divides his time between walking, running and the odd cycle ride.

This is his first book.

187 223
219 226

The Journey in Between

A 1,000 mile walk on El Camino de Santiago

Keith Foskett

www.keithfoskett.com

The Journey in Between

By Keith Fosket

(ISBN: 978 - 1480176393)

www.keithfoskett.com

Front cover photo by Keith Foskett

Rear cover photo by Terry Abraham
www.terrybnd.blogspot.co.uk

With love:

To Mum, who never doubted any of my crazy adventures and always shared in my excitement.

To Dad, for passing on the Foskett walking gene.

To Bam Bam and Nan, I know you are both always with me.

Other books by Keith Foskett

The Last Englishman

(ISBN: 978 - 1480169111)

A 2,650 mile hiking adventure on the Pacific Crest Trail

Coming in 2013

Balancing on Blue

(ISBN: 978 - 1480176416)

A 2,178 mile hike on The Appalachian Trail

Acknowledgements

In my preparation for El Camino and during the actual walk I made new friends, and they, along with existing friends, all helped me in various ways. Some steered me gently in a new direction, others offered help and advice. Some people come into your life for a fleeting moment, some you know for a few months or years and some are with you for life. The following are in no particular order but they all deserve a mention for assisting me in the walk, helping me write this book or for just being someone I value.

Thanks therefore to:

Mum for never doubting anything I have done or aspired to do, no matter how crazy it was at the time, and for always encouraging me to do what I wanted, and to realise my dreams.

Dad for "eventually coming round" after a bit of persuasion, for his advice and concern and for passing on the hereditary walking gene in the first place.

My sister Tracy and nephews Thomas and Liam, who spurred me on with the well-worn question, "How's the book coming on?"

Cherry, for your belief in us.

Gabriella for providing me with a paradise where I could write and her hours spent in front of my laptop digesting the drafts. "You only have to ask, and the universe will provide."

Ziena for her help, even if it meant that I couldn't quote her.

Trish, I have so much to thank you for, but that would be a book in itself.

Ingrid Cranfield for editing the text.

Ryn and Christina, who turned a simple request for assistance into a personal mission.

Mano for the translations.

Lesley, I hope you are happy where you are.

Spencer Vignes from The Observer.

Obs the Blobs for his work on the photos and manuscript.

Nikki Johnson for her word processing skills.

All my friends who proofread some of the work and gave me their views: Sparkers, Lotty Wotty, Agapi, Baz, Maggie Moo, Moneypenny, Mumfa, Amy Lou and Grovesy.

All the pilgrims I met and became friends with along the Camino: the French Canadians (Gérard, Chantal and the names I forget); Jeannie, Bernard, Gare, Reginald, Tania, Pascal, Antonio, Sean, Roberta, Pierre, John, Yetty, Warren and Kylie.

And God forbid I have missed anyone, but if I have, thanks anyway: you surely know who you are.

Introduction

Clarification

I could blame it on my parents but that wouldn't be telling the whole truth. My Dad is mainly responsible for my walking passion. My Mum was never a huge walker but did pass on some interest. My Granddad on my mother's side was responsible for the wanderlust. He was more of a cyclist but I have heard crazy stories of him cycling from Sussex to Derbyshire just for the hell of it.

So I figure Dad's walking gene is 70% to blame, the rest from Granddad and my mother, in that order. I can imagine those genes sitting down over a coffee somewhere in my frontal lobe discussing future walking plans and prospects, when was the best time to release their full potential, where to go, for how long, etc.

I have fond memories from my early teens of family holidays which entailed driving to Wales or Dartmoor in a sky blue Triumph Herald, with my sister or, when she got bored of such things, a best mate. I was more into skateboards, girls and Abba at the time, but Dad would cunningly con us into walking somewhere a couple of hours away because there was a great ice-cream place half-way or Mum would promise to give the new skateboard thing some serious consideration. So, most of the time I found myself walking and running about with my mate over hillocks, through streams, getting filthy and having a great time, oblivious to the fact that we were only, really, walking.

At around fourteen I discovered tents, not so much because it meant spending a night in the woods but because it meant a night away from home, a grown-up thing to do. I was, however, getting hooked on real walking, as opposed to an occasional ramble with the folks. When Dad suggested I try the South Downs Way with a friend, which at around 160 kilometres isn't too easy a prospect, I jumped at the chance for my first real adventure. It was close to home, so if there were any problems there would be a bus or a train somewhere, some of the landscape and route were familiar, and the weather forecast promised a great outlook.

I roped in Andrew Boyd after dismissing some poor objections, such as missing his favourite TV programme and being away from his girlfriend for that length of time (even though I knew she was seeing someone else). I thought his lack of actual interest in walking, which was the main problem, might be rekindled by the great outdoors. Besides, all my other mates were not interested, on holiday or listening to Spandau Ballet.

Dad dropped us off around South Harting one evening. Our tent was so flimsy, it would have fallen down in mild breeze. Our sleeping bags took up most of our packs, leaving just about enough room in mine for Mum's saucepan, a Camping Gas stove, several cans of baked beans, numerous Mars bars, a couple of T-shirts and a rain jacket. As long as it didn't rain or get windy, we'd be fine.

Four days in, on Kithurst Hill above Storrington, it did both. We had pitched right on top of the Downs and the expedition was going well up to that point. I noticed some alarmingly black clouds and a slight breeze just before I zipped up the tent, but had full faith in our little shelter. I woke up about an hour later with Andrew screaming and a rain-lashed canvas slapping me in the face. Every few seconds lightning lit up the scene and all I could see was my mate wrapped around the support pole down one end of the tent, with petrified eyes, looking like a cat up a lamppost with a dog underneath.

"Hold your tent pole!" he screamed. "Hang on or the whole tent's gonna go!"

Thunder crashed all around us for two hours as we battled

to keep the tent upright, terrified that one of the poles would be hit by lightning. It felt as if we were in the centre of the storm itself. Every so often, when the lightning illuminated everything, I expected to look down the other side of the tent and see a pile of charcoal briquettes where Andrew had been struck. Then the water started to trickle in. After thirty minutes we were paddling around in two centimetres of it, very cold, scared shitless and with arms hurting so much from holding the poles we couldn't actually feel them.

By the time the storm had finished with us it was daylight. We struggled out of the tent, sopping wet, tired and thankful to be alive. We caught the train back home, both of us silent as we gave camping out some serious reconsideration.

I completed the South Downs Way the following summer with another mate. It never even threatened to rain on us once and I remember thinking that the elements owed me one.

In my twenties, cycling took over as my main activity. I travelled to various countries and indulged in the occasional hike here and there, just to remind the leg muscles that I might call on them again. I took part in the Three Peaks Challenge four times (climbing up the three highest mountains in England, Scotland and Wales in under 24 hours) and developed a deep admiration and fondness for the mountainous areas of this country. I made regular trips to Wales, the Lake District and Scotland. I dabbled in mountaineering but became frustrated at the mechanics of it. The need to wear harnesses, use ropes, tie knots and other distractions frustrated me. It took away the simplicity of putting one foot in front of the other, so, whenever I went up a mountain, which I loved, I chose the route that could simply be walked.

The uncomplicated act of walking is one of the appeals. I have never been one to require an in-depth understanding of something to appreciate it. If it works, then I don't question it - the simpler the better. Walking is the most natural and oldest form of travel. It is designed to get us from one point to another with the minimum of fuss and at a pace that allows us to notice things that we would normally miss.

We live in a world where we seem to want to make everything quicker in order to free up more time, which in turn we fill up with other stuff. When it all gets too meaningless for me, I feel the need to escape and walk. To be part of the outdoors, with all your belongings strapped to your back, to be able to camp wherever takes your fancy and to have no decisions to make other than where and when to sleep and eat clarifies, simplifies and puts the world in perspective.

Late one summer, I decided my world was in sore need of a little clarification . . .

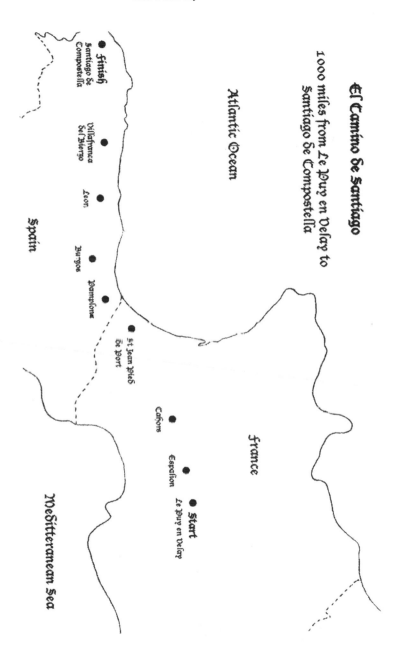

Chapter One

Getting to the Start Line

People lose it at airports. Excitement gets the better of them, frustration makes them pick arguments with someone they have never met and say things they would not normally say. Throw in some rage, fear, sadness and it's a crazy mixture. People cry, laugh, get upset and you can observe it all from a suitable vantage point. Emotion spotting is the new Train Spotting. Order yourself a cappuccino, grab a seat and take it all in.

I sugared my coffee and considered adding more, but I was on a health phase. The sort of health phase where you try, but never really do anything of any importance. Like having one less sugar, but then having another coffee. Or changing your brand of cigarettes and fooling yourself into thinking the new ones are better for you.

I took a sip, let the frothed milk sit on my tongue so I could just taste the chocolate top and glanced around the Lyon airport terminal. A young woman was trying to settle two children who were throwing a tantrum. Her expression was one of near boiling point and complete frustration. The children were stamping their feet up and down and raising hell outside the Duty Free. I observed their faces, a mixture of mischievous contentment when they thought they had got away with something and then exasperation when they discovered they hadn't. A man bearing a striking resemblance to Jack Nicholson was trying to cut his croissant in half but appeared to be having trouble because he was still wearing sunglasses. I always struggle to understand this practice of wearing shades inside. It makes no sense. A young couple were kissing and groping with a sense of urgency but also tenderness as his hand brushed away a stray curl of hair from her cheek. I was trying to decide if they were soon to be parted or had just been reunited.

People from all walks of life milled around, business people clasping laptops under their arms, budget travellers leaning precariously forward, almost dragging hands on the floor like a Neanderthal to counteract the load of a rucksack. Passengers running to catch flights, couples gesticulating over who forgot the tickets. Drivers and chauffeurs were waiting at arrivals holding up cards with clients' names on them. I could tell the companies that were efficient and well organised, as the names had been printed neatly, with the company logo just underneath. Even the drivers were well turned out, with name badges and pressed clothing, their shoes reflecting the airport lighting. Then there were the cab drivers. Fags dangling from their mouths, hair greased back, stubble casting a grey shadow, and shirts unbuttoned as far as they dared. They had pulled a piece of box out of the bin and scribbled something indistinguishable on it. I had always harboured a strange desire to be one of those drivers just so I could hold up a board with someone's name on it. As the client saw me and walked over with a smile of recognition, I would promptly turn it over so they could see the back which read 'Only joking'.

I had arrived from London that morning with my possessions stuffed into a bright yellow backpack, sweating the spirit of adventure, and slightly the worse for wear after a very dubious ham and salad roll courtesy of the airline. My stomach sounded like a cement mixer churning thick porridge. As I clutched my stomach with one hand and puffed out my cheeks, I must have looked like a walking advert for indigestion tablets.

I was in the middle of an eight-year period of 'sporadic travelling'. This entailed working, usually as a temp, doing whatever was available from filing to emptying dustbins. I would scrimp and save for a few months and when I had collected an amount of money that was nowhere near enough for the next trip, I would head off again. A few months later I would return to England and start the whole process over again. It was unpredictable but that was the attraction. I had spent most of the summer working at a yoga centre in Greece. Having finished earlier than expected and still with a relatively moderate bank balance, I realised I still had some of the summer left to plan a trip. So I found myself back at my parents' house, holed up in my old eight-foot-square bedroom. It was the middle of August and I wondered what I was going to do for the rest of the season. I didn't really need to work, which was a blessing because that's a serious waste of good weather. I had thought about flying to America to do a long-distance hike, but it was too late in the season and I would have encountered snow, making the going difficult. Options on the other side of the equator such as Australia and Latin America were impractical because of the cost of flights.

Then I remembered a conversation from a couple of years earlier. A traveller I had met briefly in a Greek hostel was telling me about a walk in Spain. I recalled sitting on a café chair, riveted, while he told me of a walk he wanted to do. His description and hand signals were animated. There was genuine excitement in his voice and a look of almost enlightenment on his face. I covered my eyes with my hands and propped elbows on the desk as I tried to recall the name of the walk. It wouldn't come. It was somewhere in France and Spain so, grimacing, I gave a search engine the few clues I had. As I flicked down the list of options, familiar words appeared and it was then that I then recalled the traveller saying them. 'The Camino de Santiago'. It all started to flood back.

As I gleaned what information I could, it began to emerge as the perfect walk which ticked all the right boxes. It was the right distance I was looking for, about 1600 kilometres. This translated to about three months' hiking. With luck the weather would hold right up to October and November. The flight was inexpensive, and the Spanish make damn fine red wine. Not to mention those Latin women.

Over the next couple of days I sat by the pc surrounded by empty cups with black treacle on the bottom where coffee had once been. Crumbs dotted used plates and pieces of A4 littered the room with scribbles and notes. I left the room only to bond with my cat and explain why I was leaving him again after having just got back.

Eventually, succumbing to tired eyes and an aching spine, I leaned back in the chair with my hands clasped behind my back and smiled. The walk was on. I had no maps, just a guidebook from the local shop with what seemed like reasonable directions. Anyway, it had a really nice picture of a bridge on the cover.

The ancient path I had chosen to walk came under many guises. As well as the Camino de Santiago, it was also referred to as El Camino, the Way of St James, the Way of St Jacques or the Pilgrims Way. To confuse the issue further, pilgrims, as walkers on the route are fondly known, could choose from numerous starting points. In fact, a true pilgrimage by definition starts at one's home. From the south coast of England to the north-west coast of Spain would have been a great walk, but I had limited time before the first snows fell over the Spanish mountains. Most pilgrims start their trek from Saint Jean Pied de Port in France. This small town nestles at the foot of the tail end of the Pyrenees, about a day's walk from the Spanish border and about 750 kilometres from the finish at Santiago de Compostela in north-west Spain. It is easy to get there, has many facilities, and thousands of potential pilgrims start there each year. Novices choose this as their starting point because they feel there is safety in numbers.

Other starting points include Paris, Vézelay, Arles and Le Puy in France, or Seville in Spain. But don't let that fool you. Walkers can start from wherever they choose. There is no rulebook of the Camino saying you must begin at any one particular point. Indeed, to qualify for the coveted Certificate of Completion at the end of the walk in Santiago cathedral, you need actually walk only a minimum of 100 kilometres, a little more if you choose to cycle or ride a horse.

I had, literally, as much time as I wanted. However, walking in cold weather has never been my idea of fun. So, I had blessed myself with three months to complete my mission and this pretty much determined my starting point for me. Le Puy en Velay, the guidebook assured me, was two and a half months' walking to Santiago de Compostela. This would get me to my destination before winter gripped northern Spain, and give me a couple of weeks to boot as a buffer zone. I was sorted.

El Camino is old, very old. If it were a person, they would have had their bus pass for twenty years. If it were a movie, you would be watching through a lens and winding a handle at the side. The first documented journey along the route was made somewhere around AD1145 by a certain Amery Picaud, a French cleric, and pilgrims had already been walking the route for many years before that, well over a thousand, in fact.

A religious pilgrimage is the primary reason for doing the walk. I'm not religious, but a brief acquaintance with the story of the walk is enough to whet anyone's appetite.

The legend began after the death of Christ. One of his disciples, St James, travelled to Spain to try to spread the gospel, with little success. He returned to Jerusalem, where Herod obviously took a dislike to him and had him beheaded some time around AD44, making him a martyr. Disciples took his body and brought him back to Spain, where they buried him in a tomb on an empty hillside.

For the next several centuries, no one held any knowledge of the burial site, until a hermit named Pelagius received a vision of the location of the grave, guided by a star. I guess St James figured if it worked for Jesus, he might as well have a go. The remains were exhumed and identified as those of the saint. A church was built on the site, and grew to become the present-day Santiago de Compostela, although the grand cathedral now towering there was built much later.

As news spread of the find, the location began to fulfil all the criteria of a potential pilgrim site. It was difficult to reach, over rough terrain, requiring the crossing of rivers and mountains. The trail was riddled with such dangers as bandits and wolves. The prevalence of disease in the area, coupled with the fact that Spain was at war with the Moors, compounded the difficulties and meant a true pilgrim would have to endure suffering to reach his goal. Regardless of what the history books tell you, my understanding of a pilgrimage is a very long, difficult journey where there's a reasonable chance you'll get killed.

Towns and villages began to grow along the route. Accommodation, food establishments, hospitals and all manner of amenities appeared to service the pilgrims, and the route became more famous as each year passed. It follows, therefore, that the Camino is rich in history, culture, sights, energy and an unusually high number of churches. When pilgrims first started walking to Santiago, it was said that the churches were their map and guide. The route stretches east to west. They could tell which way was west by the sun and other simple navigation aids, so their method was to look in a westerly direction for a church spire. A church spire would mean a village or town, and they would be pretty sure that was the direction they had to head in.

Pilgrims in the past walked in simple sandals, one long item of clothing like a cloak, and perhaps a hat as shade from the fierce sun bearing down on them. A staff would help their balance and provide friendship, aiding their climbs up as they leaned on it and supporting them on the steep descents. Perhaps tied to this would be a small bag containing food or water. Provisions were procured on the trail by buying, trading or begging. And of course dangling around their neck would be a scallop shell, the emblem of the Camino to this day.

Supposedly, when the boat carrying St James originally landed on the Spanish coast, a man was riding on horseback along the beach. The horse was startled by the boat and plunged into the sea, from where both rider and horse eventually emerged covered in the shells. Even to this day, many of the beaches in the area of Galicia are strewn with scallop shells, particularly the curved white sands at Finisterre. And it is a sure way to spot a pilgrim from a day tripper when you see the shell stitched on to their pack or swaying from their staff or neck. Although Santiago is the true finishing post, many then walk the extra five or so days to Finisterre on the Atlantic coast and I had promised myself to do the same.

So, why walk 1600 kilometres? Or even 100? Why do some pilgrims come from as far away as Canada and Australia? Why strap your life on your back to walk for three months? There are several reasons.

The obvious first choice is religion. It is the same principle for Christians, Catholics, Jews, Hindus and all faiths, to make a pilgrimage to a place of great importance in their faith. After all, St James was a disciple of Christ. The Camino ranks as high in importance as Jerusalem and Rome. Individuals make their way to the cathedral at Santiago to kiss the statue of St James, and feel safe in the knowledge that they have 'suffered' to make the trip.

Spirituality also plays a big role. Various books have been written on the Camino, fuelling this aspect. Many pilgrims make the challenge in the hope of maybe receiving enlightenment or enjoying some spiritual experience. It is true the Camino is full of natural energy lines, known as ley lines, following its course from east to west. These lines date back thousands of years and, although we know they exist, we have not been able to explain their importance or even how they work. When in proximity to one, especially for extended periods, people have noticed an increased 'awareness' of their surroundings and a feeling of being happier, closer to feeling 'complete'. It is true that some experience events of the kind they were hoping for and I think it is fair to say everybody emerges as a changed person. I didn't experience anything of cosmic proportions, although I encountered many nights with two, three or maybe four vivid dreams, one of which was a premonition of events happening the following day. Most people I met looked happy and content; you could argue that anybody would if they had a couple of months to partake in something they love. This is true, but it was certainly more than satisfaction. I was certainly aware of an energy, an energy that made me feel free, with little to worry about, and had a regular trick of putting a smile on my face.

In the Middle Ages people were sent to walk the Camino as a punishment for a crime and a chance to repent when they arrived in Santiago. Some pilgrims journeyed as a way of gaining merit and improving their standing in society, earning respect. Some even completed the walk for others. The wealthy of the day would pay lesser mortals to complete the pilgrimage for them. I hoped that method was still being used, as my funds were a little limited. If I could just find someone to pay me for doing it, I'd be laughing.

Me? As I said, I'm not religious. I would admit that I was hoping to receive some sort of spiritual encounter, maybe an insight into the meaning of life. I certainly wasn't undertaking it as a punishment (although at times it seemed like one). I wasn't even after any merit, and I never did find someone to pay me. I just simply fancied a long walk.

I ambled over to the Airport Tourist Information Office, a place I have never held in great esteem. I concede they are a mine of information and extremely useful. However, first, they label me as a tourist, which I hate. Even though most of the clientele, myself included, are indeed of this breed, to me it's a dirty word. It reeks of someone looking lost and confused, with a Kodak dangling around their midriff, white socks and sandals, scratching insect bites and with the unnatural glow of a lychee fruit. Even though I suppose I was a tourist, I cower from seeing or even hearing the "T" word.

Secondly, you take your chances with the character found on the other side of the counter. The ones that appear the most intelligent are usually the most ignorant. Light travels faster than sound. This is why some people appear bright until they actually speak. They are either extremely helpful, with a genuine smile, or they would rather be somewhere else. Unfortunately, as usual, I got stuck with the latter. I was secretly wishing her companion would become available first, as she seemed a little more natural and perhaps helpful, but there wasn't a lot separating the two of them.

I dispensed with trying a little French as that would have only confused the issue.

"Hi, can you please tell me how I get to Le Puy?" I enquired. I had pronounced Le Puy the way I thought it should be, as 'Le Poo'. This simple, innocent error cost me valuable minutes.

"Le Poo?" she replied, looking very confused.

I thought eye contact would improve the situation, so I removed my sunglasses.

"Yes, Le Poo. I need to get to Le Poo. Can you tell me the best way to get there please?"

"Ah, you mean Le Pwee!" Her smile and expression let slip that she found my ignorance a little amusing.

"Ok," I said, "Le Pwee. How do I get there?"

"The quickest way is the bus to Lyon train station, and then the train via St Etienne. You can get a ticket for the bus just behind you at the desk. There should be one every 15 minutes. Enjoy your time in France".

The securing of the bus ticket was, thankfully, trouble-free. As I stepped outside the air terminal, the mid afternoon August sun rushed over my face like the breeze on opening the window of an air-conditioned car in mid-summer Miami. I looked up and squinted as numerous postcard-perfect clouds streamed overhead. Lyon was visible a few miles to my left as the occasional church spire broke through the skyline. Cars stopped, people alighted. It made me feel somehow that I was on the verge of escaping all the commotion of modern life, as though my journey was starting and my pace was slowing down. Like driving for an hour on a motorway, then turning off down a country lane. For the first time since deciding two weeks before that I was going to walk El Camino, I felt a little uneasy about the task. My knees wobbled a bit, I sighed and bowed my head. Not out of sadness, you understand. I was looking forward to the whole experience with relish. The little pause for thought was just to try and comprehend actually walking 1600 kilometres. I could board another plane and fly to Santiago and back all in that same afternoon. It was possible to visit the Avis desk, sort out a nice little sports coupé and spend a couple of weeks doing the trip in air-conditioned luxury. But no, it was the actual walk that was the challenge. That was the reason I was here, and if it hadn't been the Camino, it would have been somewhere else.

The coach stopped at the kerbside and hissed as the brakes were released. I dodged through passengers retrieving luggage and threw my pack into the hold and then waited patiently as the amorous couple from the airport tried to negotiate the steps on to the bus without letting go of each other. They took their places; he had the aisle seat while she sat next to the window. As he became more affectionate, kissing her harder and clutching her waist, he pushed her up against the window. Like a cartoon character that hits a wall high up, and then slowly starts to slide down to earth, she began to slide up. I saw a guy walk past outside the coach grin as he observed two squashed buttocks stuck to the pane. I was about to advise amorous guy that he should take a rest so I could have a go when the bus kicked into life.

We sped along the motorway for thirty minutes, making occasional stops. Nothing outside looked like a railway station but I kept asking the driver just in case.

"Station"? I asked, raising my eyebrows.

"No," and he would make some sort of gesture to his watch suggesting more time.

When we did arrive he turned around and smiled, revealing an alarmingly big gap in his teeth, and gave the thumbs up. I disembarked and had to quickly bang on his door as he began to pull away again so I could get my bag back. The station was huge; it seemed bigger than the airport. It was all I could do to keep my eyes ahead of me as I entered this massive hall: I just wanted to look up as though I had just entered a church. People were milling about everywhere, spilling out of little cafés, tapping their toes with folded arms as they waited in line for a sandwich and shuffling forward inch by inch to a roped-off area that was the horror of the ticket line. Think of banks on a Saturday morning, multiply by 20, and you have some inkling of the picture. The roped area wound back and forth like a concertina. It reminded me of Philadelphia airport a few years previously. The queue for passport control was so long, they had kindly built a room for the sole purpose of dealing with the influx of visitors. There was enough rope winding back and forth in that place to kit out the rigging on a small ship. At Lyon they had also thoughtfully installed the system with the little black, electronic sign that flashes up a number in red and a directional arrow when a desk becomes available. The Post Office back home loves those toys. When I get to the end of the line, there always seems to be two counters with staff behind them doing absolutely nothing. They just look into space, and when they see me looking at them with an "Any chance you can push your button?" look on my face, they bury themselves in a pile of tax discs. At least 50 people appeared to be contemplating suicide as they stared into space waiting for a counter. The line was painfully long, and I wasn't looking forward to communicating my needs in French. There was a small tourist office with a cute French girl sitting behind it. It was a real dilemma, a long queue or the "T" counter. I went for the counter and it proved the right choice. Not only did she speak word-perfect English and give me the platform number, time of departure and arrival, but she also smiled and offered to supply me with the ticket. "Result!" I thought as I walked past the other queue with a smirk on my gob. I was starting to like France.

The train carriage was like a blast from the seventies, and actually, it probably was. Brown plastic fabric covered the seats, trying to imitate leather. The lino on the floor had been reduced to a strip of wood in the middle where it had played witness to thousands, probably millions of commuters, and looked so worn in places that I feared I may actually fall through to the line whizzing by underneath. To my surprise, people were smoking. Not that this bothered me, it was just a pleasant change to be given the choice of a smoking compartment when nowadays signs adorn most establishments telling you that you can't. Unlike the English rail system, this one actually worked. The train left when it was supposed to. There was no "The train at platform 4 has been delayed. We apologise for any inconvenience caused." It wasn't exactly Concorde, but it worked.

I arrived at St Etienne to change trains, a place name somehow evoking romantic ideals. There were a couple of hours before my connection so I did a short scout of the area outside the station. I sat down in the park and wondered where the population had vanished to. The place was deserted. A few people walked their dogs, but that was it. The shops were shut, traffic was non-existent, even the birds were on a tea break. Drizzle started to fall so I sat under an oak tree and played with my Dictaphone. A shop door rattled across the road as the owner unlocked it. Small bells tinkled as she jammed it open and placed advertising clapboards in the street, which reflected perfectly in the puddles. I wandered over, paid for a couple of EEC regulation-shaped bananas and walked back to the tree. I wasn't hungry, just needed something to break up the monotony of a damp, lifeless afternoon in the big town. An overcast blur streamed past overhead. Trees swayed in the wind, and a fine spray smoked across the park. The black path was broken up with mirrors of water as I made my way back to the train station for my connection to Le Puy, reminding myself that some day I would return to St Etienne to see if anyone actually lived there.

The remaining section of the journey was uneventful save brief glimpses through the trees of a landscape dipping and curving, a result of volcanic activity thousands of years before. Valleys, gorges, rivers and hills littered the area and the greenery seemed more intense and vivid. Le Puy straddled this unusual scenery as it rippled up and down. Rocky peaks dominated the town, rising up like stalagmites, some topped with statues or buildings. They were long, tall, slender, and dwarfed everything else. One was topped with the Chapel of Saint Michel d'Aiguilhe, and another with a statue of Notre-Dame de France. It was like surveying a giant sand-coloured cardiograph.

I neglected to bring a guidebook to France, apart from my one on the Camino, reasoning that I needed to save weight. So, standing outside the entrance to Le Puy station, I wondered where to stay. Under normal circumstances, I would have checked the guide, decided whether hostel or campsite would do the trick for the night and make my way there. Without the guide, I had to find out for myself. A wave of jealousy washed over me as I watched loved ones being collected, kids being ushered to waiting cars and more couples kissing and groping each other. It's one of the few aspects of travel that doesn't appeal, finding a place to spend the night. First it's a case of deciding which offering would be most suitable based on criteria such as location, distance, price, and whether they let females in the male dorms. Then it's a case of finding them.

A sign on a building opposite promising 'Cheap Hotel' tempted me. However, budget mode kicked me firmly in the arse, and I began studying the town map decorated in cigarette burns, which had melted the plastic covering, rendering 'Campsite Bouthezard' as something indistinguishable. Nevertheless, I calculated a quick stroll of about 40 minutes and I would be checking in. Sure enough, I found the place beautifully nestled among poplar trees, resting up between two rivers. Thirty French francs secured me a shady spot underneath one of the trees, among a smattering of other tents and caravans.

I had expected more walkers, as Le Puy was one of the main start points for the Camino. There was a handful scattered around, but not many. The rest of the campers were a random mix of nationalities, with random modes of transport. German cycle tourists had cordoned off one section of the best grass and set about making it their own. A precise washing line doubled as a boundary fence, as the male positioned each piece of laundry with fanatical attention to prevailing wind direction and the sun's position. His girlfriend was sorting equipment on the ground with such precision that I thought any minute she would inform him that they were missing a rubber band. An Austrian couple were near to me, and seemed to be in more of a holiday mode. Far from being organised, they were just slouching in two deck chairs and sinking Kronenbourgs like they were going out of fashion. The obligatory English couple plus two kids were doing the "family holiday" thing. Mum was peeling the spuds while Dad was trying to figure out why the barbecue was too hot. As he lifted up and peered with upturned nose at the hard, black slab that was once a hamburger, I think he had pretty much decided that they were dining out tomorrow.

French campsites have always amazed me. The French love and place great value on their camping expeditions and traditions. The grass is always plentiful, soft and springy. There is always a toilet and wash block, and while they do vary in cleanliness, they are generally well presented and have everything a camper should require. I had last camped in France as a teenager on a cycle trip, and remember being grateful for the camping facilities then. After all, in those days, £18 a week wages from working in a supermarket didn't get a traveller very far. We English could learn a few lessons from our French counterparts about communal campgrounds. Back home, I would by this stage have no doubt endured a delayed train journey, and found myself in a field in the middle of nowhere, that was pretending to be a campsite, full of cow shit, boasting as many amenities as, well, your average field.

After washing off the rigours of a day's international travel in the shower, I spent the evening just lying on the grass by my tent taking it all in. I cooked some pasta and then lay on my back, drinking fresh coffee, courtesy of my new camping percolator, watching my cigarette smoke curl up and out of sight. I thought about the little planning that had got me here, my complete lack of training and my limited financial supplies. Odds were a little stacked in the Camino's favour but I had one ally, and a powerful one at that, determination to succeed.

I gazed up at the leaves on the poplars, which appeared to sigh as they lifted up gracefully, then relaxed as the passing breeze caught them unawares, like that last, deep, breath we take before falling asleep. The sun had slid under the horizon for another day, leaving only a colourful memory of golden hues streaking above me. A rainbow was arching gracefully over the Chapel of Saint Michel D'Aiguilhe, teetering on a fulcrum at the hill's apex, providing a colourful and stark contrast to a deep black, merciless cloud mass bubbling behind. The whole vision was still curing, still maturing, and improving by the second. I took it as an omen that the Camino was sure to be beautiful, but there would be difficulties under the façade. I zipped up my sleeping bag, listened to a few raindrops explode on the canvas inches from my head and dozed off with that secure feeling of being safe and warm whilst the elements stirred around me.

The Camino was always going to be an unknown and invisible journey in that I did not know what would be around the next corner. I had few expectations of what it would hold. Most of them were to be surpassed. All of them were met with conviction. I did not know whom I would meet, what I would see, smell, hear or taste. It would be a pathway hiding its secrets and surprises, a journey along the line of fate. It had a beginning and it had an end, but those were the only aspects of its character that were certain. Everything else was ensconced between these points waiting to be experienced. The unpredictability was dangerously exciting.

Tomorrow I would start walking sixteen hundred kilometres to Santiago de Compostela.

Chapter Two

Breaking Myself in

I awoke the next morning with an enthusiasm eager to be released. The little rain during the night had dispersed, to be replaced with perfect walking weather, as if it knew my journey was beginning. White clouds gently socialised with a small breeze, resisting the urge to be moved on. The sun was already gliding along its east–west journey, sending shafts of light through the clouds, which cast shadows on the grass like moving apparitions. A squirrel jerked up and down a nearby oak tree, flocks of birds swooped and rose almost as though they were riding waves. Ducks flapped in desperation, trying to take off, while silver water droplets tumbled off their ochre feathers.

I felt wide awake but my eyes were having difficulty opening, as they often do at the start of the day. I entered the camp site bar searching for a caffeine fix. It was empty except for a woman resting on her side of the counter reading a newspaper. I offered a feeble "Good morning". She paused on the football results and looked up just in time to catch me peering down at her cleavage. Smiling, she adjusted her left breast, took one look at the narrow slits where my eyeballs had once resided and started fiddling with the dials on the coffee machine. It hissed and spluttered and eventually she handed me a very strong espresso accompanied by a stale croissant.

My memories of previous visits to France were all returning to me as I walked through Le Puy. Battered old

Citroëns belched out black clouds as they bumped down uneven streets. Old men sat outside rustic cafés, sipping their coffees and brandies, a Gitane stuck to their bottom lip wafting up smoke the same colour as their ageing hair. They conversed with their mates while throwing elaborate gestures with arms and hands to emphasise certain points, all interspersed with eruptions of laughter. I stopped to savour the tormenting aroma of fresh baked bread from one of numerous bakeries. Shop shutters clattered noisily as they were pulled up. A couple were engaged in an animated, heated exchange: in most countries this would draw disapproving looks, but in France it was part of everyday life. Everyone seemed relaxed and in no hurry. Assistants in shops laughed with customers; even the estate agents seemed genuinely busy.

Before I could truly get going, I had to obtain a Pilgrim's passport, or *créanciale*, for the Camino from the Cathedral. The *créanciale* is a piece of card about the size of a usual passport, except it is folded like a concertina and when opened out stretches from hand to shoulder. Your basic details are written on (name, address, etc.) and the rest of the card basically consists of about eighty printed, matchbox-sized squares. Each one of these sections is designed to be stamped at certain establishments along the route with their own particular design. The *gîtes* (in France these are cheap, hostel-like accommodations) and their cousins the refuges in Spain were the main source for these stamps, along with some restaurants, bars, museums and even shops. The primary purpose of all this is to provide proof to the Cathedral authorities in Santiago de Compostela that the owner has actually completed the route he or she claims to have walked and is thereby eligible for the coveted "Certificate of Completion". The *créanciale* is not a "good idea"; it is considered a necessity. It also rewards you with cheaper accommodation than your average tourist gets and discounted meals at establishments displaying the "Pilgrims' Menu", although at times that was not necessarily a bonus. All the walkers I met had one. You just don't walk El

Camino without it.

Classic architecture stared back at me, proud, intense, almost arrogantly boasting its heritage. Streets and alleys split off randomly and aimlessly around me, as if I was standing in a hole in a broken pane of glass, the shatter lines radiating out. Attractive women meandered leisurely around me, finding solitude in shop windows displaying the new autumn fashions. There were a few pilgrims peering into their guidebooks and squinting anxiously at street names. Locals were picking at breakfast on wrought iron tables, which spilled on to polished cobbles. Tourists were strolling around, hands clasped behind their backs, bending over to get a closer look in souvenir shop windows. I felt somehow different, even famous. I wasn't part of those people on holiday for two weeks. I was on a different mission. I felt like crying out, "Look at me! I'm gonna walk from here to the Atlantic coast," but I doubted anyone would have listened.

I made my way to the Romanesque Cathedral of Notre Dame, where my research had assured me I could obtain the passport. The steep streets and steps up to the cathedral had me seriously questioning my sanity before I had even set foot on the actual Camino. My lungs were exploding from three weeks of inactivity. I felt like I was wading through knee-deep snow hauling an oil tank behind me. By the time I reached the top of the steps leading to the cathedral, I was a wheezing wreck.

The huge wooden doors were ajar. I entered to feel a rush of damp, moist air surround me. A gloomy corridor wove around the main seating area. Polished wood panels adorned the walls, giving way to a bleak stone floor; I could almost feel the coldness of it rising through my boots. I found a small souvenir room at the rear of the cathedral, where, judging by a small number of pilgrims, the elusive *créanciale* was there for the taking, but it didn't prove that easy. I approached a very rotund nun sitting behind a desk. I have nothing against people with a larger frame, but it was hard not to stare. Her chin hung down in several layers like molten lava, her attire was at stretching point. I half expected her buttons to ping off, or the stitches to fray and snap any second. If she were wearing high heels, she would have struck oil.

I found we had a serious language barrier. I always assumed that I could get by in France by letting roll with a sentence containing predominately English words, with the odd French noun thrown in, and mask the whole mess up with a crap accent. Well, it seemed to work last time I was here.

"Excoos eem mwoir Madame, I em lookeen fur le creanceearlee por Le Camino." I realised as soon as I said it that my theory stood about as much chance of success as a fart in a hurricane. I knew the reply before it even came.

"Pardon?" she replied with a smile that suggested customer service was not her main priority. I managed to communicate what I was after by pointing to a small pile of *créanciales* on the desk in front of her.

"Ah, oui, oui!" she said, a wave of enlightenment rising up over her face. "Moment." She pointed to some chairs positioned around the room. I spent the next hour alternately sitting down and wandering around the room looking at the exhibits. Every once in a while she would look in my direction, nod her head and smile. All the time, she would be dishing out passports like they were cakes going cold. With a mixture of impatience, and perhaps thinking she had misunderstood me, I made my way to the desk again. A young chap bearing a striking resemblance to Adrian Mole ambushed me in mid-stride.

"Sir, I eem sowee for le wait, my friend speaks no English. Perhaps I can elp you." He peered at me through small, round glasses. His hair was slicked back with oil so all the comb marks were visible like furrows in a field, and it was so shiny I could see the stained glass windows reflected in it.. He stood nervously playing with a hanky and occasionally jerking his right arm. At least we were making headway and the language barrier had been pushed to the cloisters.

"Yeah, hi. I am walking the Camino, and from what I understand, I can obtain a *créanciale* here to assist me, a pilgrim's passport," I explained, doing a double take when I saw the diminishing pile on the desktop.

"Oui, Sir, we do provide *la créanciale*. Please, first I must ask a few questions."

Now, I am a laid-back sort of guy. It takes a lot to rattle me. I was, however, reaching a point. I had been waiting for nigh on two hours. In that time walkers had come and gone after receiving their passport. I was tired, in desperate need of a smoke and so hungry that everything I looked at was starting to resemble sweet pastries.

Luckily, Mr English speaker processed my request relatively smoothly, although I did have to provide some basic information such as name, address, age and sex. I also had to promise that I was not looking to acquire the passport by means of deception, or to use it for any purpose other than that for which it was intended. I paid a small fee, and also purchased a small neck pendant depicting the church for my neck chain.

By the time I got outside, I was drawing on my cigarette as though I was trying to suck a pea through a straw. I took a couple of photos, had an argument with the straps on my rucksack, and stumbled off towards town, and the start of the Camino.

"This is it," I said to myself. "This is the start of all my lack of planning." The start of twelve weeks of walking. Twelve weeks! I still couldn't wrap my head around the prospect of travelling by no means other than putting one hiking boot in front of the other for that period of time. Sixteen hundred kilometres! That's like walking from my parents' house to my sister's, and back, three times!

It was August 18th. I walked back down the cathedral steps, along Rue des Tables, left at the Choristes fountain and on to Rue Raphaël. I emerged into the Place du Plot, considered the traditional starting point for the Le Puy pilgrim, where the weekend market had already been plying its trade since the early morning. Wooden tables filled the square and buckled under the weight of local produce. Mushrooms lay jostling for space among blood-red tomatoes and white papery garlic. Onions tied in strips were dangling from rain covers like plaits of ginger hair. Apples the colour of blood looked ripe and juicy and nestled among green pears and rich black plums. Vegetables had been groomed to perfection, displaying virtually every hue of the spectrum. Colour was being thrown up everywhere; it was like a paint-box riot of colour. I felt obliged to buy something, even though I didn't need anything. Then I remembered an umbrella. I had waterproofs and a cover for my rucksack, but it took ten minutes of delving into its furthest caverns to retrieve them and put them on. By which time, invariably, it had stopped raining. An umbrella, I figured, would literally be worth it for those short showers.

Perhaps, subconsciously, I was thinking of Nicolas Crane, walker and author, who traversed from Spain to Turkey a few years back, entirely on foot. "Que Chova" was the name he had christened his friend to shelter him from the rain and to fend off a few dogs. I felt like I wanted to be part of the experience he had written about, the careful search for the perfect companion, the perfect umbrella. In the end, all it amounted to was picking the lightest and cheapest version. I squeezed in the shop, hitting people with my rucksack and sending postcard stands spinning. I wasn't in the mood for shopping. That was one of the horrors of society I had come out here to escape. I pondered the thought of christening it with some well thought-out, profound name. Several options came to mind, like old friends, relatives and pets, all of whom had meant something special to me at some point in my life, and who would perhaps bless this umbrella to look after me in the coming storms. Something meaningful, something different and something unexpected. After deliberating this for several minutes I eventually settled on "Brolly".

Boulevard St Louis merged into Rue des Capucins, and then rose steeply. The buzz of the market faded to just a colourful memory. Le Puy en Velay was shrinking each time

I turned around. It all merged into one brown and grey mass; the only redeeming features were the church spires breaking the blot. Soon I was encapsulated in a kind of meditative walk. My feet were on autopilot, and I was just lost in my own thoughts. The steep hill out of the city eventually flattened out and merged into the French countryside. I stopped, slid my rucksack on to the grass on the Camino's edge, retrieved my peanuts and lay with my back in the grass looking up at the sky as thousands of pilgrims before me had done, perhaps in this very spot.

The sun was hot, burning my exposed flesh. I had expected hot days, but I was still thankful. Sun to me is sometimes the very essence of a good walk. To take advantage of a beautiful day and to walk while the sun disperses its heat. I felt as though I was the luckiest person on the planet. I had a little money; everything I needed to live on was squashed, in no particular order, in my rucksack. I did not have to suffer an intrusive alarm clock for three months, and my life consisted of a stony track weaving in and out of classic countryside. Things were exactly how I liked them, uncomplicated. After my initial fears about the distance I had to walk faded, I came to realise it wasn't going to be so much of a walk but more of an experience. You can admire the peak of the mountain, but it's the journey up that holds the real pleasures.

As I heaved my rucksack on to my back and the fabric moulded into the ridges and curves of my spine, I realised something that I had missed during my walking meditation. My rucksack was seriously heavy. I had packed with care, two pairs of socks and liners, two pairs of underwear, two T-shirts, a pair of light hiking trousers, shorts, waterproofs and the usual camping equipment one would expect to take. So why, when I had placed it down on the scales at check in, had I been horrified to see sixteen kilos displayed? Some pilgrims I had seen in Le Puy had rucksacks so small that I would have struggled to squeeze in a food allowance.

I do pack carefully; I had packed carefully. I was thorough and had omitted some items that I normally would have taken. However, I need certain "comfort" items that always come with me; I think we all do. Some people make do with a cup of instant coffee in the morning. I wouldn't go near the stuff and for years scoured the hiking shops for a small, lightweight piece of equipment that brews proper, fresh coffee. I ended up securing an insulated mug with a built-in plunger while travelling in Canada a few years before. I probably didn't "need" the umbrella, but had grabbed it, again for comfort. I would rather have an extra half-kilo and know I could sleep at a beautiful spot, and pull out my stove for a hot coffee. The thing is, if you want to have a light load, you do have to be careful about packing. Every single item has to be looked at for its merits. I've seen people pay ten pounds each for a titanium spoon, fork, and knife. Fine, they have saved weight. If they put a modicum of thought into it, however, they would realise that you need only a spoon to cook and eat with, and they would have a cutting edge on their pen-knife. I have seen people pack hairdryers, three pairs of shoes, four pairs of trousers, six pairs of underwear and even a CD radio cassette player, and then complain that the load is too much for them. I end up somewhere in between. I buy lightweight gear, and then ruin it all by taking too much of it. I'm the sort of guy who goes into an outdoor shop for a pair of socks, and comes out with two carrier bags full of useless crap.

Then you get the extremists. I'm talking about people drilling holes in the handles of their spoons, cutting their toothbrushes in half, and pulling off the metal lace loops on their boots. The truth is, the harsher you force yourself to get about the whole weight issue, the lighter your rucksack will eventually be. It's just a case of finding the right balance and the right choice of equipment for you. It's also worth noting that many people on the Camino, in fact most, at some point stop to post equipment back home because they need to lose some weight. In the end, I decided to carry as little food as possible and buy provisions few and often. The heaviest items a walker carries are usually food and water. I would become fitter as the walk progressed anyway, and if I was still struggling later on, then I would post some equipment back home to Nerve Centre HQ, better known as Mum.

I passed my first *balise*. These markers direct pilgrims on the correct route, like a wooden footpath or bridleway sign back home. To find them depicted on a sign is a rarity. Instead, I think someone did a lot of walking with a brush and paint pot and marked any suitable medium vaguely found in the right place. Rocks, fences, trees, houses, walls all got the treatment. These soon-to-be-familiar logos were to become my friends over the next few weeks, until I reached the border with Spain, where they changed into the Spanish version. They consisted of a horizontal white rectangle on top and a red pointer underneath. The white rectangle remained the same always, a red rectangle running parallel underneath signifying that the pilgrim should carry straight on. The other two variations, where the red segment would point left or right, were self-explanatory. The last option consisted of the white rectangle on a diagonal, with the red crossing it on the opposite diagonal, your basic cross on its side. This proved to be invaluable, as it advised that the pilgrim had taken a wrong turn and should reverse back to where he or she had seen the last sign. I started to say "Thank you" every time I saw one. And when I needed one, I would ask, and the Camino would oblige. One seemed to appear at exactly the time I was most in need of it. I carried on this method throughout the entire Camino. I don't know why I started to be grateful, but it worked. Except for a few times when the trail was confusing and seemed to give no clear direction, my thanks and requests were always answered.

I walked gently and deliberately that first day. I wanted to break my body in gently, but more importantly I wanted to establish a rhythm. I needed the Camino to be a memorable experience, not a physically demanding mission defined by schedules and plans. It was more of a stroll than a walk. I spent time studying and surveying what was around me. The track itself varied from well-worn stone ruts, with grass lining the middle, to shingle on the newer stretches.

Occasional small bridges hopped over busy brooks, grasses caught in the soft current like long, flowing locks of emerald hair. Fields of corn the colour of sand stooped over in the breeze. Irregular-shaped meadows were patched with clumps of oak trees, like spots on a Dalmatian.

I turned around to check my progress and caught site of another pilgrim on the trail, about a kilometre behind me. I wasn't in any hurry, so he soon caught me up. He was walking as if he had just robbed the bank in Le Puy and the police had let out the sniffer dogs. I wondered what his hurry was, and why he wasn't taking his time and savouring the experience. When he got to a few feet behind me, I turned around, smiled and said "Bonjour". He said nothing. No eye contact, no facial expression, no body language. I repeated the greeting in case he hadn't heard me, but still he didn't respond. He just walked on with his head down, without a word. "Nice to meet you too, and I hope you enjoy the rest of the Camino," I shouted after him, making damn sure that he did hear me. I wasn't expecting a response, and I didn't get one. I began to wonder what his problem was and even got paranoid, for some reason, that the church had forgotten to impart some vital piece of information, that pilgrims were not supposed to speak. What if I had to walk all the way and as a penance to God I was not allowed to utter a word while I walked? I was very relieved when, shortly afterwards, I passed a pilgrim sunbathing and he smiled and said "Bonjour".

I had decided to camp out the first night. I would just pick a nice spot and set up camp away from any prying eyes. However, after about five hours and fifteen kilometres' walking, I passed the small hamlet of Montbonnet. It was quiet, unobtrusive and just seemed to exist, doing its own thing and not bothering anyone. There were a couple of farms, dogs were running around in the yards on chains, chickens pecked at whatever small morsel they could find. There was the odd hum of a tractor in a nearby field, harvesting the fruits of the summer's labours. The only disturbance to the tranquillity was the occasional 2CV zooming past on the small country road.

I always have good intentions to camp out and when I do, I don't regret it. Sometimes, however, my brain accelerates towards logical mode and demands I seek a little comfort. But I do love getting back to nature. I enjoy finding the perfect spot to pitch camp. Maybe by some water, a nice flat area for the tent, some firewood close to hand. On clear nights I rarely pitch the tent, preferring to sleep out. There are not many simple experiences you can have these days, such as lying on your back picking out the constellations (I can recognise two now), snuggling down in a sleeping bag, and feeling a chilled waft of night air brush you cheeks. Not to mention crapping your pants when something moves in the bushes a few feet away from your head.

A voice in my head offered: "Fozzie, why camp out in a miserable field when there is a *gîte* a hundred metres down the road? Why get into your sleeping bag when you're filthy, when they are sure to have a piping hot shower? Why make do with your provisions when they will probably have food to buy and a cooker to rustle something up on?" I relented, swerved a sharp right along the road, and then turned right again into the small farmyard. Perhaps I had subconsciously asked for shelter, and if I did, how would I know this was the right place? I got my validation immediately. Two border collies came bounding out, tails on overdrive, tongues slapping with a look of devotion in their eyes. "This will do nicely," I thought.

I knocked on an old oak door studded with lead rivets. An attractive woman of around thirty five answered with a genuine smile and an expectant look on her face, as though she thought I should speak first.

"Er, bonjour, Mademoiselle. Avez-vous une … place to sleep?" I offered. She giggled sheepishly and put her hand to her mouth.

"Excuse me," she replied, "I do not wish to be rude, but that's the worst French I have heard in a long time!"

"Well, that is good news. Yesterday it was really crap, so I'm glad things are improving."

She looked like a cross between a catwalk model and a housewife. Wavy, blonde hair tumbled down the sides of her face like dangling party streamers. Her only make-up was a subtle pink lipstick, which highlighted her tanned skin. She was perspiring in the heat a little and her white vest stuck to her. Moisture droplets winked back at me from the nape of her neck as they caught sunlight. Flour marks smudged a blue apron and her hands. She left a little on her nose as she brushed off a fly and blew a lock away from her eye.

In the space of five minutes she had given me the guided tour. There was indeed a good kitchen with a few groceries to buy. Hot showers were on tap, so to speak, and the rooms were dormitory-style. I opted to camp in the grounds as a compromise and save some funds. She offered breakfast of bread and jam plus juice and coffee, which I accepted, and I watched her slink back to her house, tossing her hair and sending it rippling down her back.

After showering and watching any fatigue I did have swirl its way down the plughole, I rustled up some soup and rice, and blagged two boiled eggs and some bread off a couple of French cyclists. The French are generous like that, always ready to dish out some provisions if you show them what little you have with a resigned look. I went outside and played with the dogs for a while, and chilled out with a coffee and a smoke. It was about seven p.m. and the sun was still up, and still warm. I remember thinking it would be quite a change two months down the road. The sun would have already set, it would be chilly, probably raining, maybe even snowing in Spain. But for now I was content, very content. Fifteen kilometres in a day was hardly breaking any records, but I hadn't intended to. I had done what I had wanted, a casual, gentle, easy first day of breaking myself in. My back and shoulders felt fine and, most importantly, my feet showed no signs of any blisters. Sure, I was tired, had been hungry and needed a long night's rest. And as I squeezed out my toothpaste I realised my toothbrush was cut in half.

Satisfied with both my pace and my fitness, I dwelt once

more on what was in store; and it brought a huge smile to my face.

By the time I had finished daydreaming, the sun had set. I ran for my tent as a few fat droplets of rain began to land around me. I hurriedly zipped up the shelter and looked up to see clouds the colour of soot racing up as though someone was drawing the blinds over the sky. They were billowing over me with frightening ferocity, transforming a star-splattered arena into a shade darker than night itself. There was a storm building.

Chapter Three

Pushing Too Hard

The elements had indeed stirred last night, a vicious thunderstorm kept me awake for an hour. In the end I opened the zip of the tent and lay there taking in the spectacle. The electricity lit up the French countryside every few seconds like a million fireworks, illuminating the surrounding hills and providing a split-second glimpse of the dark sky overhead. Each thunderous clap made me cower as if expecting a lightning strike to pinpoint my safe little haven. Raindrops smacked on the grass, transforming the area into a waterlogged mess. The ground appeared to move and become alive as the drops collided and sent up a myriad of small splashes like explosions. It was an awesome, energetic display of Mother Nature at her cinematic best.

I awoke after sunrise and clambered outside. France had received a spring-clean. Everything was wet and glinted in the sunlight. It smelt fresh and moist. I went into the farmhouse breakfast room, which the family had long since left for another day's toil in the fields. The lady of the house welcomed me again, and invited me to eat as much as I could. There was fresh coffee, orange juice, limitless crusty baguette and homemade jams, the classic continental breakfast. A woman joined me. Shoulder-length grey hair curled around the sides of her face, disguising the outline of her face and giving her a soft appearance. She was probably in her sixties, and wore glasses with frames so big that she might have been able to see what was behind her. She looked in good shape and I got the impression she was a walker. She ate carefully and attentively, seeming to savour each portion as if it were her last meal. I had not noticed her last night, perhaps preoccupied with my thoughts.

She spoke a little English, and we chatted about the Camino, for she too was on her second day after starting from Le Puy en Velay. The conversation followed what was soon to become a familiar pattern every time I chatted to pilgrims. Where we had started, where we were going, where we were from, and the reasons for succumbing to El Camino's lure in the first place. She left before me. I was in no hurry. I was to meet this woman several times over the next few weeks. I never did ask her for her name and I don't know why. Usually when I am introduced to someone, I forget their name straight away, and end up asking them again. It didn't seem to matter with this woman, who showed an equal lack of curiosity about my name. I spotted her walking past the window shortly afterwards, smoking a cigarette. I decided to call her the smoking woman.

I settled up with the owner, the grand sum of about five euros. She bade me farewell as I strode off. It was always refreshing to meet proprietors of hotels, guesthouses and the like, who seem genuinely happy. Imagine having twenty or more walkers hanging around your house every night in peak season, and still be able to appear totally relaxed, provide a warm and genuine smile, and be helpful, and then do exactly the same thing the following day. I'd go nuts if I had to do that all the time.

I left and crossed over the road and back into the countryside, through fields laid out in random fashion. Stone walls about waist height separated them and yielded to the Camino, which wove left and right and then entered a pine forest. I spotted a pilgrim through the trees in a small clearing, relaxing after his lunch and soaking up the warmth. I love pine forests: they remind me of magical, secret places, and bring back memories of books such as *The Hobbit* and children's fairytales with a touch of wizardry and the mystical. Unicorns prancing among the pine needles, medieval cavalry charging by and perhaps a glimpse of Merlin. I wanted to camp there and spend the night experiencing the atmosphere, but smiled to myself when I realised this would be just the first of many, many chances along the way.

I dipped sharply down among deep green woods. The decline was severe and because of the rain it was also slippery. Coupled with the weight of my rucksack, this made me feel as though I was taking my first, tentative move on skis. If I leaned too far forward, my body toppled forward; too far back, and it felt as though any second my feet would be snapped away, flung up in the air, and I'd land on my arse, like a cartoon character slipping on a banana skin.

I reached the pit of the mini gorge, skipped over puddles and a brook, and climbed again for a few minutes. A dog saw me and started barking wildly, straining at a chain. The entire garden of the house was fenced in, and I wondered why people take on beautiful animals and then keep them tied up.

The stones and mud yielded to tarmac. I crested the hill and arrived in the village of Saint Privat D'Allier, a beautiful place sitting on the edge of the gorge, and apparently threatening to topple over any second and drop down to the river below.

I put down my rucksack, gave myself a sugar fix with a soda and a bar of chocolate and sat on a bench to watch life go by. It was the beginning of the week, but it felt more like a Sunday. Everyone proceeded without any hurry, a practice they have mastered well in Europe. People were walking dogs, buying their bread for the day and chatting to their friends in the shop, or just strolling around without a care in the world, as if they were all on holiday. I was so drawn into the whole ambience that I just hung out on the bench for an hour or so.

I was determined to walk every step of the Camino, every single metre of the fifteen hundred kilometres. I did not want to accept any lifts, take a bus or catch a train. I knew that on arrival in Santiago de Compostela, pilgrims presented themselves to the cathedral authorities to obtain their certificate of completion. I knew they asked a few questions, which they were obliged to do to weed out walkers who tried to obtain the certificate by means of deception.

I began to play a scenario in my head. I imagined myself sitting in the square outside the cathedral, and being approached by a sinister-looking character.

"Fozzie?" he asks, clamping a clip board firmly in one hand, a pen poised in the other. He is wearing a badge displaying the words 'Fake Pilgrim Spotter', and he peers at me over half-framed spectacles. His head is bald save for some long wisps of white hair dangling from each side, and he is wearing a long, brown cloak with sandals just peeking out at the bottom.

"Yep, that's me."

"I understand you are requesting the coveted certificate of completion on the Camino from the authorities here at Santiago."

"Er, yep. That's correct."

"I am sure you won't mind just answering a few questions. We have to be careful in these situations. People have been passing themselves off as pilgrims, in order to get a certificate. First, where did you start from?"

"Le Puy un Velay in France," I would say, feeling a little nervous.

"Le Puy? That is a fine walk; you have done well, pilgrim."

"When did you start?"

"Erm, August 17th "

"Arh, I see you have progressed well. Le Puy to Santiago is a long walk, I see that you wanted to make the most of your time on the Camino. Congratulations".

"Thank you." At this point my fingernails are firmly rooted in my mouth, and taking a hammering.

"Now, let me see," he says, scanning down the paper on his clipboard and sliding his spectacles up his nose. "Ah, yes. Can you tell me if a pilgrim should turn left or right out of the campsite in Le Puy un Velay in order to start the Camino?"

"Well…he would turn…lef…No! Sorry, right."

"Excellent, excellent," he says. I smile, thinking maybe this isn't so bad after all. But then he continues the inquisition.

"Very well, imagine the Camino descending out of Conques. Please enlighten me as to the name of the river you cross before the sharp incline."

I shift nervously, looking down at my feet. "The river? Conques? The river, the river, the river…there isn't one! Hah! Trick question!" I spit, feeling immensely proud.

"Actually, it's not. It's called the river Dordou."

"Oh…shit. I knew that. Really, I did. Have I failed, then?"

"No," he says, with the same malicious chuckle that my maths teacher would have been proud of. "We would not expect 100%. That would be unfair."

"Oh, great, 'cause it was just a lapse of concentration. I knew there was a river, really."

"One incorrect answer is available to you. Let us see how you acquit yourself with my other questions. You are sitting by the river in Espalion. A fine bridge, quite possibly my favourite. Please tell me what you see on the other side."

"Huh! Now that *is* a trick question! I need to know what side I am sitting on before I can tell you that!"

"Yes, excellent, well spotted. Let us say, the north side, looking south."

"O … K … I would see the park on the other side, poplar trees running right to left along the path. There are a few men playing boules and some laughing children near by. There is a football pitch with a grandstand, and if I look through the seating, I can just make out the café." I sit back, smirking.

"Good … very good. Now, one more question, answered correctly, and I can leave you in peace, Mr Foskett."

"Please call me 'Fozzie'. Would you like a cigarette?"

"No, I do not smoke. Cast your mind back along your route. Follow from the beginning to the end, and observe. Tell me how many churches you visited."

"Oooh … five?" I offer, a bit hesitantly now.

"Five? FIVE? Is that all? I cannot be expected to authorise a certificate to a pilgrim who has visited only five churches on the entire route! That is ludicrous!" And the man, becoming more and more the villainous accuser with every passing moment, roars with laughter.

"Wh ... wha ... what do you mean? There's nothing in the transcripts that dictates I must visit a certain number of religious establishments. Excuse me, but that's nonsense.'

"I beg your pardon?" He stares at me.

"If you're gonna fail me on that question, then I demand to see your manager ... now!"

He opens his mouth to reply but is cut off before he can do so by another, kinder-looking man, who towers imposingly over both of us.

"Manuel! There is no need to question this poor man any further. Please leave, I will see you in my office shortly. Go!" Manuel cowers like a trapped dog under the glare of his master.

"Mr Foske ... sorry, 'Fozzie' Please accept my sincerest apologies for the behaviour of my colleague. He takes his job a little too seriously at times."

My daydreaming was interrupted when I caught sight of the smoking woman sitting by the side of the trail.

"Cigarette break, huh?" I smiled.

"Oui. It is one of a few weaknesses," she replied, squinting as she looked up at me.

"Nothing wrong with a few weaknesses. I'm guilty of a few myself, smoking included."

We exchanged a few pleasantries and I continued, through tunnels created by stumpy oak trees curving over me and the familiar stone walls cluttered either side. I reached the small hamlet of Rosiers, having walked a total of around 18 kilometres that day. The soles of my feet felt strange. It was a feeling I had experienced when hiking before. It felt like blisters, but I knew it was just soreness. My shoulders were also aching from the constant rubbing of the rucksack straps. I should have stopped, checked out the situation and stayed there for the night. Foolishly, however, I decided to carry on to the large town of Saugues, where I told myself I could check out my aches and pains, and spend the night in a cheap, communal *gîte*. I was also low on food, so I would be able to stock up in the town.

This turned out to be a huge mistake. I had walked too much, too early. My body was still being run in. I should have been building my distances up slowly and resting often. By the time I reached Saugues I was in agony. I was barely hobbling and my shoulders felt as though someone was rolling his knuckles up and down on them. I must have looked like a runner who had just crossed the finishing line in a marathon and collapsed into someone's arms.

I winced my way to the first *gîte*, which was full. Then to the second, also full. I stocked up on food and limped down to the last communal *gîte* by the river Sauge. As I leaned over to one side to take off my rucksack, something gave in my right shoulder. I yelled with pain, much to the bemusement of the guy sitting at reception.

My shoulder felt as though someone had driven a skewer straight through it. I couldn't move for about five minutes, and was stuck there, standing but leaning over to one side, bent forward, scared even to breathe, my face contorted with the excruciating pain.

This was it, I thought. My attempt on the Camino was over, after just three days.

After a while I eased my body upright, which seemed to take forever. The pain, still intense, seemed to abating slightly. I booked in for two nights, somehow tentatively hoisted my rucksack on again, then struggled for another five minutes to the communal room where I would spend the night with three other pilgrims.

My shoulder, I was to discover, was one of two problems. I had deliberately delayed looking at the soles of my feet, for fear of what lurked there. I knew it was bad because it felt bad. Whatever the problem was, it was minor compared to my shoulder. My feet seemed like a mere distraction.

My morale, which up until now had been good, dipped to a low and it was an effort to snap myself out of a bad mood and try to convince myself that the day's events were just a hiccup.

I knew deep down it was blisters causing the pain, I just couldn't fathom out why. My boots were well worn. They had been broken in over the course of a year's worth of weekend hikes, and I had worn them while working in Greece for four months that year. I had good socks, and wore thin liners underneath. I washed my feet religiously every night, and gave them a good massage to ease away the aches. It couldn't be blisters.

I sat on the edge of my bunk and eased off my boots, then slowly peeled off my socks as one would carefully peel a plaster off an open wound.

"Bollocks," I muttered to myself as the full picture was revealed on one foot. It was worse than I had imagined. On the sole, a line of skin running parallel to my toes, stretching from my big toe to the third toe, had pushed up into a ridge, like a chain of mountains rising out of the plains. There were also blisters on my little toe and on the sole of my heel. My other foot was pretty much the same.

I was out of action, at least for tomorrow, and decided to take a rest day to see if things would improve.

I remembered reading somewhere once that when we get injured, our reaction to the problem and how we deal with it can determine how it heals. For example, if we take the view that the injury is disastrous or, conversely, if we consider that it is not as bad as it looks, then the body 'listens', takes heed and acts accordingly. Having a positive state of mind can affect our body's capability to make itself better.

I tried to concentrate on imagining that both the blisters and the shoulder were minor problems, and pushed my fears to one side. It seemed to work. To my astonishment, after a short time, my shoulder felt as though there had never been a problem to start with. The blisters were obviously still there, but after I had punctured them, squeezed out the liquid and patched them up, they also seemed much better. My good spirits returned.

In any case, while planning the walk, I had decided to

incorporate a rest day once a week, so the timing couldn't have been better. Filling my mind with positive thoughts, I roamed around Saugues. I was hobbling a little because the blisters still hurt, but at least I could walk. There was no way that I was going to give up now, whatever hardships. Short of breaking a leg, I fully intended to be admiring the Cathedral at Santiago de Compostela in a few weeks.

Too many times in the past I had set out on a direction, be it a job, a challenge or some other test, and failed. I always wanted to succeed but for some reason I would turn back halfway down the road. I was determined the Camino would not end up as one of those failures. Maybe I was subconsciously learning the valuable lesson that if I put my mind to something, then I could do it. I knew from the start that state of mind would prove the main problem. I was physically fit, my stamina was fine, and I knew my body was well capable of the task. I just had to persuade my mind not to throw negatives in the way.

Over the next few days, my blisters continued to cause pain in both feet. The difficult part was getting going first thing in the morning, and after every rest stop. Once I was moving, the pain subsided, and I actually forgot at times I was suffering. As soon as I stopped, however, even for five minutes, it took ten minutes of hobbling and wincing before the pain abated and I could settle into a normal stride. I was wondering how long this would go on. Unlike this walk, my previous treks had lasted only a week or so and I had rarely got blisters and at most suffered from them for four or five days. This was therefore unfamiliar territory.

The smoking woman was also in town and she had made friends with a French couple, with whom I also became acquainted. Reginald was a retired teacher. The first thing I noticed about him was that he sort of bounced when he walked. His knees seemed to be incredibly flexible, and when he placed one leg on the ground, his whole body lowered much more than you would expect, and then seemed to ricochet slowly back up to repeat the process. It was like a bungee jumper, falling quickly at first, slowing to a stop as the elastic broke the fall and then slowly rising again. It sounds very ungraceful, but believe me, if walking was a work of art, this guy was the Mona Lisa. His whole demeanour revealed him as a well 'worn in' hiker. His rucksack and equipment were soiled, but not exactly dirty. He had brought along tried and trusted friends, stuff that he knew worked, and the occasional piece of dependable new gear. He had every gadget in his bag, perhaps a little worn and grimy from years of service but in full working order.

His features were also getting the worse for wear, but still working perfectly, with oil in all the right places. He constantly had a pipe balanced in his mouth, and his teeth were tanned from the smoke. A couple of day's stubble shadowed his face.

"Your rucksack appears large," he said, peering out through 1960s spectacles and replacing his pipe in his mouth between sentences.

"Yeah. It's around 16 kilos, but I like to be self-sufficient," I explained, trying to sound convinced myself. "It's nice to be able to stop where I want to in the woods, and just set up camp. Unfortunately, I have a weight penalty for the privilege, but I'll get used to it. I can always post some stuff back home if it gets too much."

"I too like to be self-sufficient. I carry a sail from a small boat. I use it as a tarp when I camp out. It works perfectly, and weighs one-tenth of a tent," he proclaimed, as if it were commonplace.

I left Reginald in no doubt that he would bounce all the way to Santiago. He just oozed confidence.

The weather had improved. The first week or so had seen the odd rainy day. Now it was hot. It was a treat to walk in the shade, and I relished entering woods as they cut out the sun and provided a musky coolness. It was bliss to take off my rucksack and turn into the breeze so my moist T-shirt could slap my back and make me shiver. Sweat ran down my arms and on to my trekking poles. It mixed with sunblock and wove a route over my eyebrows, sometimes dripping into my eyes and making them sting. Instinctively wiping

The Journey in Between

them, I made matters worse by leaving a fresh deposit from the backs of my hands.

Because the Camino runs to the west, it was a comfort never to actually have to face and squint into the sun until the evening. Its heat would singe the back of my neck in the morning, and my left arm would receive the attack during the heat of the afternoon, but by the time it was trying to overtake me on the left side I had usually hung up my boots for the day.

I began to know exactly which way I was heading just from my position in relation to the sun. If the rays smacked me straight in the face when I was looking forward to lunchtime, then I knew the Camino had swerved to the south. If I was closing in on the day's end, and the left side of my body was stroked by the sun's warmth, I knew I was walking north. And if I set off for the day's walk in the morning and found myself squinting into direct sunlight, I knew I had not had enough coffee, was still half asleep, and had begun walking the wrong way.

The actual surface of the Camino varied greatly. Parts were sandy, some were gravelled. Some areas wove across fields of deep green, which was always welcome as it was kinder on the muscles. Sometimes sunken boulders and slabs broke the surface and I'd amuse myself by hopping from one to the next. I became aware when certain stretches of the Camino boasted some sort of heritage. I could tell that it was the original way just by the look and feel of it, the way it wove and the buildings and landmarks it brushed against. Over the centuries, the Camino has been redirected in places, mainly because of land ownership. These new stretches are sometimes just gravelled over. Other parts I could see had been renewed through a swath of recently cut trees. The original Camino just had a feeling about it. It's difficult to put into words. You just know. The surface was littered with large cobblestones, about the size of a telephone directory. Thousands of feet had sand-papered the tops into smooth slabs, the edges rounded and sleek. Grass sprouted and eased through where it could, and a classic stone wall on one or both sides usually accompanied the path.

The tarmac stretches I soon learned to enjoy. At the beginning, I just relished the chance to walk on old tracks, and be rid of the black bitumen. However, it had its advantages. First, it was smooth, with no obstacles. Some stretches threatened sprained ligaments if I didn't keep both eyes on placing my feet carefully. When I reached a road, I was able to look around me all the time without fear of tripping and falling on my face.

Second, roads usually meant that a town or village was approaching. Occasionally, I would be ambling down a leafy dirt lane, and be surprised to emerge into a hamlet without warning. That wasn't the norm. My guidebook would usually indicate when I was coming near to civilisation, and that was almost a relief when I was hungry and a road would appear, winding down to a bakery or small shop.

On some occasions when I reached a road, there would be no sign, and my guidebook would be sketchy as to the correct direction. I only had to look at the verge of the road, and I could see a clear line, a slightly lighter shade of silver green, where the blades had been flattened by passing pilgrims. And sure enough, when the way left the road again, the grass would return to its upright position.

I reached the highest point of the French section when I came into Chapelle Saint Roch, at an altitude just short of 1,300 metres. There was nothing here except a small shelter for bad weather. I had mistakenly thought it may offer some facilities such as beds or a stove, so I carried on seeking a *gîte*. Further on I detoured down the D987, which the guidebook assured me would take me to three *gîtes*. The first of the three had a bad vibe. I meandered around the rear of the old house, to come face to face with a rather stern-looking Madame.

"Hi, is it possible to camp here?" I enquired sheepishly. She thought about my request for a few seconds, running her tired eyes up and down me.

"Eeeer, oui," she replied eventually, unconvincingly. I waited for her maybe to add directions or to point out some spot in the yard where I could be remotely near some facilities. Nothing, she just stood there.

"Merci," I retorted. "Where?" She led me over to a fence commanding a view back up the hill I had just come down, and pointed to a spot about twenty metres into a field. I made my way back around the house, and began pitching my tent. After a few minutes, I heard her shouting something and flapping her arms around so wildly that I thought it was some sort of warning, as if the local bull had spotted me. She then began to point further up the hill and made motions with her arms as though she were pushing a car.

"Great," I thought to myself, "as if moving another fifty metres up the hill is going to make that much difference." So I picked up my gear, plodded over to the area she had indicated and continued. After another few minutes, a pilgrim who had already booked in came over to me in the field.

"I think she wants you to move to the next field. There is some sort of problem if you pitch tent here," he said.

"Thanks. Do you know exactly where she means?" I said, scratching my head and laughing.

"Yes, I think she means up there," he said. "Come, I will show."

I followed him back up the hill, clutching all my equipment beneath folded arms, and tripping over dangling guy ropes trailing on the ground. He showed me a small area next to a rundown garage. It was bare of any green, full of cow pats, and I would have had to negotiate a barbed-wire fence every time I needed to get out. The whole place looked as if it might be advertised in the local 'Land for Sale' column of the paper as 'To clear'.

"Look, thanks, but don't worry," I said, feeling a little stupid that he had taken the trouble to show me the spot, and now I was going to reject it. "I think I'll walk on into the village and look for something else."

I mooched further into La Roche de Lago, and after a while I stumbled across the *gîte* logo swaying from one nail, dangling on a dark green picket fence. It looked perfect. I was tired, hungry, needed a shower and my blisters were complaining. I made a deal with myself that if I couldn't stay here then La Roche de Lago just wasn't meant to be and I'd go camp in the woods.

As I unlatched the gate, I caught sight of a robust and challenging figure of a Madame watching me curiously from the kitchen window, like a guard dog itching to pounce. She opened the front door and came down the path using the same arm flapping routine.

"Monsieur, le gîte est complet," she cried dramatically, as if she was auditioning for a part in a movie. My heart sank. All I wanted was hot water tumbling over my sore limbs. I went for the "This is my last resort, or I will die here" routine.

"But Madame, I have une tente," I implored. I pointed to the green bag squeezed between tie cords on the back of my pack. I gave her a classic puppy-eyed look with upturned palms and slouched a little to swing things in my favour. To my astonishment, the woman had understood my word-perfect French. She beckoned me to follow, somehow squeezing her large frame between the house and a wall running up one side. My tent plot was secured among rampant chickens, basking in the last of the sun's warmth. Madame and I communicated somehow and it was arranged that she would cook a meal for me if I came to the house in two hours. Success!

After a reviving torrent of hot water in the shower and some relaxing, I made my way back to the front of the house and knocked on the door. She beckoned me to take a seat at a huge wooden table dominating a traditional, rustic farmhouse kitchen. I didn't know what to expect. In the end she just busied herself around an old cast iron stove, tinkering with this pot and that, checking the oven and clanking about.

First she served me an entrée of vegetable soup, then salad, rice with a steak, a mountain of cheese and fruit to finish, all accompanied with limitless crusty baguette, red wine and water. It was all in perfectly sized portions, as if she knew my stomach storage capabilities and I finished the whole lot, feeling extremely satisfied.

She gave me a steaming cup and I sat on a rickety old bench outside sipping sweet coffee. The night was still being born, still encroaching on the last orange glow of the sun on the hills opposite. The crickets had started their chorus, the stars were intensifying, and the ambience was becoming more and more serene.

"Good idea to come here," I thought as I laid my head on my folded-up fleece and snuggled up inside my sleeping bag. The chickens gradually stopped scratching about and the light on the tent changed from the orange of a sinking sun to the silver of a rising moon. "Today was a good day."

Chapter Four

The Bag Rustlers

Saint Alban sur Limagnole appeared below me, its terracotta rooftops forming a patchwork of patterns all over the town like a chequerboard as the bells of the church of Saint Alban cried out the midday call. I followed the route carefully, occasionally looking up to familiarise myself with the town's layout. After what seemed an endless descent from the hills, I emerged from an alley on to the quiet main street. Smack in front of me was a pharmacy, which no pilgrim could fail to notice. The owner would appear to have been the ultimate marketing ace, as the whole front window proudly boasted a display of a leading brand of blister patches, known as 'second skin'. He must have been making a fortune.

He also had perfect timing, or, rather, I did for, as I turned left on to the Grand Rue, having stocked up on supplies, my left leg buckled as I felt another blister squelch. I meandered down the street past a couple of small cafés. Someone called my name.

"Fozzie! FOZZIE!" It was Hans and Louise, a Dutch couple I had met in Saugues.

"You want a coffee? You look like shit!" Hans had a knack of quickly getting to the point.

"You must have read my mind! That would be fantastic," I replied. I sat down between them, slouching rudely, and let the sun wash all over me. We discussed my blisters and the fact that they appeared to be getting worse.

"Where are you staying?" I asked.

"There's a campsite about three kilometres out of town," said Louise, "with a bar and a swimming pool."

That was all I needed to hear. I had to sort out my feet once and for all, and if that took several days, so be it; I didn't have any deadlines. I followed them out of town on the road and they left me to check in as they strolled off to their pitch. I checked in for two nights and erected my tent between three trees, on a spot commanding a great view over the whole site. As I wouldn't be doing much moving about for the next few days, I figured I might as well entertain myself with a good view of everyone else's business.

After trying and failing to hitch a ride, I walked all the way back to town to stock up on supplies for my convalescence from the local shop. The store chain was called Casino, very apt when you take into account that's it's a gamble whether they actually have anything you want.

That evening 'Operation Blister' began. It was a delicate procedure, requiring a deft touch. There was actually a far better method of dealing with blisters, but unfortunately I would not learn this for another week or so. The secret was to keep everything clean and sterile. First, I prepared my faithful Swiss army knife, holding it in the flame of my lighter to sterilise the scissors. Then, while I propped myself up in a very poor half lotus position, I snipped each blister in the middle and let the liquid ooze out on to a tissue. I then had to carefully cut four lines radiating out from the centre to the edge and snip off these four bits of skin so as to leave just the tender, pink skin underneath, which looked like a piece of raw beef. At one stage, when I lost concentration, I inadvertently plunged the tip of the scissors into the exposed area. I tried desperately to stifle a cry, but it got the better of me. I grasped my foot and rocked back and forth, cradling it like a baby, wincing with eyes shut tight.

Once the pain had subsided, I realised that my sterile wipes had run out. I looked around. There was an old French couple staying in a tiny caravan next to me. First I tried to get the woman's attention by waving, looking helpless, and calling out. No luck. So I hopped over to her, pointed to the hole in my little toe and, from memory, muttered something like "sterilisation". Amazingly, she opened a cupboard door and produced a bottle of sterile cleaning fluid for wounds. That's one of the great bonuses of campsites, you can blag just about anything.

Teeth gritted and one eye closed, I gave blister number one a generous squirt. It was like squeezing lemon juice on an open wound, excruciating. This time I managed to stifle any obscenities until the pain stopped. Instead of applying a blister patch, I used a plain strip of gauze. This enabled me to keep dirt off the area, but still let air get to the wound, as my priority was to dry the wounds out.

At night I removed the gauze and let the blisters breathe fully. Each day I cleaned and changed the dressing, just as the nurse tells you to do, on each of the six blisters. And each day I would stay next to the tent, moving only to pee or shower, or sit by the stream. Wherever I ventured out, I had to balance and walk on my heels, much to the amusement of the camp residents, who would nudge each other and nod my way with stifled giggles.

A friend had emailed me with an interesting method of dealing with blisters that he had been taught in the South African army. These unfortunate recruits would have to fill a syringe with methylated spirits, pierce the wound and squeeze the liquid in, forcing the ooze out. The meths apparently dried out the skin, made it tougher and it was of course sterile. I did consider this method, but, knowing my luck, I'd be smoking at the time and end up with third-degree burns everywhere.

Saint Alban sur Limagnole eventually became my home for four nights. It got boring at times: there's not much a guy can do when he can't really move. It got to the stage where I was actually looking forward to having a shower because it killed a few minutes. I did eat well, though. I love cooking and eating anyway. Now I had been gifted with plenty of time, I made the most of it. One night I produced sausages, fried onions, mashed potatoes and peas with gravy. Not bad with one camp stove.

I went to bed early and got up late. Other interests that kept me occupied during the long days were reading chocolate wrappers, feeding my new friend, a baby chick I named Rachel, guessing what my neighbours were cooking from the smell, staring into space and convincing myself that I wasn't going senile.

On my last day I decided to go into town for a lunch treat. Luckily, as I waited by the entrance to the campsite, I got a lift. I chose the same place where I had drunk coffee with Hans and Louise and found the locals tucking into some reasonably edible-looking offerings, so I sat down and ordered a cold beer. After amusing myself for a bit trying to translate a discarded French newspaper and look like a Frenchman, I called to the waitress, who resembled someone from the eighties Gothic era.

"Bonjour, mademoiselle," I smirked, "s'il vous plaît le menu?"

"Oui, monsieur," she replied, bounding back inside.

I waited, and I waited some more. Every time I tried to attract her attention, she would be looking the other way. Eventually she arrived. No menu, but she did place a plate in front of me containing a slice of pizza and a very attractive parsley garnish. By the time I could react, she had bounded back off again. So I ate it anyway, and very tasty it was too. I thought it no use trying to explain the misunderstanding when she arrived back at my table to take my empty plate, and just went for dessert.

"Une crème brûlée," I said.

The waitress pointed obligingly to a woman at the next table eating a crème brûlée and asked me in broken English to confirm if that was what I meant. I replied it was.

She then nipped off again and after a few minutes, she came again, leaving a plate in front of me containing a portion of French beans, pasta twirls and a steak. I ate that too and, although I eventually did get my crème brûlée, I had to stifle a laugh when a pilgrim appeared and asked for 'le menu'. I was just leaving when he received a mixed salad. I learnt a few days later that my misunderstanding came about because the menu in French is 'Carte'.

After the fourth night I decided my feet had improved sufficiently, and I was desperate to get back into the swing of the Camino. All the regular faces I had become accustomed to seeing would be a few days ahead of me now, so I would be making new friends. For a brief second while I walked the bridge over the stream out of the campsite, I was sorry to be leaving, but I put that down to a minor lapse in concentration. I needed new scenery, different trees, a different-sounding river and unfamiliar birds. Rachel chirped and looked very sorry to see me go.

The countryside was advertising the end of summer. The hay was piled up into cone shapes in the field, and the air full of the sweet smell of the harvest. Tractors bumped along ungracefully, and dusk advanced just that little bit earlier each day.

I had been trying, unsuccessfully, to locate a camping gas cartridge, as my existing canister was nearly empty after my unscheduled rest. The village Aumont Aubrac promised great things, but didn't deliver. There were numerous shops selling everything the average hiker didn't need and nothing that he did. If you required meat, the butcher would oblige. Those in need of a trim would be spoilt for choice by the four hair salons. I could even purchase a hunting knife that would have made Rambo jealous.

In the end I decided it was an omen that I wasn't meant to find the cartridge. As I left town I decided to camp in the forest, and make a fire to cook on. I found a great spot on the edge of the trees in a small field. It had a good supply of firewood, was blocked from prying eyes on the Camino, and faced east to capture the first of the sun in the morning. Before long, the crickets were in chorus and my fire crackled and sprayed out an orange glow, which matched the setting sun behind it. The pines were becoming silhouettes, and my only reminder of the modern world was the gentle hum of traffic on the road a way off.

I lay on my back while soup bubbled on the fire, and

looked up at the void of black spread out above me, splattered with the constellations. I picked out the Big Dipper and the North Star, directing travellers as it had done for thousands of years. Orion was visible, guarding the sky. The tips of the pines swayed from side to side, almost choreographed, and creaked from time to time. It was great to have new scenery at last.

One of the great experiences of the Camino is the history. It just sort of smacks you in the face. Because many of the villages, towns, hamlets and even cities sprang up to cater for the ever-increasing numbers of pilgrims, you encounter aspects of the culture at every turn. The buildings in this area of France use huge, rectangular blocks of stone for the walls. The bottom of the roof tiles are curved as a decorative touch. Farms are common, indeed, many of the so called hamlets are in fact just a couple of farm buildings. Cow dung is cemented to the road and farm animals still pull carts and plough fields. Wherever you go, you hear wildly barking dogs. Timber beams protrude from walls, awnings lean out perilously, and everything looks as if it might collapse at any moment, although it had clearly been like that for centuries.

Iron crosses on top of large stone foundations reminded me I was on the right track. Some were constructed from wood, others had been elaborately forged from iron, the strips curled and wound by some expert blacksmith of years gone by. Some were barely waist-height, some towered over me, almost demanding attention by their very stature. Virtually every settlement was blessed with a church, a necessity for the pilgrims who travelled the Camino when religion was the law. Some were small and simple chapels, usually growing in grandeur with the size of the town. In places I could look at my surroundings and imagine I was in the Middle Ages. Few, if any modern distractions intruded; even the planes overheard seemed silent.

I had stopped at a café called Chez Régine in the small hamlet of Les Quatre Chemins. I ordered a Coke and a croque monsieur because that was all I could understand. I sat outside and looked around. No one was hurrying. An old tune wafted out from a radio, sharing the breeze with fragrances from the kitchen. Plastic Coca-Cola tables, faded from red to pink from the sun, broke up the small area at the front. I wrestled with the sunshade for a while and kicked my heels in the dust while over the road geese cackled and chickens pecked. Apart from the occasional clang of a saucepan from the kitchen, it was quiet.

That café marked the start of the Aubrac plateau. After diving in and out of forests and woods since the start, the route suddenly emerged into an area devoid of trees. The scenery reminded me of Dartmoor in south-west England: no trees, tracks meandering in no particular direction pinned in by waist-high granite walls, tall grasses bent over in the breeze. The ground was a rich chocolate brown, and occasionally I would have to skip over and around boggy areas. I remembered, when I was about ten years old and on one of our regular family holidays in Dartmoor, the feeling of the peat giving under my feet, the stiff breeze stealing the sweat off my forehead, and the rolling hills rising like the folds of a big blanket dumped on the floor.

There was still the occasional clump of trees, and as I walked through one, a sign led me to a spring with an old iron table and a couple of chairs. I shivered and gritted my teeth as I ducked my head under the cold water. It tasted somehow sweet and I must have taken a litre without coming up for air. As I was resting on one of the chairs, a French couple joined me. The woman spoke good English and we chatted as her companion gave my trekking poles a test run.

I had not used trekking poles before coming out to the Camino, but they had proved to be a godsend. At first I was worried I might look like a skier, but I soon felt lost without them. On the few occasions I forgot them after resting somewhere, I needed to walk only a few paces before I knew something was missing. On the flat terrain they were really just a means of rhythm. My arms would have something to do as well as my legs, and it felt good. I became accustomed to the click, click, click as the carbide tips hit the ground and I nicknamed them 'Click' and 'Clack'. On the descents they provided stability and balance. Some sections of the Camino are very steep and riddled with stones and boulders, sometimes wet and slippery from the rain. Add to this the weight of your pack, and you come to realise how treacherous some areas are. One slip could have meant the end of the walk for me, and Click and Clack held me up.

The real bonus was going uphill. Imagine how much easier it is if there is a banister to hold on to when you are climbing stairs. Click and Clack were my handrails: I could really lean into them and almost pull the rest of my body after. Sometimes, just to remind myself what a blessing they were, I used to stop using them suddenly, pulling them abruptly off the ground and parallel with the road, like a downhill skier. Immediately my pace would slow down, and I had to make more effort. I don't think I would consider hiking anywhere without them again.

The French guy seemed impressed as well, to judge from his approving nods.

"Why are you walking the Camino, Fozzie?" his companion Floret asked me.

"I'm not too sure," I replied. "Several reasons, I think. Spiritual energy, spare time for an adventure, for a nice, long walk, and maybe just because it's here."

"It is interesting that you say spiritual energy," she said. "How would you describe the energy you feel here?"

"I just feel great to be alive. Doesn't everything seem more colourful out here? Don't you notice the birds and the insects more? I can't explain something like that, I just know."

She smiled. "Yes, I know exactly what you mean. I feel it too, everybody feels it, and some notice it more than others."

I wondered why Floret was walking the Camino.

"I lost my husband some thirteen years ago. It was a hard time for me, and I realised then that I should have done something like this. A space as vast as this gives you opportunity to think about what has happened, and where you are going; it provides you with somewhere for your grief. And this is why I am walking with my friend: he lost his wife three months ago. I remembered how I felt, and suggested he walk here as I should have done. I came for him, really, but I am loving it."

I turned to him. He spoke no English so was not aware what we had been discussing, but I could tell from the look in his watery eyes that he didn't need a translation. I felt mine well up a little as well, and we smiled and nodded at each other to recognise understanding.

"I'm sorry," I said. He nodded that he understood.

"He is much better," she interjected. "The walk is doing him good. We have been walking for only two weeks, but already I notice the change. But what do you mean 'Because it's here'?"

I laughed. "I guess it's an English expression. Mountaineers say it about why they climb mountains. It means we do something simply because we can, maybe to prove to ourselves we are capable of it."

"I understand," she said. "I wish I could walk all the way too."

"What's stopping you?"

"Oh, you know. The house, bills, leaving my town, family."

I tried my best to encourage her. "Everyone is capable of travelling. What we think are obstacles are just inconveniences that can be overcome. First, you can let the house. The tenants are then responsible for the bills. Your friends, will be there when you get back, and no doubt extremely proud of you. I have seen lots of the world, and I will see more. I never wanted to get to the stage of being old and having regrets about not seeing anything that this planet has to offer. The number one issue for you, and anybody in your position, is having the guts to get up and make the decision. The rest is easy. I have been where you are, so I know how you feel. Sometimes, our problems are just up here," I said, tapping my head.

She smiled in agreement. "I know you are right. It is getting past the comfort zone of your normal life, and doing something out of your usual routine. It's a little scary."

"Well, I hope you have a great time, and I hope you both come back next year and finish the whole thing."

As I entered the town of Nasbinals, I decided a comfy night in a *gîte* was suitable reward for cranking out 29.5 kilometres that day, the most so far. There was a street market careering all over the road, just packing up for the day. I bought a slab of salami and some cheese to supplement my dwindling food stocks.

The *gîtes* were generally of a good standard, and this one was no exception. I found a spare bed in the upstairs dormitory and headed off for the shower. I had just soaped up when I was interrupted by a rapping on the door and someone calling, "Hey, man!"

I turned off the shower, and keeping my eyes shut because of the shampoo, called back, "Hello? Yeah? What's up?"

"Man, stop using the shower, it's running all down the stairs!"

"OK, hang on a sec." I turned the shower back on, knowing it would cause a commotion when they heard it outside, but I had a head full of shampoo and a body covered in soap that needed to come off. Sure enough, there was a rapping on the door.

"Hey man, turn off the shower!"

I carried on, the whole rinse procedure taking little more than thirty seconds.

"Hey! There's water coming out! Turn off the shower! Can you hear me?"

"Yeah, I can hear you," I said, tearing open the door and coming face to face with a French Canadian guy. "What the fuck did you expect me to do? I had a head and face full of shampoo. I had to rinse it off, I couldn't see a fucking thing, MAN!"

"Look, I'm sorry, I thought you couldn't hear me," he said, backing off a little.

"No worries". I shook his hand, smiled to disperse any friction, and helped him and a couple of others mop up the mess.

His name was Gerard. He was in his mid-forties with a

little grey hair poking through above his ears. He had a penchant for saying "Man" like some time-warped hippie from the sixties, made all the more amusing by his French accent. His casual gear was hiker branded material; he liked the best – and liked to advertise it. He was walking all the way from Le Puy to Santiago with his wife Chantelle and four friends. Other French Canadians had tagged on and the group had swelled to about ten.

After the little contretemps of our first meeting, Gerard and his entourage were a regular sight on the Camino and I used to look forward to seeing them, which happened at least every couple of days. Often I'd come across them sitting in the grass munching on their supplies, and Gerard would always greet me with, "Fozzie, hey, man, how's it going?"

The following morning I was rudely awoken at 5:15am. The plastic bag rustlers were out in force. A lot of pilgrims set out on their walk as early as possible, any time between 5:00 and 7:00am, so that they can finish the day's walking by midday, avoiding the higher temperatures and having the afternoon to recuperate. It makes perfect sense, I know, but logic does not apply when you are woken up at the crack of dawn every day by walkers stuffing their belongings into supermarket carrier bags. These familiar, innocent-looking holdalls seem the perfect solution to keeping gear dry and sorted. In fact, I used them myself. But that irritating daily rustling noise was starting to grate on my and others' nerves and was greeted by moans and angry faces and the wrapping of pillows over heads by those still in bed.

At first, people were genuinely concerned about waking other pilgrims. However, no matter how hard they tried, it was impossible to move those bags quietly. Eventually the rustlers, acting on the principle that everybody was awake already, just did their packing more loudly, ramming clothes into bags, ramming the bags into back packs, and so on, until the anti-bag-rustling lobbyists were almost ready for armed revolt. Why the hell, I wondered, didn't the early starters pack their shit the previous evening?

Although I was usually awoken early by the bag packers, I

would eventually drop off again. I have never really been an early riser. I resented having to get up at some unearthly hour to go to work and the phrase "So, we'll make an early start then!", far from rousing me to enthusiasm, generally did the opposite. I get up when my body feels ready, and if I find I am struggling to wake up or get out of bed, then I assume that it is plainly too early to be attempting it.

Five o'clock in the morning for me is no-man's-land, a twilight zone, an area I don't mess with. I usually got up around 8:00, slapped some water on my face, breakfasted on whatever I found in my food supplies, drank three cups of strong coffee, smoked a few roll-ups, threw my stuff in my pack and headed off around 9:30. So, I would be walking in the sun, so what? I would rather be walking in sun than darkness for the first hour. It would be hot. So what? Rather hot than a bit of a chill. So, I would finish around 3:00 or 4:00 in the afternoon. So what? That was ample time to wind down, eat and maybe go and do some sightseeing. And, to all potential pilgrims who read this, it would provide ample time to pack my kit before I went to bed!

Chapter Five

Finding My Pace

Some days I would remove my watch, a simple act, with interesting results. I would have to rely on my body to tell me when I needed things and take more notice of how I was feeling. Out on the Camino, I had no real need for the time. My watch had a compass, an altimeter and a barometer, which I used on occasion and came in handy, but mostly they were just toys.

During the early days of my walk, I would take a break for a cigarette after an hour, stop around one o'clock for lunch and set a goal to finish the day's walk around four. Without my timepiece it was different altogether. I went for a couple of hours without even realising I needed a cigarette.

One day, I decided I would stop for lunch when I was hungry, and when eventually I did stop to eat and check my watch, I found it was three o'clock. The pleasure of that surprise soon waned when I felt the familiar pressure of blisters again. It had been ten days since my improvised hospitalisation at the campsite at Saint Alban sur Limagnole, and despite the odd twinge, my feet were holding up well. I had walked only seventeen kilometres that day, but couldn't go any further. I had asked the universe for a solution several times: this was the day it was to arrive.

The town of Saint Chély d'Aubrac was very cute, but I was too angry and full of self-pity to notice. As I was sitting on a stone wall with a coke and a cigarette, I heard someone say my name.

"Hi, Fozzie." It was Walter. I had chatted to him briefly a few days earlier. He was walking with his wife, Barbara, and a friend called Oulie.

"You ok? You look a little down," he observed.

"Yeah, I guess so. I've got bloody blister problems again, can't seem to get rid of the things."

"Tell you what, Fozzie. I have to go into town to get some supplies. We are staying at the *gîte* here. I'll be back here in thirty minutes and I will take a look at your feet for you. I am a doctor of medicine".

"Fantastic!" I said, smiling broadly. "That's really good of you."

When he came back, he bade me follow him to the garden at the rear of the *gîte*. Barbara and Oulie were reclining on iron chairs, chatting and sipping on lemonades under low trees. If there had been a few amply bosomed females in long, white lace dresses daintily carrying parasols, the scene would have passed for something out of *Pride and Prejudice*.

I lay back on a sun lounger and slipped off my socks and boots. Wincing, I pulled off each of the six or so blister patches on each foot, and waited for the worst.

"Fozzie, this is no problem at all". I was a little taken aback by his initial prognosis.

"Are you sure?"

"Certainly. I thought your blisters may have been hurting because they were infected." He was checking each one with the precision of a watchmaker. "I am pleased to tell you that these are the cleanest-looking blisters I have ever seen, even cleaner than mine." I felt a strange little flush of pride.

"So why do they hurt so much, why do I keep getting them, and why won't they go away? I even rested for a few days a week or so ago to let them heal."

Walter's answer came as a big surprise. "That was probably the worst thing you could have done. The best advice I can give you, and I tell you this from experience of my walks, is to keep walking. Grin and bear it. If you stop to rest them, then the skin will just soften, which is the main problem in the first place. The trick with blisters is to keep plodding on. The more you walk, the more your skin toughens up and adapts to the task that is being asked of it. The human body is a wonderful thing, it can deal with lots of things, and sometimes it just needs a little time. Sometimes you just have to trust it."

His advice was starting to make sense.

"Each evening," he continued, "pierce them with a sterile needle and squeeze out the juice. You might want to give them a squirt of antiseptic liquid to be sure. Just make sure they are clean, and repeat the process the next evening. I guarantee you that your feet will take care of the rest. After a while the skin will become hard in the problem areas, and you can leave them be."

"Thanks, Walter, I feel better already." The way he explained things was wonderfully reassuring.

"What are you doing tonight?" he asked.

"Dunno. Why?"

"Come to dinner with us. There is a nice little restaurant in the main street, our treat."

"Look, I appreciate the offer, but I couldn't ..."

He brushed my objections aside. "We'd like your company, and it looks like you could do with some cheering up."

It was a good evening: the first real meal at a decent restaurant I had encountered on the Camino. We communicated in French, German, English and Greek. The wine flowed, the food was great. No cooking, no clearing up. We exchanged email addresses as we parted and I wobbled, a little worse for wear from the wine, back to the *gîte*, where I tripped up the steps and woke a few people up, including three French Canadians in my room. However, they were inveterate bag rustlers, so I drifted off to sleep, contented with a little revenge.

The following morning I was raring to go. Although the blisters were still painful, I was confident about Walter's advice. It was a beautiful morning. As I made my way down a hill out of town, the early morning mist was still clearing. I passed over a small bridge spanning the river Boralde and up past the cemetery dominating the hill. The Camino entered a silver birch wood set halfway up a long slope. It was eerily quiet. The sun's rays spliced through the damp air from my left, like a torch shining through the smoke from a fire. The ground was soft and I felt good, really good.

According to the guidebook, this was gorge country: no huge ravines, but rocky outcrops littering the area. Trees clung to cliff edges, their exposed roots grasping helplessly to the edge like giant hands. The clear waters of streams meandered around millions of polished stones, gently shelving into the water like a series of small beaches. Sunlight lit up leaves as the branches swayed and cast constantly moving shadows and the beautiful smell of damp, peaty earth reached my nostrils from time to time.

I joined a small side road for a while. A sign intended for vehicles boldly warned of a T-junction – three kilometres ahead! "Good God," I thought. "What are we supposed to do, start to brake now?"

I started to climb. I hadn't really encountered much in the way of steep inclines up to this stage. This one wasn't very long, perhaps a kilometre or so, but when I reached the top I was dripping with sweat. There was a farm, boasting a fridge, which looked completely out of place by the side of the trail. It was stocked full of sugary goodies – cans of Coke and other fizzy mixtures, chocolate, mini cakes. A sign on it asked pilgrims to take what they needed and leave the money in the basket. There was even a notepad to sign. I picked out a few treats and wandered off, munching. This, I thought, must be the only known fridge in the Western world equipped with a visitors' book.

At lunchtime I wandered into a small grocery store in Saint Côme d'Olt. My salami was perspiring alarmingly, and the cheese was sprouting furry stuff. It was one of those classic places that specialised in nothing, but had pretty much everything, including the elusive camping gas cartridge, just visible over the side of a box tucked into a corner. My existing one had lasted longer than I had expected, even though for the last few days it had been running off fumes.

As I shuffled through the aisles, something else took me by surprise. "Well, fancy seeing you here," I said to myself. "I never expected to see you in the middle of France." But there she was, a tin of Heinz Baked Beans, her head covered in a layer of dust, nestling among inferior friends. I took her to the till, feeling her coldness in my hand, paid and tucked her safely in my pack.

That afternoon I crossed the river Lot, where the locals frolicked in the water to escape the burning temperature. The river on my right kept me company for a couple of hours. To my left, huge automatic sprayers sent curving jets of water over the tall, thirsty parallel lines of maize that loomed over me. Before long, the Pilgrims' Bridge over the river came into view as I reached the striking town of Espalion. Medieval buildings with emaciated beams from years of weather abuse leaned perilously over the river. The park was alive with the clinks of boules, children yelled, fisherman cast nets into the shallow waters and lovers strolled. The place just beckoned me to rest there the night. There was a *gîte*, somewhere, but it looked so tranquil by the river that I decided I would sleep rough.

I crossed over the bridge, turned right and wove through narrow streets until the river appeared again. A small area of water by the bank was calm and devoid of any current, hemmed in by some strategically placed stones, perhaps as a swimming area. I took it as a hint that I needed a bath and stripped down to my boxers, then, realising that most of the locals must have seen a naked bottom at some time, removed them as well. The relief was enormous as the water momentarily chilled me and washed away the day's sweat and filth. It felt fantastic. As I surfaced, I caught sight of a couple of old ladies chuckling at me from the other bank.

What would have been the reaction in other countries I wondered? In England, I might have received a few disapproving glances, some finger-pointing and some stifled chuckles. The Italian police (my personal favourites) would have eventually moved me on politely, but not before stopping for a chat and bringing me an espresso and offering me a smoke. In India, I probably would have had several hundred locals for company also washing and doing laundry. In America, I probably would have been arrested, first for indecent exposure and then for loitering, with "probable intention to dive dangerously" thrown in for good measure. Here, the inhabitants of the town just walked their dogs at dusk, smiling an acknowledgment my way, giving me the odd wave. With the river tumbling a few feet away and some good fresh air, I enjoyed the best sleep I'd had in days.

In the morning, I wanted to check my emails, but discovered that Espalion was devoid of any public internet facilities. Internet cafés, I was told by the woman at the tourist information desk, can be found only in the larger towns and cities like Paris.

"Jeez," I muttered, checking my guidebook on the way out. "There are 5,000 people living here, how large do you want it?" But I could sympathise with their wish to hang on to their culture and I would rather have a town full of character with no internet café than the reverse.

Some people go as far as to refer to hiking as meditation. Others simply like it as relaxation, some as exercise. To me it provides all of the above. I got lost in my own thoughts many times on the Camino, and often when I stopped for a rest, I would realise that I remembered none of the past few kilometres.

Walking does this to me. I get into my own mind: where I am going, where I have been, the next step of my life, plans, ideas, goals, etc. It gives me the chance to sort out my life. Dreaming like this on the Camino, I would miss direction signs and have to retrace my steps to find the way. Other times I would forget when I saw the last marker, and have no idea when the next one would appear.

Sometimes, exercising my mind became more conscious. When it was a bleak and boring stretch of walking, for example, I played games to pass the time. A song might pop into my head for no particular reason, and I would end up singing it for the rest of the day. Back at home, that song of the day was usually the first song I heard on the alarm clock in the morning; it would worm its way into my subconscious as I struggled to emerge from under the duvet. Out here, I had no source to feed me tunes, except the odd radio. There were the obvious favourites that I had accumulated over the years. And there were also those dreadful songs that you might hear on a pub jukebox – offerings from Abba, early stuff from Madonna, maybe even the Bee Gees. On exceptionally corrupt days, my desperate subconscious really came up with some crap. Trouble is, as hard as I tried, once embedded, that song of the day is nigh on impossible to root out. There was little I could do when I realised I was humming along to "Showaddywaddy" or doing a rendering of "This Ol' House" by Shakin' Stephens. Today, however, I plummeted to new depths, involuntarily humming the theme tune to "Cagney and Lacey".

Autumn was approaching. I could sense it, even without the obvious visual reminders. The air smelled different, night trespassed a little earlier each day, bringing the occasional chilly spell. Leaves started to change from summer greens to browns, yellows, golds and rubies, and each day there would be a few more fluttering about on the ground. The sun seemed to take a little longer to heat the air and on some mornings a mist hung low, obscuring the countryside like a translucent window. I love the summer; I dislike winter. Autumn is that pleasant interim period where I am sad that the hot days have passed, but am not yet quite dreading the cold ones. If summer was a fresh chocolate éclair with cream oozing from the sides, and winter was a cream cracker, then autumn might be a jam doughnut. It was pleasant security.

I reached Golinhac late evening after climbing for what felt like hours, although in fact I had probably covered only about ten kilometres. I pitched tent in the grounds of the *gîte*. There I met a Dutch guy called Gare, who was finishing his two weeks on the Camino the following day and who plied me with offerings that he no longer needed: blister patches, antiseptic cream, needles, medi-tape. The true godsend, though, was some herbal cream, designed for aching feet. Gare demanded that I try it there and then. I tell you no lies when I describe this stuff as foot orgasm in a tube. It was awesome. The harder I rubbed, the better it felt, if you'll pardon the pun.

I had decided to head for Conques and take a day's rest. I had heard much about this historic medieval town, itself a national monument along with many of its buildings. Here I could recuperate in classic surroundings, with some good food, a hot shower – and, I hoped, the chance to see the World Cup soccer qualifier between England and Germany. Boy, would I be pissed off if I missed that one.

Conques lived up to its reputation and then some. It was touristy, but as it was the end of August, the numbers were dwindling. I had deliberately left only fifteen kilometres or so to walk in the morning, so I would arrive relatively early, have a leisurely afternoon, and make the most of my rest stop the following day.

The village clung to the side of a small, tree-choked valley, blocking the view of the river. Conques seems to have become caught in a time warp, resisting change. Not only were the streets cobbled, probably with the original stones, but there was even straw here and there, spilt off the back of a cart.

Little stone channels in the middle of streets ferried water away after a passing storm I had just missed. The uneven stone surface still glistened with the moisture. Moss stuck in the cracks glowed a radiant green. Medieval buildings unscathed through the centuries displayed dark timber beams and ancient stone and brickwork. Stairs disappeared up and down. Alleys wound back and forth. The whole place was a maze, a labyrinth of pristine comeliness. Handpainted signs in black and gold dangled over shop doors. Small, cosy, smoky cafes plied for trade. Children giggled, as though the serenity of the locality affected them too.

It was futile trying to catch a glimpse of a telephone wire or a satellite dish. Not that I wanted to see one: I just wanted to catch someone out, who might have overlooked something.

It was almost as if Conques had survived from the eighth century, through countless battles, because the enemy couldn't bear to destroy it.

Conques was blessed with two relatively economical places to stay. Gare had advised me to take advantage of the lodgings at the Abbey of Ste Foy (Saint Faith), rather than at the *gîte*. I passed the *gîte* on the outskirts and took a look out of curiosity. It was clean enough, but there were no facilities to cook or even eat. The beds were so close together that if you were to turn over in the middle of the night, you would probably end up on top of the person next to you. So I carried on down into the village centre to seek out lodgings in the Abbey.

It took a while back tracking down streets and back passages to locate it. I couldn't exactly miss the Abbey, which loomed out of the centre as if it was attempting to grasp the clouds. As usual, when all else failed, there was security in following the other pilgrims. They were either heading out on the Camino or looking for somewhere to stay. I walked down past the tourist office, down some steps to an inner courtyard with a well in the centre, where laughing kids were trying to fish money out of the water. Passing under a stone archway, I saw the path lead up to a door, which swung open, revealing a glimpse of an inner yard through another archway. A map displayed the route of the Camino, and as I went for a closer look, a voice floated over from an office on the left. I turned and saw a woman looking at me, confirming she was talking to me.

"I'm sorry," I said to the middle-aged lady behind the desk. "I don't speak French. Do you speak English?"

The woman smiled and pointed to a seat in front of her. She called to someone in French, and after a while a man appeared, who took her place behind an old wooden desk, smiled and adjusted his glasses.

Before he could speak, I heard a voice saying, "Please, I really want to." I glanced over my shoulder to see an American woman, perhaps in her early twenties. She looked despondent.

"No, I told you, first you must finish the Camino. I'm sorry, that is the way we and all of the *gîtes* operate. There are no exceptions. Now please, I have to help this gentleman." He motioned to me, and she puffed her shoulders and stormed out.

"She stayed here for a week," the man explained, turning to me, "fell in love with the Abbey, and with Conques, and wanted to volunteer to work here."

"Is that a problem?"

"No, not really. We get many requests each week, offers of work. We have a rule. People who want to volunteer here, well, we need to know they are serious, and not just out for a summer of free lodging, even if they are working. They need to know what it is like to have finished the Camino. They need to be able to answer pilgrims' questions. How far it is to there, what the terrain is like, where to stay. But most importantly, to prove to us that they are willing to complete a goal to contribute to what we do here."

"I see," I nodded.

"If she is serious about helping here, she will be back. We already have applications from pilgrims who have finished the Camino to work here next year. All the positions are taken, and we have more applications waiting to hear. Anyway, I presume you want to stay here?"

"Yes, for two nights please. I am taking a day's rest tomorrow."

"This is not a problem. We have plenty of space. Do you want any meals? We have breakfast and evening meal."

"Er, no thanks. I'll be fine."

He looked genuinely concerned.

"I don't want to force you into eating here," he said, "but Conques is expensive, very expensive. It is teeming with tourists, and the restaurants know it. We have great staff and they really do a fantastic meal in the evening, several courses. Breakfast is all you can eat, coffee, orange juice, muesli, toast. The…"

"OK, OK. You persuaded me. How much is it?"

"One hundred and eleven francs. That is your bed and meals for one night. So, two hundred and twenty-two francs for the two nights."

It was about twenty-two pounds. I would struggle to find even bed and breakfast for one night at that amount back home. He led me up a stone, spiral staircase to the dormitory, giving me a mini guided tour as we went. It was a beautiful place. The stone had softened over the years to a series of curved edges and pastel shades. Windows and arches offered glimpses of the village and valley, and closed doors made me wonder what was on the other side.

"By the way, I want to see a soccer game on Saturday night. Do any of the bars here have satellite TV, or do you know of a place where I might be able to see it?"

"I don't think you will have much luck," he said. "There is no satellite reception here because the dishes go against planning laws. There are a few bars that do have TVs, but they will probably show the French game. It may be worth asking."

The whole place was scrupulously clean. Old and basic, but spotless. Even the tiles in the washroom gleamed, with not even a streak mark. My dormitory room held about fourteen bunk beds. Large windows were open and a cool breeze wove through, rustling papers, playing with clothing hung on beds and cooling me off. My window looked down on a small garden on the edge of the village. All I could really see was plants and trees and the valley tumbling away. I could have been in a cottage, alone in the middle of nowhere.

There must have been fifty pilgrims eating that night. It reminded me of the school canteen: long tables with people facing each other, rubbing their hands in anticipation. Before the food was served, the man who checked me in gave a small speech welcoming us all. Then we all joined in to a communal song, the lyrics of which had been written on a board. It was called Ultreya and although in French, I could tell it was a hymn of faith of some kind. That song stuck with me for the rest of the Camino, becoming my "song of the day" several times, and I often heard others humming and reciting the words as they walked. The words were written in visitors' books everywhere, it was sung around meal tables and I even saw "Ultreya" written as graffiti on walls by the side of the road or in the dust on the trail. I didn't need to know the translation. If there was one word that meant El Camino, it was "Ultreya". We walkers only needed to see the word somewhere, and we would grin and relive our experiences of the past few weeks. It was not until some five years later that a friend told me that "Ultreya" was a Spanish word derived from Latin, meaning *Onward!* It was in common use by pilgrims to greet and encourage one another along the way.

That evening I did a tour of the bars to find out if any planned to show the England game the following evening. I'm not a hard-core soccer fan but for me the world stops when England plays, especially if our opponents are Germany. And I'm not alone: passions fly, tempers fray, emotions burn and pride matters. Short of falling of a cliff, I was determined to watch.

The responses were not good. Wherever I went, I was told they would be showing the French game, not the England game because of the lack of satellite dishes. Dejected, I realised I would have to leave Conques and seek out some hotel where I was assured coverage.

Leaving Conques was hard, but I made an early start for once and followed the Camino down to the valley floor, where it crossed over the River Dordou. As I turned around a breath of mist was creating eddies over and around the Chapelle Saint Roch perched above me. The outline was silhouetted by the early morning sun. It was beautiful, eerie, and an awesome farewell.

I had reached the first day of September, the day I had I always regarded as the end of the summer and the start of autumn, at least back home. There was a definite chill in the air and I hoped I could make it to Santiago before winter really took a grip. I also passed the two hundred kilometre mark on leaving Conques, which, I calculated, meant I had done two-fifteenths of the total distance of the walk. I had been going for sixteen days. That put me bang on course for three months to complete the trip. I felt a little surge of excitement. Perhaps I would actually do this thing! I had two cigarettes on my break to celebrate.

I arrived in Decazeville early afternoon, a disappointingly ugly town with all the trimmings of the twentieth century. Most places were shut until around three, so I treated myself to a burger and fries and a chocolate éclair, all washed down with a Coke. Good staple, healthy nourishment …

At the tourist office, a middle-aged woman peered up at me from behind the counter. Thick, bifocal glasses made her look like a cartoon character realising a train is about to run them over.

"Bonjour," I said. "Parlez-vous anglais?" My French lessons at school had never covered the possibility of asking for a hotel room for the night with cable facilities capable of showing an England international game.

"Yes, I speak English. How can I help?" she responded. Things were definitely looking up.

"Erm, well, it's a bit of a strange request, really. I need a room tonight, but I need to watch a football game that will only be on cable or satellite. Somewhere cheap, as long as they have this facility."

"Ok. I don't think it will be a problem. There are two or three places that come to mind." She leafed through a booklet and circled two options. "These two are around two hundred to two hundred and fifty francs. They both have cable. Would you like me to call one of them to confirm, and make a reservation for you?"

"That would be great, thank you."

A few minutes later I was bounding along with a serious spring in my step humming "Football's Coming Home". What made the game that much more important was that if we did not win it, England had very little chance of qualifying for the World Cup.

The Hotel Foulquier was set back from Avenue Victor Hugo and from the outside looked like an American motel.

The interior was like a throwback from the eighties. The colour scheme was pink and black. Flowery curtains clashed with striped wallpaper, all bottomed off with a grey carpet. At least it was clean, and at least it had a TV. I made a pre-game sweep of the channels. Eurosport was available, as well as a French sports channel which would certainly be showing the French game, but might offer highlights of the main match. These were two promising options. I restrained myself from becoming too excited, but did manage a small smile of anticipation.

The art of watching football is that you get up only once during a match to stretch your legs, at halftime. This means all necessary requirements must be to hand. There is a syndrome known as "absent scoring". Most fans will confirm that the moment you get up from the game to have a pee or make a coffee, someone will score. This is why it is imperative to visit the toilet, make your drink, kiss your girlfriend and apologise for the ensuing abuse of expletives, and do whatever else needs to be done, before you sit down. I had prepared well. My meal from the hamburger joint lay beside me. Several cans of Guinness nestled within easy reach of my right hand. Popcorn was at the ready. I had even rolled several cigarettes before so I would not have to avert my eyes. It was perfect.

The TV flickered to life. Sure enough, the French game was the main offering. I turned to Eurosport, shut my eyes, then slowly squinted through the cracks in my eyelids hoping to see little men running around a green pitch. No such luck. What were they showing? Clay pigeon shooting! Bloody clay pigeon shooting! I was furious, seething. How could the management of a European cable company insult me with that crap!

I suffered two hours of clay pigeon shooting on one channel and the French national team on the other, hoping in vain they would tempt me with some highlights. I eventually managed to grab a report from CNN around midnight. At least we won, 5:0. I was ecstatic. It took me a week to get over it.

Pilgrims don't just walk the Camino, although that is easily the most popular method. I saw many riding bicycles and a few on horseback. Bernard, whom I met one day, had different ideas. Plodding alongside him was a donkey, which carried all his gear, so Bernard was able to afford a few luxuries. All he carried on his back was a day pack containing a few sandwiches. Donkeys do have drawbacks as well as benefits, he told me.

"For starters, they walk slower. I cannot walk ahead because he would get lost. So I have to walk at his pace. It's frustrating at times but I have got used to it. After all, I am not in any hurry. Secondly, he needs food. And by food I mean prime hay. He can nibble on grass during the day for his snacks, but he needs his hay fix in the evening. If he doesn't get his hay, he doesn't go anywhere. Thirdly, he knows his distance. When we hit twenty kilometres at the end of the day, his built-in mileage gauge kicks in, and he just stops. I can't budge him, he's there for the night. So I am limited, but we have a pattern now. After all, he is doing me a favour. It's only right I should indulge his little whims."

For some reason the approach to Figeac was lacking in water supplies. Usually I would pass a couple of water sources each day, which was all I needed. By lunchtime I had run out. As I walked past a house attached to a large barn, an old chap was cutting his whiskers, holding a small hand mirror.

"Bonjour, Monsieur," I called, asking in pidgin French whether he had any water and pointing to my empty water bladder. This was a mistake. If my French hadn't confused him, then the water container with a tube dangling around my knees certainly had. He came down and, holding the bag gingerly, with two fingers, peered in and smelt it as if it was some sort of enema equipment.

I tried to explain, making glugging noises with my throat, and imitating turning a tap with my hand and holding the bag under it. I was just about to crawl along the ground holding up a pleading hand like a soul lost in the desert when he smiled and led me up the stairs to his modest two-roomed flat. He filled the bag for me, and gave me two glasses of first-rate French plonk as a bonus. I remember thinking as I left him that I should practise this method more often. Not only was this a genuine opportunity to obtain water and to get to know some French people, but I might also even get the odd titbit of food thrown in. I spent the rest of the day practising my French, pulling hungry and thirsty facial expressions, and generally trying to look weary for my next attempt.

If I had known more about plants, I could probably have survived the whole Camino living off the land. There were blackberry bushes everywhere. Hedgerows groaned and stooped over and walls disappeared as the season's fruits, sprouting from all locations, tumbled and draped over them. Mint plants poked their heads through grass at the side of the path. In fact, I could smell them before I saw them. I was reminded of my grandmother, who used to throw a handful of leaves into the pot of boiling new potatoes. In autumn, chestnuts turned the path into a shimmer of mahogany. The fields were full of sweetcorn, tender and bursting with freshness. I could have dined on mushrooms and fungi and in Spain there were even cumin plants, releasing an inviting waft of curry into the air, which puzzled me until I finally figured out where it was coming from. Rosemary bushes, huge and deep green in colour, had me scrambling over walls to retrieve a small stock. I would 'steal' a few potatoes from the edge of crop fields, and boil or roast them with mint or the rosemary. Apples were regular friends, plums glistened in the light like precious stones. Indeed, the whole Camino was one mammoth outdoor fruit and vegetable market.

Chapter Six

From a Good Plan to a Bad Plan

"Nirvana" had been rolling around in my head for a couple of days. I rarely know the titles of songs; I just know the ones I like. When someone asks me about an album I'm fond of, and what my favourite track is, I usually just say, "The third one is great" or, "I love chilling out to track eight." "Nothing on top but a bucket and mop, and an illustrated book about birds," went this song. I just hummed the rest because I couldn't remember most of the lyrics either.

I was on the approach to Le Causse, a limestone plateau with scrubby vegetation and scruffy, stunted trees. I stopped at Gréalou. My food stocks had dwindled pathetically to a cereal bar and enough rice to produce maybe a portion of sushi. The épicerie promised in my book was long gone. The only option was a bar café. It would have meant more than my budget would allow, but the craving in my stomach was overriding the logic in my head. A pilgrim walked out.

"Hello," he said. He was French but somehow knew I was English. His name was Gérard.

"Hi," I said.

"If you are looking for something to eat, I wish you good luck. The Madame has been left on her own. Her assistant has gone off somewhere, so she is doing everything by herself. Cooking, drinks, being a waitress, and she is trying to have her lunch as well. She is a bit stressed."

"Thanks, I'll watch my back," I said, smiling.

The place was empty except for a group of four pilgrims and another couple flirting in the corner. "How hard can it be to run this place with six customers?" I wondered as I approached the bar. After waiting a while, I "accidentally" dropped my loose change on the counter to attract some attention. There was movement and the owner appeared through a doorway. She approached in a menacing manner with a hard stare, sort of like a boxer eyeing up the opposition. She stopped by me, wiped some stray lunch from her mouth, put both hands on the bar and looked at me, saying nothing.

"Bonjour," I offered. For some reason I derive great pleasure from toying with people who are already annoyed. It's like playing with a lighter and fireworks at the same time. I smiled and let a silence hover for a few seconds to get some sort of reaction.

"Oui!" she spat.

Wiping the spit out of one eye, and giving her another annoying smile, I scanned the bar.

"Une Coke. And ... er ... avez-vous a menu, please?"

"No menu," she stammered and then volleyed off a few, rapid sentences of which I understood nothing.

"She said she only has a meat sandwich, a kind of salami. I had one myself, it wasn't good, but it's edible if you're hungry." One of the pilgrims, who I later learned was called Bernard, had come up to the bar to help, as he knew I would have problems with my limited French.

"Thanks," I replied. The look on his face suggested he was enjoying watching her suffer too. I ordered a sandwich and a packet of crisps.

As she opened the fridge, most of the contents crashed over the floor. She released a hurl of abuse so frightening that half the customers cowered under the table.

I escaped outside with Bernard and his wife joined us. He offered me the rest of his wine as they were heading off.

"Thanks for all that," I said.

"No problem," he replied. "See you on the trail."

The salami in the sandwich resembled old leather, but it

tasted OK. The Coke was barely cold, and the crisps were stale. I was too hungry to care. I berated myself for letting my food supplies dwindle. There is nothing worse than having nothing to eat and nowhere to buy anything. I remembered a cycling trip through Europe a few years earlier. It was Saturday, and the shops all closed on Sundays, so I had procured all the necessities to last me the weekend. On the Saturday evening I settled down at my campsite to cook up a stew with the fresh vegetables in my bag. It was then I realised my stove was out of fuel.

Le Causse was, indeed, a strange area of France. The plants and trees seemed stunted somehow, as though they were trying to grow but a huge hand was pressing down on them. The trees were mainly oak, but barely managed a height of ten feet. A type of gorse bush grew everywhere, tugging on my clothing as I brushed past. Chalky rocks protruded from reddish soil. My guidebook had given me the impression that the trees on Le Causse were sparse, as on the Aubrac plateau. On the contrary, however, most of the landscape was taken up by these diminutive trees. It was eerie, even scary at times.

Part of my mission on this walk was to hone any spiritual "skills" I had, to become more in tune with my feelings, to take more notice of events and their meanings. I wanted to be able to experience what was going on around me. I did succeed; after all, I was blessed with plenty of time to practice. I walked into a wood and immediately felt ill at ease. It was dark, the sunlight struggled to make any inroads and it smelled damp and musty, not a pleasant dampness, more a stench of rot. The trees were stunted, twisted, misshapen. Plants were pathetic shades of green, flowers limp and with incomplete petals. There was no breeze, nothing moved and it was silent. I felt as though not one but many people were watching me, like in those cartoons when someone is walking through the dark and little white eyes appear behind them.

I began to walk faster. I felt as though I was being chased, as though if I looked around something would be running after me. Eventually the trees thinned and I reached a small road. I crossed and entered another similar wood, but I felt totally secure there. Everything looked the same, but there were noises, a breeze would ruffle my hair once in a while, it felt safe. So what had happened? To this day I wonder. I just knew something bad had happened in that place. It was as though a hundred souls had been lost in there.

In the early days of the Camino, the route was riddled with bandits. They would pick on pilgrims, and they knew the most productive areas to lie in wait. Woods and forests were ideal. They could hide even a few feet from the path and be totally hidden from view. Many pilgrims were robbed of what little possessions they carried. Many were murdered. Had that wood been such a place? Was it still harbouring the energy of what used to happen there? I have experienced similar emotions in certain places in the past. However, it never felt as strong and certain as it had done that day in that place. I was sincerely glad to get out.

I carried on churning out the kilometres. By this stage I was so attuned to my walking speeds and distances that I knew exactly, almost to the minute, when I would arrive somewhere. My natural speed, I calculated, was about four and a half kilometres an hour. I could push up to as much as seven kilometres an hour but I hardly ever needed to. I wasn't in a hurry, and there were very few occasions when I had to be in a certain place at a certain time. It also damn near killed me every time I kept this pace up. However, it was interesting experimenting.

By now I was even confident enough to question the guidebook. The author, quite rightly, had based her calculations on an average speed. So, when I read about a detour of "seven hundred and fifty metres, or about eleven minutes", I would say to myself, "Actually, that's only about ten minutes". When other pilgrims said they were aiming for a town to rest overnight, and they would be there at five o'clock, I knew I would probably be relaxing on my bunk when they arrived, as my pace is just as little faster than other people's. Not something to be particularly proud of, just the way I'm made.

Cajarc appeared below me as I crested a hill. As I carefully made my way down the remaining thirty minutes or so, it became clear how beautiful not only the town was, but also its setting. It was completely encircled by chalk cliffs, like the sides of a volcano crater. If this place had ever come under attack in the past, it must have been easy pickings. Any opposing army would simply have set up their trebuchets on the surrounding hills and flattened the place.

The campsite was ideal. Neat little trimmed hedges bordered each plot; it was like having your own garden. Most of the tourists had retreated back home in time to get their children to school for the new term. I had stocked up at the shop with lots of goodies to replenish my aching limbs and now badly needed a carbohydrate fix.

A French guy had set up camp in the next "garden". After he had tinkered with his motorbike and finished an hour-long conversation on his mobile, he came over.

Christoph, who spoke good English, was a motorbike mechanic on two weeks' biking holiday. He had a friendly demeanour, and we sat and talked for a while as potatoes bubbled on my stove.

"You want a beer?" I asked after I had eaten.

"Sure, we can go into town," he said, looking excited and rubbing his hands in anticipation.

Cajarc was spookily quiet. I realised that most of the locals were tucked up in the bars that dotted the centre. We chose a suitable spot and sat down outside. Although it was the beginning of September and well into the evening, the nights were still warm. Christoph sipped on a vivid yellow drink that I had not seen before.

"It is called Suze," he explained. "It is brewed from the roots of a plant that grows in this region. You may have seen them, the flowers are yellow and it is quite common, about so high." His hand indicated his waist.

"Yeah, I have seen them. How does it taste?" He let me have a sip. It was very sweet, with a taste so unusual I was unable even to describe it, but it was damn good.

We chewed the fat for a couple of hours, talking of the Camino, motorbikes, the weather and McDonald's. I am not a huge fan of the great burger chain, but I do succumb to the odd Filet-O-Fish. Since my arrival in France they had been few and far between.

"They are here," Christoph began to explain, "but we put them where they belong, a good couple of kilometres out of town."

"Because you want to keep your villages as they are, your heritage intact?"

"Yes, exactly. We do not want to become part of this Westernisation process, where all the local businesses are forced to close because a large garden centre or supermarket has opened up. We do not want huge shopping malls dominating our culture, destroying our villages and towns. In the large cities like Paris maybe, but not in places like this."

"It's a good attitude," I said. "I feel the same way about England. We are slowly destroying our small village businesses and shops by letting the large chain stores take over. It saddens me too."

"Here in France," he agreed, "we value what we have. Look at this square here. We still have the butchers and the bakers. You can buy your vegetables fresh every day from the greengrocer who is trading with the local farmer. The cake shop continues to bake as it has done for years. It is how people like it; they are comfortable with it. If the council receives an application from McDonald's or some DIY chain to build in the centre, it is often rejected or, at best, given permission to build out of town, but they know that is not the ideal spot, so sometimes they give up. We don't need change. We just want France to retain some sort of individuality.

"We still keep the same opening hours, nine to twelve and two to seven, or thereabouts," he went on, warming to the theme more and more. "People here don't want to be able to go and buy an electric chainsaw at ten in the evening. We don't need a twenty-four hour pharmacy. If we need a new carpet, we call Pierre, the carpet guy. Maurice services our vehicles and Claude deals with the plumbing. It works. Why do people feel they need to change it?"

We staggered out of the bar around midnight. I lost count of how many times we both tripped over something, laughed out loud at something not really that funny and generally behaved extremely immaturely, as only two drunks know how.

I woke in the morning fully clothed with both legs inside the tent and the rest of my body outside, resting on the grass. To my surprise, I had no hangover, which I put down to the Suze and dangerously made a mental note that it was acceptable too drink too much of the stuff.

I am a "glass half full" sort of guy but I'm also a realist. I know the law of averages dictates that it is highly unlikely that anyone can walk 1600 Kilometres without at some point falling over, or at least coming close. That morning, walking out of Cajarc, I proved myself right.

It was innocent enough. I was merrily walking down a narrow track pinned in by bushes at head height when they suddenly cleared on my left to reveal a small, stone wall. On the other side some family had obviously spent the fruits of their labours on their dream cottage, renovated to perfection. Beside the swimming pool lay an extremely attractive, bikini-clad woman, soaking up the sun. Her legs were endless, her tanned skin glistened with droplets of perspiration, and she ... well, you get the picture. After three weeks of meeting backpacking women clad in hiking boots and ridiculous sunhats, you can imagine how I felt. My pace naturally slowed a little. It slowed a lot. In fact, if I had been going any slower, I would have stopped. She looked up. I looked at her. I smiled, she smiled. We held each other's gaze, still smiling.

It was like that scenario you see in the movies sometimes. Man and woman lock eyes, man walks into lamppost. There were no lampposts here, but there was one hell of a huge boulder. As my right foot smashed into it, I felt myself going over, the weight of the pack pushing me forward. My arms flung and flapped around for anything to grab on to to save falling. It was all happening in slow motion. God only knows how it must have looked from her angle. One minute there was a torso bobbing up and down behind her wall, the next moment it had disappeared.

Somehow, I didn't hit the deck but ran on all fours trying to retrieve my balance, and eventually I did. I popped up behind the wall a few metres further on, to see her hand over her mouth and her breasts in sync with her giggling. I bowed, she applauded, and I walked off to save further loss of face.

I was getting fitter, feeling less tired as each day passed and climbing hills like a man possessed. I felt good, really good. Muscles were starting to bulge in my legs where I didn't even know there were muscles. Even my upper body was firming up from using the trekking poles. My breathing was less laboured. I had always considered myself relatively fit. I cycled, on occasions I went to the gym, I jogged, and I swam. But the Camino was giving my body newfound energy. My daily distances were slowly creeping up too. At this stage I was averaging around twenty-two kilometres a day, although I knew I was capable of doing around thirty.

One day I was slumped on a bench under an oak tree in the little hamlet of Bach, pencil in one hand and notebook in the other, totalling up the distance for the day. I had two surprises. First, I had finally managed to break the elusive thirty-kilometre barrier. To me it was like completing a marathon. I had come close before, twenty-seven, twenty-nine and a half. Better still, I had reached the milestone without much fatigue.

Second, as I wrote my journal that night, it hit me that, after walking for nineteen days, I had covered over three hundred kilometres, one fifth of the total distance of the Camino. At first I was elated with the realisation that I was actually capable of doing this thing. Then my excitement waned as I took in what a small dent it actually was. Twenty percent, it was nothing really. The pros and cons twisted round in my head. I was proud of my achievement to date, but battering their way through these positive feelings was the memory of those tough days, all those monotonous stretches that I thought would never end and the knowledge that I had a whole lot more to get through. I couldn't figure out why these negative thoughts insisted on pushing their way forward. I concluded that I was just making the challenge tougher than it was, to prove to myself that, for once in my life, I was capable of reaching a goal. I was determined not to be beaten into submission this time, not to take the easy option. I was becoming stronger, learning to take the route that might be more difficult but that offered bigger rewards.

I woke to a serene morning. As I crawled out of the tent, a veil of mist undulated over the field as though an artist had just painted it, his brush merely glancing the canvas. Dew shone in the grass, each blade bent over with the weight of a moisture droplet. The toll of the church bell in Bach seemed hushed as though it was embarrassed to break the silence, and horse hooves clattered a way off. I arched my back and stretched, trying to find some sunlight through the trees to warm myself. While my pan lid rattled over the boiling water, I rummaged around in my food bag and tore off pieces from a stale baguette. I cleared up, hoisted my pack and wandered away, my mind occupied with thoughts of nothing more than a day's stroll.

I had been wondering why, during the past couple of weeks, a lot of the *gîtes* were booked before I even got there. I was one of the first to arrive but the owners usually shrugged their shoulders with a resigned look. Several times I had been forced to walk out of town and camp, not that this was a problem but a shower and a restaurant always lifted the spirits at day's end. A French pilgrim I met enlightened me.

"I have my mobile with me. I stay at *gîtes* every night but I call and book three nights in advance," he said.

I had purposely left my mobile at home, horrified by the thought of it ringing and beeping and disturbing the ambience of the Camino. I had come to walk precisely to escape such modern distractions. It seemed wrong to me that those of us who didn't carry a mobile were being deprived of a bed for the night by those who did. Where was the camaraderie in that? I looked forward to arriving in Spain, where the refugios, as the lodgings are known, do not accept bookings. It was at it should be, first come first served. I am not saying that everyone should leave their mobile behind. To a lone pilgrim, this little device may provide a lifeline in an emergency. In the meantime, I was content with camping out for five or so nights a week, and taking my chances at the *gîtes* when I got there.

Other walkers had GPS units. If you are lost in the middle of the Sahara or in an uncharted jungle, then they are a necessity. What would we need them on the Camino for? You're never more than a day's walk from anywhere, and there's a nice little track in front of you, with markings on it to tell you where to go. It made no sense to me. One American I met was the proud owner of one of these units. According to the guidebook, one stretch of the Camino was four kilometres long.

"Actually, Fozzie," he said with pride, "I consulted my GPS because I thought it seemed longer. And it was. The actual distance was six kilometres! Imagine that!"

"Imagine that, indeed," I replied, trying to look interested and wandered off to the nearest bar.

I had been walking over ground resembling moor land for an hour or so. As I crested the brow of a hill, the large settlement of Cahors appeared below me. It was tucked up in a huge loop created by the river Lot, which I had been following on and off over the past few days. The famous Pont Valentré was just visible spanning the water on the outskirts. It was an impressive sight. The whole panorama was laid out like a huge map on a cartographer's desk. I could even plot my way through town and out again from my perch.

I descended into the town, crossed the Pont Louis-Philippe, walked up Gambetta, and before long I had paid for two nights' lodgings at the hostel on Frédéric Suisse Street. I immediately warmed to Cahors. It was friendly and clean, and the locals looked as though they were genuinely happy to live there. It was alive and bustling, but never overwhelming. In the busy cafés circling Place Aristide Briand, tobacco smoke and freshly brewed coffee smells caught the breeze as did peals of genuine laughter.

I recognised a guy sitting outside the hostel tending his feet. We hadn't met but I had seen his face a few times. His name was, appropriately, France.

"Blister problems?" I enquired.

"Yes, nothing until now, and then this," he replied, pointing to the offending bulges on the small toes on each foot. "I took my boots to a cobbler to see if he could adjust them. He did, but it has made no difference." He stuck a pin in one of them, making me cringe as the liquid oozed out and dripped on to the ground. "Blistering", as I now referred to it, was a regular sight on the Camino. Because everyone assumed that everyone else was in the same boat, most pilgrims would tend to them, regardless of where they were, or in whose company.

I passed on Walter's advice, happy that my blisters had gone to be replaced by hard skin, so hard that I could actually tap it.

Although I'd never suffered from insomnia before, my sleeping patterns now were a chaotic tangle. Since day one of the Camino I had been experiencing the most vivid dreams, on occasions two or three a night, waking after one and falling asleep again until the next woke me. I presumed it was something to do with the Camino's energy and the ley lines. I began to write the dreams down, but could never make any sense of them.

My lack of sleep was starting to bother me. I would go to bed around ten or eleven, much earlier if I was camping. By two in the morning I had probably managed one hour of shallow slumber, tossing and turning and becoming more frustrated with each minute. I usually slept OK in the tent, in the fresh air, but not at the *gîtes*. It was starting to annoy me.

By three in the morning at the hostel in Cahors, I had given up. I got up and wandered down to the TV room, where I found a French teenager drawing on a joint and clearly stoned. I sipped a coffee (probably not the best solution to insomnia) and smoked. He turned around and constantly tried to converse with me in French, waving the TV remote around and looking at me through bloodshot and distant eyes as he brushed ash off his arm. I decided after five minutes that lying awake in my room was the more attractive option and told him in English that he looked like a Jack Russell, that he should get a haircut and that the French can't play soccer for shit. He nodded his head in approval and waved goodbye.

The following day, miserable for lack of sleep, I deliberately stayed out of everyone's way and concentrated on cheering myself up with some alcohol and food. I found a little café down a side street and sat down to three courses with wine at lunch, then sat by the Pont Valentré for what seemed like all afternoon. It is a beautiful piece of architecture stretched across the water and its fortifications must have been a formidable sight for enemies approaching. The shimmering water, the grass on my back and the breeze tickling my legs improved my mood considerably.

On the way back to the hostel I stopped at a phone box and called a friend in Greece. I had spent most of the few months before the Camino on Crete and made some great friends. Trisha and I shared a hunger for adventure that needed constant feeding, so we would head off around the island on our mopeds just to explore and we found all the best tavernas, the most beautiful walks and the most deserted beaches.

She sounded confused but excited. We had talked in depth about starting our own vegetarian restaurant on Crete. For the time being, she was finishing her time at a yoga retreat, and we were both looking for a reason to return to Crete the following year. She had spoken to a Greek taverna owner who was planning to go to America at the end of the season, and needed someone to take over the following year. It sounded perfect. Trish would be given free rein to experiment with the menu and make her mark on the place.

"Go for it, Trish!" I said enthusiastically. "If that's what you want, and it means you are where you want to be next year, then do it."

"Fozzie, I know. I'm just a bit lost. There's so much to sort out if I do it. My head's all screwed up. You need to be here. All the money stuff and the legal angle. I'm all wobbly just thinking about it all."

I spent the rest of the evening wandering around in a daze, wondering if I should have asked the question that I wanted to ask. I phoned her the following morning.

"Fozzie, what are you doing calling me in the morning? You usually call in the evening. You were lucky to get me."

"Trish, are you asking if you want me to do this thing with you?"

"Yes."

"Well," I said, "the answer is yes, but I can't make any promises to get out there before the end of the season. My priority is to finish this walk first, you know that, and that will take until the beginning of November, sooner if I can increase my distances. Then I could get out there for the last two weeks of the season, see everyone, and we can talk to this guy and sort it out. How's that?"

"I think it would work, Fozzie."

I replaced the receiver. The full impact of what I had done suddenly hit me, and I didn't like what I felt. I had inadvertently given myself a schedule. From being in the position that I had leant over backwards to be in, having no timetable to keep to, walking as far as I wanted to each day, resting when I damn well wanted to, I now had to complete by a set date, the middle of October. All these freedoms lay in tatters on the ground by the phone box. I cursed. I was feeling excited at the prospect of returning to the island I had fallen in love with, but frustrated too. I cursed again.

According to my original plan, to finish by early November, I would have needed to walk an average of twenty-seven kilometres each day, six days a week. It was a loose plan, based solely on the weather. If the Spanish winter was late or mild, then I had the option of extending the trip.

If, however, I were to finish by 10th October or thereabouts, I would have to walk thirty-five kilometres each walking day. It wasn't exactly out of the question, but it was difficult. It meant eight or nine hours of walking each day. Throwing in an hour for lunch and a couple of breaks, I would need to start no later than eight thirty in the morning. I would be up with the bag rustlers.

Up to this point I had finished each day tired but not exhausted and, once revived, ready to do the same the following day. To increase my distance by ten kilometres meant I would be a physical wreck each evening. Although I hadn't made a promise as such, I felt I had an obligation to fulfil. I began blaming myself for getting into the position to start with, of ruining the Camino I had been blessed with. Nevertheless, I decided to give it my best shot. I would aim for thirty-seven kilometres each day, two more than I needed: that way, perhaps, I could do a little less one day a week, say twenty-five.

As I left Cahors, a place I resolved to revisit some day, and crossed the Pont Valentré one last time, I encountered the steepest section of the entire Camino. It was only about three metres long, but it was pretty much vertical. There was another option, a footpath that curved around and finished at the same spot, but this looked more fun. If there had been no metal grab rails plunged into the rock, it would not have been possible. I hauled myself up, my pack doing its utmost to haul me back down again. It was fun. It may have only been a minute's worth of mountaineering, but it got the blood squirting around my body.

I came up behind a guy loudly singing, "Ultreya", as if he didn't care who heard him. Pierre, who came from the north-east of France, was in his sixties and had short, grey hair that was ruffled and untidy from the breeze and sweat. He was the first real pilgrim I had met who completely took his time and relaxed on the Camino. He ambled along, humming and singing and looking all around him, often stopping to take a closer look at a plant or the view.

When he heard click and clack on the tarmac, he turned

round and said hello. We introduced ourselves.

Are you walking all the way to Santiago?" he asked.

"Yes, all the way."

"You walk very quickly," he smiled.

"Long story, which I won't get into. Unfortunately I have given myself a time limit."

We talked only briefly. I kept making false starts before he would say something and I felt obliged to pause and answer. I ust have looked stupid and awkward. I felt strangely a little angry at him for having the freedom that I had surrendered.

The schedule I had set was still fresh in my mind and for most of the day I concentrated on nothing but plugging out the kilometres, head down, trying to keep my speed up to six kilometres an hour, checking my watch at lunch breaks and making sure I didn't overrun. If I had only thirty minutes for lunch, I could relax a little. By the time I hit Montcuq in the early evening, I was a wreck physically and mentally from straining to be at a certain point at a certain time. The soles of my feet were on fire. I literally had to lift them off the ground with my hands and rest them on top of my pack. The only time they didn't ache was when I removed my boots and socks and exposed them to the air. My right calf hurt, and threatened to get worse. I had even had two fresh blisters on my ankles. I hadn't taken the least notice of what was around me because I'd been focusing on a point two metres in front of me all day, watching my step. I was destroying myself, and my Camino.

Chapter Seven

The Trail Telegraph

It always amazed me how and where I bumped into familiar faces on the Camino. Some people I saw almost every day, other people once a week, maybe once a month. The French Canadians were regular sights. Sometimes I would overlap the people I had come to know, at other times they would overlap me. I might see them resting in a field, looking at a church or drinking at a bar. I knew then I was ahead of them – not that it was a race, everyone just developed a need to know where all their friends were at a given point. Sometimes we would lose each other.

"Fozzie, have you seen Pierre?" someone would ask.

"Yeah, two days behind," I would reliably inform them.

"What about France?"

"Last time I saw him was Cahors; he was taking a day's rest. I left a day before him, so he's about a day behind."

I guess we all developed a mental map of the Camino. Mine took a bird's eye view, covering perhaps a week's walk in length. Dotted along it would be other pilgrims, marked by little flags with their name on them sticking out of the packs. It was easy to find out where a particular person was, or how they were doing. As I passed someone, or they me, I would update my mental map.

Then there was the "trail telegraph". As most of us didn't have mobiles, messages and information were passed from person to person until they arrived at the intended destination. You would imagine such a haphazard method would prove unreliable but in fact it was surprisingly successful, perhaps because it was a pleasantly different way of communicating. On any given day hundreds of messages would be moving along the Camino at various stages, waiting to be delivered to the right recipient, whether it was 'Tell Gerard that I've got his spoon, he left it at the *gîte'*, or 'If anyone sees Chantelle, can she meet me at the church in Lauzerte lunchtime tomorrow?' You could even pretty much arrange an evening meal for ten at a certain town on a certain day if you sent out the messages a week before and gave them plenty of time to reach your friends.

I encountered my first day of rain. I had been camping and it must have started in the early hours. For the first time, I had to walk in waterproofs, which I hate: even with today's 'breathable materials', you end up being cocooned in a mini sauna. They keep the rain out, but if your body is working even a little hard, you get damp from the sweat anyway, so why bother protecting yourself from a little moisture?

If you bear in mind we lose a litre of water just when we sleep, you can imagine how much we lose in a summer rainstorm with sixteen kilos plugged on your back, walking up a hill. When the rain eventually stopped, I would peel off the layers at the first opportunity. My T-shirt would be wringing wet and stuck to my back and my shorts would have damp blotches over them as if I had failed to make it to the Gents on time. Others on the trail would be doing the same, frantically whipping off their outer clothes as vapour rose off them like morning dew on a wall when the sun hits it.

My pack also needed protection. At the first sign of rain, my usual course of action was to go under the nearest tree to see if it would only last a few minutes. If this was not the case, then I would commence "Operation Keep Dry". First, I had to drop my pack and find the waterproofs. As it rained quite rarely on my walk, these items were classed as "not used often", and therefore at the bottom under everything else. Hence, "everything else" would have to come out – and inevitably also got wet. Trousers would go on first. They had zips around the ankles so that you could, in theory, put them on without removing your boots, only some idiot designer had obviously not taken into account the actual size of hiking boots, so they would have to come off anyway. The jacket thankfully was pretty straightforward. After that I had to fix on the "one size" rucksack cover. I am always wary of anything described as "one size". No matter how I adjusted it, how far I pulled it over the top or stretched it over the bottom, there was always some part not covered.

And I am not exaggerating when I say that seven times out of ten, by the time I had gone through this rigmarole, it had stopped raining anyway. I need not explain "Operation Remove Waterproofs", let alone "Operation Throw a Huge Tantrum". By this stage I had no umbrella: brolly had snagged on a tree somewhere after Cahors.

I seemed to be the only one who used this method on the few occasions that it did rain. The humble poncho is making a comeback and all because of its wonderful simplicity. I watched with a mixture of admiration and intense jealousy when other pilgrims hit a rainstorm. They would stop, retrieve their poncho from a side pocket, stick their head through the hole, and let the whole thing just "fall" over them, and their pack. The poncho didn't need to be particularly breathable because all the air circulated underneath it. It was a miracle of design, and got me wondering how they ever went out of favour in the first place.

Sunflowers grew everywhere in this part of France and I often walked through fields blazing with their yellow faces. I reached Lauzerte, a historic fortified village dating back to 1214. It sits on top of a hill, giving uninterrupted views for miles all around. It was my birthday and birthdays mean indulgences, in this case, food. The obvious choice was the village centre. The cobbles looked as if they had just been varnished after a passing shower. Pigeons cooed and flapped around, sending the local cats into frenzied bouts of frustration. I wiped off a seat at the café that seemed to be drawing a larger crowd than most. My policy of eating at establishments that were busy had served me well, up until this point at least.

After a good fifteen minutes of deliberately avoiding eye contact with me, the young waitress eventually came over. A greasy slick of hair flapped against her face and she wore a permanent frown. Pencil poised over her order ticket, she stood, bored and resolutely unhelpful, squinting through ultra-thick glasses.

"Can I use your glasses as an ash tray?! I asked. I knew she didn't speak English, as one of the other guests had given up on that venture.

She looked puzzled.

"I said, if I ordered breakfast now, would that be enough notice for you to get it to me on time?"

I'm not that rude really. It's just that she was treating the whole café like a waste of her time. She was ignoring everyone, taking a decade to bring out orders, and kept tutting all the time, as if everything was an imposition.

The table with the English tourists had heard me. At first they looked at me in astonishment, then they just started to giggle. I winked at them.

Smiling now, I ordered a Coke and a croque monsieur. She scribbled down the request and sauntered back to the haven of the kitchen.

I waited for forty minutes. Eventually I went into the bar and gave her the money for the Coke.

"Monsieur, le croque monsieur?" she said, surprised.

"Well, where the hell is it?" I stammered. "I ordered the bloody thing forty minutes ago. It's your basic cheese on toast with some frilly extras. You know? Cheese on to toast, under grill and there you go. What are you doing? Milking the damn cow?"

If it wasn't for the fact that when it arrived five minutes later it was the best-tasting croque monsieur I had eaten on the entire Camino, I would have gone off to one of the other establishments. I can't remember the name of the place, but, for all future pilgrims entering the market place in Lauzerte, it's the one on the far side in the corner, with the red chairs.

Try the one with the nice yellow chairs on your left instead.

I stumbled into Moissac that evening in the dark after walking thirty-eight kilometres, literally incapable of going any further. I still had to find somewhere to sleep and something to eat. What a birthday! I soon stumbled across a café serving up such delicacies as hot dogs, chips and burgers. There were photos of the options lit up above the serving area. I realised my hunger was borderline dangerous and ordered two huge baguettes each stuffed with three hamburgers. The cook raised one eyebrow slightly, smiled and muttered something about pilgrims as he slapped six hamburgers on the grill. I collapsed into one of the chairs outside and devoured the food like a wolf with a chicken.

"How far is the campsite?" I asked the waitress.

She replied that she thought it was closed for the season. I had forgotten that some French campsites shut at the beginning of September. It was time to sleep rough again. And it needed to be close. On a trip with a friend a few years previous, we had slept rough most nights. It was obviously cheap, which was a major concern at that time, and we became experts at finding pretty comfortable places to spend the night. The knack was to have your amenities on hand. We referred to potential locations as "hotels" and graded them according to the facilities near by, which were, in order of importance, shelter, lighting, toilets, water, seating, privacy and ground comfort. Shelter essentially meant anywhere where we would remain dry if it rained, such as a bus stop or even some trees. Lighting could come from a street light or a window. If there were public toilets, we didn't have to rely on restaurants. Water was a tricky one. It could always be obtained from somewhere such as a bar or by calling at someone's house but far better was a tap or water fountain. We could use our sleeping mats as seating, but preferred a bench or seating area. Ground comfort ideally meant soft grass as opposed to concrete. A poor "hotel" would offer one or two of these amenities; if we found three or four we were usually quite chuffed, fives were a rarity and sixes and sevens happened once in a blue moon.

The place I had found rated about four and a half, the half coming from the fact that there was light, but not very strong. There was a bench to sit on and toilets a short stroll away, so I could have a wash and get water to brew coffee in the morning. Top marks went to privacy: my actual sleeping location was a hollow hedge and people, such as the occasional dogwalker, could be a metre from me and have no idea I was there. Unfortunately there was no shelter, but thankfully it didn't rain that night. This just goes to show that the best hotels don't necessarily come with roofs and a bathroom.

Moissac was a large town, but somehow still retained that sleepy feel about it. I walked up Rue de la République and came into the main square flanked by the abbey of St Pierre. I studied the portal, with the apocalypse depicted in the stone, and marvelled at the time it must have taken to carve it.

It had been at least two weeks since I had seen her, but now I spotted the smoking woman limping towards me and looking a bit sorry for herself.

"Hey," I said and gave her a peck on the cheek. "You look a bit sad. What's the matter?"

"Big problem with my leg. I see doctor and he tell me not good. Must go easy and rest. So, I go to St Jean Pied de Port by a train, and walk from there. Then I still can do Camino but walk slowly." Dejectedly, she looked down, like a naughty child waiting to be punished.

St Jean Pied de Port was just before the border with Spain, and about halfway to Santiago. It was, give or take, seven hundred and fifty kilometres from Le Puy and the same distance again to Santiago..

"I'm really sorry," I said. Even though I still didn't know her name, and had not really met or talked to her many times, I liked her immensely. Not only did she occupy a special place in my affections, as she was the first pilgrim I had met, but to me, she glowed with courage. She was perhaps in her late sixties, and less capable than most of us, yet she had struggled to be here and she had made it with determination and grit. I wished I had half her determination and hoped that when I reached that age I would still be capable of walking such distances.

"I wish you luck. I'm sure Spain is as beautiful as France, if not more so. And it sounds like a good plan you have. Just take the rest of the walk at a slow pace, don't rush it, and make sure you rest. Muscles heal with rest. By the way, what is your name?"

"Ann, my name is Ann. Yours?"

"Fozzie."

"It is nice to know your name at last. I used to call you the smoking man. Good luck Fozzie."

She turned and walked off before I could reply.

That's one of the things about the Camino people don't really take into account. It's great to be determined, to set your eyes on the goal of Santiago. But anything may happen. We can trip or fall, be injured, get ill. That would be the end of the walk, at least until the next attempt. There is a memorial in Spain just past the village of Salceda. A bronze sculpture of two bronze boots set into a wall reminds pilgrims of Guillermo Watt, aged 69, who died there in 1993. He was one day short of Santiago. That is why, when people said to me, "Fozzie, you will make it," I always used to reply, "I will accept I have made it when I know I am there."

France also appeared in the square. He was always glad to see me, and I him. He sat down and we talked for a while over a coffee. I went over to the church portal to take a photo and when I returned he had gone. I went to pay but the waitress explained that France had already met the bill. I looked down the street to see him gleefully waving and running away, smiling back at me. I knew I'd see him again to thank him, and he knew it too.

As I have explained, pilgrims on the Camino carry a card called a *créanciale*, which we can have stamped at various establishments, as proof for the cathedral authorities in Santiago that we have been to the places we say we have been. The *créanciale* is also a unique souvenir, but mine was looking decidedly empty.

I was under the impression that I could obtain the stamps only at *gîtes* and churches. I stayed in a *gîte* maybe once a week and as I am not a religious person, my "churches visited" collection was skimpy, to say the least. When Pierre unfolded his card and showed me his impressive collection of stamps, about four times more numerous than mine, I thought maybe it was time to do something about it. He explained I could also obtain stamps at 'T' (tourist information) offices, and even at some restaurants and bars.

From then on, I went all out on a mission to fill up my card. It was like being a kid again and trying to get my entire football album filled up with stickers as fast as possible. I even started looking for inky pads in the public toilets.

A welcome sight greeted me as I left Moissac. The terrain ahead, which I calculated was a couple of days' walk, was flat. Oh, joy of joys! No hills, no inclines. The builders of the canal had spotted this also, and for most of the day the Camino clung to the bank. Although it was pretty much dead straight, it was a beautiful walk. The water was still like polished steel, broken only by the wake of an occasional boat or a fish jumping for a fly. Trees stood to attention on both sides like symmetrical soldiers guarding the entire length. Sunlight filtered through chinks in the foliage and there was a pleasant smell of damp earth. It was peaceful, and a distinct and pleasant change to experience such uniformity after such irregularity.

I had noticed my calf muscle was becoming more painful, but I had resolved to increase my daily distance travelled. Inevitably, whenever I started walking again after a rest stop, I was hobbling for fifteen minutes before the muscle loosened up and the pain abated. Logically I knew I should rest it for at least two days, preferably three or four, but if I did that, I would lose valuable time. Again I cursed myself for putting a restriction on my adventure.

"I'll tell you a short story about my experience, Fozzie", said Fabian at the *gîte* at Saint Antoine. Fabian was a Frenchman on a mission to complete the Camino in super-quick time. He ate at the same speed, shovelling spoonfuls of ravioli into his mouth and storytelling at the same time. It was a dangerous practice for anyone sitting opposite him.

"I pulled a ligament too. Like you, I ignored it because I had a schedule to keep. I must keep going, I thought. Eventually it became so painful that my friends had to issue threats to get me to rest. I rested for two days and continued. It wasn't long enough. After a few days, the problem had returned tenfold. The consequence was that I had to hole up in Conques for a whole week. Rest it now, Fozzie. You will lose more time if you don't."

"OK, I hear what you are saying," I said, wiping a piece of ravioli from my forehead. "I know it makes sense. I'm gonna give it two days and see what happens. If no improvement then I will rest. Where are you heading to tomorrow?"

"I will make Condom tomorrow evening," he replied.

"Condom!" I exclaimed, looking at him as if he were deranged. "That's sixty-three kilometres! Are you crazy?"

"I am doing about sixty kilometres every day," he explained. "It is long, I know, but I too have a schedule. I have to return to Paris to study, and this is the distance I need to walk each day to complete. I would rather do this than not walk at all. Besides, I walk with no pack."

"So where is all your stuff?"

"There is a courier service. You pay them 100 francs and they take your bag on for you, pretty much to anywhere."

I was puzzled. "Don't you think that is like cheating? Don't you feel a little guilty?"

"At first yes, but I have little choice. I cannot walk these distances in a day with my pack."

He slept in the reception area, so as to make an early start around six o'clock without waking others. Unfortunately the other pilgrims staying at the *gîte* did not have Fabian's considerateness. The noise of rustling plastic the following morning sounded as though someone had thrown an epileptic octopus into a skip full of carrier bags. As the last culprit left, a Canadian pilgrim obviously had reached the end of his tether and literally manhandled him back into the room, pointed to the light switch, then to the fluorescent light blinking on the ceiling.

"I've listened to your noise for the last half an hour. Please have some respect for others next time you wake early in the morning. We would appreciate it. And make sure you turn the fucking light off when you leave!"

There was a definite chill in the air at eight in the morning. In fact, it was cold. As I left St Antoine I was tempted to put on trousers and a fleece, but I knew after half an hour I would be too hot. Sure enough, as the day progressed I was comfortable. The air was crisp, with an autumnal chill that lasted just that bit longer each morning before the sun burnt it away.

I had decided to meet Fabian's policy halfway. I would walk for a day and if there was no improvement in the calf that evening, I would rest for two days. I imagined Fabian shaking his head and wagging his finger at me.

For the last two weeks a white butterfly had been keeping me company, appearing every day for a few minutes. It seemed as if he was egging me on, giving me the enthusiasm to go that extra mile. I used to wonder where he was every day if I hadn't seen him, but sure enough, at some point, I would catch a flash of white out of the corner of my eye, look over and there he would be. Sometimes he would dance around my head, at others fly alongside and rest occasionally on plants. I pretended it was the same butterfly every day; whether it was or not, I looked forward to seeing him and felt reassured by his presence.

My calf was showing no signs of improving and Fabian's warning was ringing around my head for most of the day. I decided caution was the best option. The town of Lectoure seemed perfect for a two-day, three-night recuperation stop. It had everything I would need: a couple of supermarkets to buy food I could cook for myself, and the *gîte* even had an oven! There was a collection of bars, cafés and restaurants and remarkably, the post office had internet access.

Everyone seemed to rally around. When my buddies

found out I was resting for two days because of my calf, all manner of remedies appeared. I was plied with pills, lotions, oils and every piece of advice available. I thanked them all but told them I would rather work on the problem myself, hoping my mental strength was enough to sort it out. That and a bottle of a very fine rosé each night to aid the healing process.

To pass the time, I checked my email, ate, drank and took more photos than was necessary. In between times, I wandered around aimlessly, hoping that something would catch my attention. I do not like wishing days away, but I was going a little crazy having to stay put, however attractive the place. And my body had become used to churning out twenty-five kilometres every day and didn't seem to know what to do with all the stored-up energy. I was surprised by how much I missed the walking, but in a good way.

I escaped the town's confines, as planned, on the third day. My calf had improved, which made the decision easy, although boredom had played a big part. I managed an early start and before long my waterproofs were on. They didn't come off for the day, as it rained on and off and was cold too. Autumn was starting to take a grip.

Pulling off the way at Chapelle Sainte Germaine to search for water, I spotted a little old lady feeding chickens in her yard. She must have been over a century old, and spoke no English at all. Even my routine with my water bag produced puzzled looks. I found a tap (which was not working) and held the bag under it. That seemed to do the trick. Why she didn't give me water from her house I don't know. Instead, she led me up her drive and pointed to the top of the hill. As we were walking, she passed wind three times extremely loudly and never batted an eyelid. Her apparent total ignorance of what had happened had me creased up with silent laughter, and I had to get away quickly in case she thought I was being rude.

It was a great day and I felt extremely content just to walk. Putting aside the issue of distance, I went back to how

I had been walking at the start, a month before, taking my time, looking around me, noticing every scene and sight. My calf was giving me no pain at all. There was a noticeable decline in the number of pilgrims, no doubt because the approach of winter made a long walk a bit of a risk. Or maybe they were all taking a rest day as well.

When I actually managed to obtain some water at a house a little further on, I carried on walking for a short distance with the full water bag in my hand, intending to place it in the rucksack when I stopped for a rest. Then it struck me. My pack was so much lighter. My water bladder held two litres, which weighed about two kilos. The lightness of my pack was remarkable. I started to ponder on the weight issue more as the day rolled on. I figured that I could send my tent and cooking equipment back home. My tent was just less than two kilos. As great as it was to camp out, did I really need it? The refugios in Spain were plentiful and cheap. In fact, many of them operate on donation only. Therefore I would have a roof over my head most of the time. Even if I did want to spend a night in the woods, the weather in the early part of Spain was still predictably warm, with little rain, so I would not need shelter anyway.

As for the cooking equipment, I was only really using it for brewing tea and coffee and could be dispensed with without too much loss of comfort. I could cook in some of the refugios with cooking facilities and if there weren't any, I would simply have a cheap meal at a bar or eat something cold. Four kilos total weight I would be able to save. That was twenty five percent of my pack. I decided to ditch the gear when I got near to the Spanish border.

I passed through Condom, which, although beautiful, did not appeal as a place to spend the night. By the time I reached the three or so houses that made up Le Carbon, dusk was falling. I was intending to make a detour of about one kilometre to the fortified town of Larressingle, but then spotted that one of the houses was empty, and being renovated. The front door creaked open to reveal rooms full of nothing but dust. I'm not keen on sleeping in dark, empty houses on my own, so opted instead for the open garage at the side, which gave me a "hotel" score of around 3.

What was also particularly pleasing was that I had broken the elusive forty-kilometre barrier. I also realised that I had completed a third of the Camino. I slept with a smile on my face.

The following day I passed a couple sitting on the grass, eating their lunch, in front of a church that was catching the full light of the midday sun. By the look on the guy's face I knew he was going to try and stop me to make conversation. I just wasn't in the mood for talking, so I avoided eye contact except for the customary nod in their direction.

"You walking the Camino?" he called.

"Yeah," I replied, not slowing my pace.

"Where you heading to?"

"Santiago."

"When you plan on getting there?" He was firing questions like a machine gun.

"Another four weeks," I replied, and waited for him to disagree.

"Four weeks! That's not possible! It's too far," he stuttered, disbelief all over his face.

I just smiled and carried on.

The vast majority of other pilgrims are a decent bunch. What astounded me was the lack of respect some walkers had for others when it came to defecating. I used public facilities whenever I could, but hey, we all get stuck sometimes. In these situations, I would walk off the Camino, a good twenty metres into the woods or fields. I did not carry a trowel, but usually picked a soft piece of ground that I could at least kick a small indentation into. Business done, I would burn my toilet paper, and cover the whole lot over.

It was a shame some other pilgrims didn't share my practices. I regularly walked past piles of foul-smelling shit on the sides of the Camino, some even in the middle, surrounding by soiled toilet paper. I failed to comprehend how people could have such a flagrant disregard for others, the countryside and the Camino. The path to me represented a way full of natural energy, where millions of pilgrims had passed, and more importantly, millions more would pass. It was sacred. How could someone desecrate it in this way? How much extra effort, when they have already walked five hundred kilometres, was it to go an extra twenty metres into the bushes?

Pierre told me of an unpleasant experience he'd had, when he had gone into the woods to take a pee. When he had finished, he picked up his pack, only to realise he had put it down in a pile of someone else's excrement. Worse, he had grabbed the bag where a prime nugget had been squelched against the fabric, and succeeded in soiling his hand in the stuff. All he could do was wipe his hand on the grass and get the worst off his bag until he reached somewhere where he could wash it.

It wasn't just human waste that was causing a problem. Litter was another. What possessed people to throw their refuse on the ground? Did they not have pockets? Had they not yet comprehended the idea of holding on to their litter until they reached a bin? Discarded food wrappers, socks, shorts, even boots and shoes were scattered along the path. Now, I don't have an exceptional memory, but I'm pretty sure I would realise that I had no boots or shoes on and must have left them behind.

I posted the tent and cooking gear at the mail office in Aire sur l'Adour. It felt as though someone had been hanging on to my shirt up until now, weighing me down, and had just let go. I had a new lease of life. I also got into the habit of filling my water bladder only half full in the morning, which made all the difference. If I were to do a similar hike in the future, I would pick and pack my equipment much more judiciously.

The landscape had changed from that of rolling hills and trees to characterless agricultural monotony. On the flat fields, large crops of maize loomed over me on all sides. There were few hedges or trees, and the pattern was symmetrical, straight lines at right angles. I got lost, had to retrace my steps for a kilometre or two, checked the book, but found it did not conform with what I was seeing before me. In the end it was guesswork. I became frustrated and grouchy, my mood worsened by the sun beating down on me. For most of the day I just walked in the vague direction I thought was right. How I made it to Arzacq Arraziguet I don't know.

To cheer myself up, I booked into the *gîte*, where the warden took me up a flight of steps to one of the dormitories. She wasn't sure if there was a spare bed or not. A woman and two guys were chatting on the stairs outside.

"Is there a spare bed in here?" asked the warden.

The three looked at each other, waiting for someone to say something. I got the impression they were a single group walking together and didn't want anybody intruding on their space.

"There may be," suggested one of the guys.

"Screw this," I was thinking to myself. "I can do without this at eight in the evening."

"Do you snore?" asked the woman, smiling.

"Yeah, I do," I said. "But only when I sleep on my back. And I fart a lot as well, especially when I have eaten beans, which I may have tonight. How about you?"

There was some giggling and banter and one of the guys assured me that she not only snored but talked in her sleep.

"Are you American?" I asked her.

"Sure am," she said warily. "Why?"

"Sorry, I didn't mean to sound condescending," I said. "I'm just surprised, that's all. You're the only American I have met on the whole Camino." I held out my hand. "My name is Fozzie."

"Fozzie? What sort of a name is that?" she giggled again.

"Long story," I said. "I prefer it to Keith, my real name,"

"Yeah, it's kinda cute. I'm Jeannie."

"Pleasure." I shook her hand. "So, can I stay in here or not?"

"As long as you don't snore or fart."

As it transpired, no one slept at all. Every time one of us even breathed, the springs on the beds reverberated around the whole room. For once, spending most of the night awake was almost worth it for the entertainment Jeannie provided with her sleep talking.

The author walking out of Le-Puy-en-Velay.

A reminder of the right direction.

Cahors. The Pont Valentré and the River Lot.

The approach to Cahors (the Pont Valentré is just visible on the far left).

The Journey in Between

Chapter Eight

In the Company of Jeannie

I had made the decision at the beginning of the trip not to walk with a companion for any length of time. A day? Fine, no problem. I just didn't want company for an extended period. I enjoyed conversation but didn't want to be in a situation where I felt I had to make it all the time and I liked being in a position where the only plans I needed to make concerned me. So, it was after much deliberation that I asked Jeannie the following morning if she wanted to walk with me that day. She appeared tired of the bickering and back-stabbing in the rest of the group, and I thought the experience would do me good. I knew she probably would not be walking as far as I did each day, but I was approaching the stage where I was tired and fed up with cranking out thirty-five-kilometre days. Perhaps, deep down, I knew it would give me the opportunity to take the Camino at a more relaxed pace. I was starting to think that I would rather slow down to my original pace and be late to Greece than continue rushing the walk. I was tired of missing out on the sights.

She agreed. We talked pretty much non-stop for the morning. It was good to talk and walk, to have someone alongside who walked differently from the way I did, and had different methods of dealing with the Camino. For one, she insisted on stopping at every church: not just for a look at the outside, to check out the inside as well. I usually peered inside each one, murmured something like, "Yeah,

111

very nice", and sat outside smoking while she carried on.

It's not that I dislike churches, but to me, if you have seen one, you have seen them all. I'm not religious either, so I had no need to go into each one and feel at one with God. It's like museums: they bore the crap out of me as well. They seem to have an atmosphere of the old school, of rules and regulations. You feel out of place if you raise your voice, and everything is static. I know you couldn't really expect to walk into the National History Museum and expect Tyrannosaurus Rex to be getting on down with the Jackson Five but at least some movement would be good. Everything is in cabinets, behind screens, ropes or barriers. That said, I respect people who are interested in museums or indeed churches. So Jeannie's insistence on making a foray into every church worked out pretty well: I would have stopped for a smoke at some point anyway, so we were killing two birds with one stone.

I tried to educate her on the wonders and pleasures of smoking a decent roll-up. She had taken to the bad habit of using Gitanes, a French brand of fierce cigarettes without filters. The rolling tobacco is also extremely strong, like taking a drag on a blowtorch. She had been using it because she was ignorant about European brands.

"I only smoke it because it's the nearest I can get to a joint. I don't really even like the stuff," she told me.

"Well, at least smoke a decent brand," I suggested and offered her some of mine. Enlightenment slowly rose up her face when she lit and inhaled. After that my tobacco depleted rapidly.

"You don't have any, do you?" she asked.

"Have any what?"

"Weed."

"No, I don't really like it. Have smoked it in the past, but don't really get a good vibe from it."

"Well, you obviously haven't had any good stuff."

"Well, let me know when you have got some good stuff," I said, "and I'm sure I'll be up for a smoke".

Jeannie was in her mid-forties. Ridiculously long red hair,

worn in a plait the thickness of a substantial bit of rope, fell down the middle of her back. She had a habit of pursing her lips as she spoke, and smiled most of the time. I liked her sense of humour. It was crude, to the point and didn't pull any punches. She told it as it was.

She had come from Florida with one of her friends, Valerie, whom I had met the previous evening, and had also started in Le Puy, intending to walk all the way to Santiago. She had left her daughter and boyfriend to look after her house, taken care of what needed to be taken care of, and accepted Valerie's invitation to join her. Things were not going as planned between them. They walked apart most of the time and didn't communicate much. There seemed to be some sort of personality clash.

"What do you do back home?" I asked.

"I'm a painter, an artist. Just starting to make a living out of it. I paint the female torso".

"Just the torso?" I asked.

"Yeah. No arms or legs, and usually with lingerie. It's classed as modern art, and I'm doing well out of it. I've had a few successful exhibitions. I've sold some examples. What do you do?"

I laughed. I hated that question.

"Well, at the moment, nothing. I've done a lot of stuff and never really had a career because I've travelled a lot. My CV is a disaster. Three months here, then travelled. Managed a year here and ... travelled. So I go home and usually do temporary jobs. I guess what I like doing, and want to do, is to cook."

The villages were becoming distinctly more Mediterranean in style, with whitewashed walls supporting terracotta roofs that shone against deep blue skies. There were vines winding over porches and frameworks, and the earth was scorched.

I was taking a few photos of the view, when my eyes were drawn up to the top of the camera frame.

"Jeannie! Jeannie!" I called.

"What's up?"

"Take a gander in the viewfinder," I instructed, pointing to the camera.

"A what?"

"A gander, a look. It's the bloody Pyrenees!" I pointed to the horizon. Just beyond those mountains, I knew, was Spain. It was maybe three days' walk to St-Jean-Pied-de-Port, that busy little town burrowed into the mountains' base, teeming with eager pilgrims ready to get going. It was a marker, a big, bold proof that I had nearly completed half the walk. It couldn't have been more dramatic, unless someone had stuck a sign on top of one of the peaks proclaiming "Halfway on the Camino, Spain this way".

No matter how hard I tried, I couldn't get rid of my dilemma about Greece. I felt I should be pushing out the kilometres, but I was enjoying walking with Jeannie. She walked more slowly than I did, but that was the attraction. Some days I would say to her that I really needed to do forty kilometres. She would just shrug her shoulders, say "OK", and keep with me for the morning, and then I would lose track of her. That made me sad because I enjoyed her company, and would much rather have stayed with her than keep plugging on. Some days I would walk a long distance, keep up a fast pace and leave her behind, then wait for her to catch me up by the evening.

I stopped at a picnic table by a river. Jeannie was behind so I ate and rested. I forget where I had purchased it, but I had an absolute cracker of a tomato. It was blood red, juicy and sweet, and together with tuna and a lump of crusty baguette, it was a match made in France.

Food was a very important part of the Camino for me. The thought of lunch and dinner provided energy to push me along. I would set myself a goal of lunch in a certain spot or town, and could taste the flavours long before I got there. It provided more than just energy. It was a goal, direction and reward. If I was staying in a place with a bakery, then I would be there at the door in the morning, smelling the flavours wafting out: baguette straight out of the oven, cheese puffs, croissants and doughnuts. I would usually buy a croissant and a pain au chocolat, Couple these with a strong coffee and a cigarette, and I was ready to take on anything.

Lunch would consist of a baguette, stuffed with whatever I had available, maybe cheese with tomato or canned tuna nestling in with some cucumber. Possibly a bag of crisps, some biscuits and an apple or banana would round things off. Then I would find a suitable spot, perhaps some soft grass or propped up at the base of a large tree, and have a short siesta. Well, it would have been rude not to, do as the locals do!

Dinner was the best meal of the day. Sometimes I would treat myself to a meal at a bar or restaurant if I couldn't be bothered to cook. Plenty of establishments would offer cheap meals if pilgrims produced their *créanciale*. The food was of variable standard, but in general pretty good. One thing you realise pretty quickly is that after a long day's walk, even the worst food tastes great.

When I did cook for myself on the camp stove, I made the effort to produce something I knew well. Sometimes I would crave potatoes, sometimes rice or pasta. It is remarkable what can be produced on one burner. In fact, I sometimes wonder why we have four burners on our conventional cookers at all. It was all a case of balancing two pans and keeping food warm while I cooked something else. At first I thought it would be limiting cooking with one pot and one burner but after a short space of time you become remarkably adept at knocking out decent food quickly. Here's a camp stove recipe as proof:

Vegetable Stew with Rice (Serves 1)

Ingredients:

Handful of rice (Basmati is good)
1 carrot
1 onion
2 cloves garlic

Dash of olive oil
Mint or rosemary to taste (procured from the trail)
1 small potato
½ packet of vegetable soup
Salt and pepper

Method:

Boil rice in salted water for required period. Set aside in pan with suitable lid, such as a plate or book, to keep warm. Fry garlic and onions in olive oil until soft (about five minutes). Add diced carrot, potato, cook for five minutes more. Add desired quantity of water and soup powder, stir. Follow soup packet instructions to cook, using the amount of powder you need for the required thickness. Throw in herbs and seasoning just before ready. Retrieve rice, which should still be warm.

Serve with bread, a summer evening and a smattering of bird song. Brew the coffee while you are eating and reserve some hot water for washing up. Easy!

Having a camp fire was even better as I didn't have to conserve fuel and could have endless hot water. I could cook stuff in the fire, such as jacket potatoes in tin foil. Or I would slice a banana lengthwise, push chunks of dark chocolate in the slit, wrap it in tin foil and place it in the ashes for fifteen minutes. When the foil was peeled off, the chocolate would have melted into the banana flesh, creating a sweet, gooey mush to spoon out. One time I pigged out on roast potatoes with onion, a rare slab of steak, peas and ice cream. OK, so I wasn't carrying a portable camping freezer, and the ice cream was a little runny, but it was still a damn fine meal.

It was a Thursday morning and I was on a final push to St-Jean-Pied-de-Port. I wanted to get there on Friday evening, and have the Saturday off to relax. That meant walking seventy-five kilometres in two days. I had done a similar distance in that time before, but I was tired of doing it. Jeannie had not kept up that morning, but was aware of my intentions, so we had agreed to meet up later.

It was a strange day. It seemed quieter than usual. I saw no pilgrims the whole time. The weather was cloudy all the time but very hot. Somehow the walk seemed to be in another country, maybe some sort of partial wilderness; it just didn't seem like the Camino I had grown used to. I followed tracks aimlessly, not caring if I was on the designated route or which direction I was taking, and I failed to take note of the *balises*. The only security I had was the sun's position either ahead of me or to the left.

Needless to say, I got lost. My list of *gîtes* promised me one in Sorhapuru. I was struggling to even find the village, let alone the *gîte*. In the end, I just took a road that felt right, and after a short walk arrived in a hamlet that was about as likely to host a *gîte* as it did an Internet bar. What I read in the guidebook seemed to bear no relation to what I saw around me. It looked as if it ought to have been in Austria or Bavaria. The residents were wearing strange clothing I had not seen before and they even seemed to be speaking in a different language. I began to imagine that I had entered some kind of time warp. I asked directions from a farmer and his wife. Although we spoke only our native tongues, the man was clearly insisting there was no *gîte* there, but advised me there was one at Larribar, another two kilometres further on.

How I managed to walk that extra distance I don't know. I stumbled into Larribar, to find that there was no *gîte*, nothing but a few houses and a church. I had no extra strength left, not even enough to walk a little further to find a place to camp. I started to look around for possible "hotels". I cursed when the door of a shed was locked, but then came to the church, where some women were cleaning the stone floor inside. They looked up and smiled.

My feet were on fire, my legs throbbing, I could feel the blood pulsing around the arteries. I sat down on the church steps and ate the only food I had, a cold can of ratatouille with stale bread. A dog kept creeping closer and closer until she finally let me pet her, bribing her with a piece of bread. The women went off into the night, chatting and chuckling.

A car parked in front of me and the occupants went into the house opposite, the children grinning shyly at me, the parents waving. The bells chimed softly, almost as if not to break the ambience. I laid out my sleeping bag in the shelter of the church porch and stretched out. It took two hours for my feet and legs to finally relax, and I fell asleep. The following day I realised I had walked fifty two kilometres.

The church bells woke me at seven. I sat up, rubbing my eyes and getting my bearings. It was cold and damp. A thick, deep, eerie mist covered the valley. Nothing moved, the sun was just poking over the hills, its rays splicing the moisture swirling around me. I yawned and stretched, my ribs cracking. Dressing quickly, I strode off, the only things on my mind being a large coffee and a pain au chocolat. They were a long way off.

I crossed a bridge above the river Bidouze. The water was clear and fresh and the bottom littered with red and yellow stones. I dropped down to the bank, cupped the water with my hands and splashed it onto my face. Above the damp track, water droplets clung to orange leaves and eventually plummeted down to join small trickles weaving their path around tree roots and stones. The Chapelle de Soyarza was visible at the summit of the next hill, a 210-metre climb away. Solitary and isolated, it seemed to mock me. As I ascended, the mist covering the valley resembled a cloak of white silk haphazardly left in a pile on the floor, undulating against the knolls and hills. Birds dived and soared on thermals like boats on choppy water, disappearing into the translucent dankness. A dog howled somewhere in a village, and soon a chorus erupted as others joined in.

The summit was quiet. I looked at my watch: it was eight o'clock. Still nothing stirred, I was on my own. Pilgrims were no doubt walking, but they would have slept in *gîtes* and be far behind me. There was a stone map carved on a granite plinth depicting the panorama in front of me. The Virgin Mary watched me from the chapel behind, her crisp, white stone contrasting against the dark oak beams around her. A small room next door for visitors would have made a perfect place to rest the previous evening if I had had the strength to make it. I wrote a message in the visitors' book to Jeannie: "21st September. 08:00 am. On the final push to St Jean, will make it today, see you there".

I was ravenous, not having eaten anything remotely nutritious for twenty-four hours. After ten kilometres I saw Ostbat Asme on a distant hill, but it seemed to take forever to get there. I entered the town as pilgrims in the past had always done, snaking my way along a path riddled with trickles of water, mud and livestock excrement. The lower part of town was where, traditionally, the poorer pilgrims would rest and take shelter. The upper town had higher-grade establishments and was reserved for those with money. In appearance at least, nothing much had changed. I reached a small square, where there was an épicerie also selling fresh baked delicacies. I stocked up on food and sat outside with a coffee and croissant, as cats played with my bootlaces and cows meandered down the street more often than cars.

Now that I had eaten, St-Jean-Pied-de-Port was within striking distance. The terrain started to roll in preparation for the Pyrenees beyond, as if someone had ruffled the landscape like a rug. The mountains, thrusting up from the depths of the earth, loomed a little closer each time I dared look at them. St-Jean-Pied-de-Port played 'catch me if you can' for most of the day. Every time I came to a cluster of houses I thought I was on its outskirts, but I was merely passing through hamlets in the approach to it.

When I did eventually arrive, the change was startling. I passed under the Porte St Jacques and came into a town bursting with Camino energy. There were pilgrims all over the Rue de la Citadelle, spilling out of cafés, talking on corners, walking in their multicoloured clothes, like a moving border of spring flowers, veterans and novices, those hardened by walking and those who had yet to discover both the trials and the splendours of the Camino. I lapped the whole scene up with relish, beaming contentedly.

I had made it half way.

One of the start points of the Camino, St-Jean-Pied–de-

Port, or St-Jean as it was affectionately known, is an attractive town and a wonderful place to rest. Somehow it had managed not to generate that tacky atmosphere that hangs about many tourist towns. Apart from the odd postcard stand outside a shop, there was a noticeable lack of cheap establishments offering out-of-fashion hats, T-shirts and fluffy toys.

The Citadelle overlooked the town, but from most angles was obscured by trees. Traditionally, Pilgrims entered the town, as I had done, by the Porte St Jacques, just down the slope supporting the fortifications. The path followed the Rue de la Citadelle, a steep, cobbled street leading down to the lower town. Bridges forded the river Nive where many a photographer had snapped the reflections of houses rising out of its waters.

I was tired and didn't know where the refuge was so asked directions from a local who obviously misunderstood me and I ended up in a small, cheap hotel. Not wanting to walk back to town I sat on the single bed to test out the comfort factor. It collapsed inward trapping me momentarily like a sandwich filling with my knees in my mouth. I chose the bottom bed of the bunk instead and was just preparing to inspect the bathroom when an extremely attractive young woman glided in effortlessly.

"You are walking Camino, yes?" she said. I always found it amazing how people knew I was English just by my looks. Perhaps it was the Union Jack boxer shorts that gave it away.

"Yes I am." She made motions to sit on the single bed.

"Er, that's not a great bed," I warned. "There's no support."

She tested it by pressing with one hand and screwed up her face in disapproval. Looking at the only other option of the top bunk and seeing my gear on the bottom one, I thought my luck was in when she announced:

"It's ok, I sleep on top of you."

Jeannie found me in the morning aimlessly walking around taking it all in.

"Hey! When did you get in?" she called from over the

road.

"Yesterday, as planned. You?"

"Last night. I got a ride into town!"

Jeannie had discovered the delights of hitchhiking. Using transport of any kind was generally frowned upon by the pilgrim masses, probably rightly; if you did, you could hardly say you had walked the Camino. We had discussed the pros and cons one day. I was determined to complete the whole distance without stepping on a train or bus, accepting a lift or indeed asking for one. Jeannie had a different outlook. She said that if she was tired or stuck somewhere with nowhere to sleep, then she would stick her thumb out. It made no impression on her conscience. I used to back her up when she came in for criticism. I guess, when all is said and done, Jeannie still walked a distance most people cannot even begin to comprehend.

"Where're you hanging out?" She crossed over the road to meet me, skipping like a ten-year-old.

"I'm at this *gîte* a little way out. It's not bad, actually, but I wish I had taken something closer to town. What about you?"

"There's this fantastic place by the Porte St Jacques. There's a lot of people there, and this old woman runs around the kitchen, grabs everyone's food and cooks it for them, whether they want her to or not! It's awesome, you should come take a look, in fact come up at seven, bring some food, wine and we'll eat and get pissed.

"Oh, and Fozzie," she called after me, "believe it or not, there's an Irish couple there. They're starting to walk tomorrow."

This doesn't exactly sound like world-shattering news. However, at this point, after seven hundred and fifty kilometres, or thereabouts, I had met no English walkers whatsoever and no Irish, Welsh or Scottish. As far as I knew, I was the only guy from Great Britain on the entire Camino. Not that it bothered me, but it would have been nice to catch up with a fellow countryman, check out what was happening back home, take the piss out the French, and so on.

I called Trisha in Greece to get the latest news on the taverna. I didn't know whether to feel sad or happy when she told me it was all off. The owner had apparently changed his mind. I moped around town for a while, walking aimlessly up and down streets, trying to come to grips with it all. Then I realised my Camino would be back to how it was at the start. Once again, I had no schedule, and anyway something else would materialise in Greece, I was sure. Gradually my good mood was restored.

The *gîte* Jeannie was staying in was a cracker. It was right at the entrance to town, on the hill. Traditionally built, it fell away on a severe slope, so that you could walk in the entrance at ground level, go down three flights of steps and emerge at street level again. I hardly recognised anyone.

"Fozzie, this is Roberta and Sean," announced Jeannie.

"Hi, I'm Fozzie. How far you planning on going?"

"To Santiago, we hope," said Sean. Roberta just lay on her bunk looking at us. It was all she could do to raise her hand to shake mine when I offered it. I just knew, at that moment, that she wouldn't make it. I doubt whether she even had the inclination to get out of bed. Sean looked more determined and enthusiastic, but they both looked underequipped. Their packs were tiny, and Sean's was more of a duffel bag, made from leather. If it rained, his gear would get soaked.

I squeezed myself into the basement kitchen with Jeannie. There were about twelve of us in there, including a couple of faces I recognised. They had all brought down their own food to cook but the old woman cordoned off the stove and cooked it all, letting no one else come near. Some found this amusing, as I did, but others scowled. As it turned out, not only was she a damn fine cook, but she knew what everyone had been intending to cook, and produced it. The German guys looked astounded when she plonked a pot of spaghetti bolognese in front of them. Somehow, in all the confusion, Jeannie managed to sneak in and whip up a salad. I don't know how she managed to get past the security, but, knowing Jeannie, she gave as good as she got.

It was one of those meals where everyone shared, where food kept coming from nowhere, and the wine flowed freely. Occasionally, a few of us would open the back door and go outside for a cigarette. The street lamps of St Jean winked back at us from below. People would leave, others would arrive. We ate whatever was going, drank whatever was offered. We laughed, talked, joked, told stories and enjoyed the atmosphere. I remember most of the Camino, but certain situations shine more brightly in my memory. That evening was one of them.

The trek out of St Jean to the Spanish hamlet of Roncesvalles is infamous, at least among pilgrims. A few had already walked it, and were back to do it again. Some had heard of it, a few had read up on the road that winds up to around 1,350 metres above sea level, but everyone was talking about it. It's by no means a huge elevation, but except for the route up to El Cebreiro in Spain, it is the toughest section of the entire Camino and is to the Camino what Everest is to the Himalayas. Named the Route Napoléon, after the conqueror himself had led his army over it, it takes the traveller over the border into Spain, and for those who start at Le Puy, as I had, it meant the start not only of the Spanish section but also of the second half of the walk. I was looking forward to it immensely.

The weather, however, was threatening. Most of my stay in St Jean had been interrupted by huge downpours, and although on the big day it wasn't raining, the sky over the pass and surrounding area was black enough to make me cower every time I looked skywards. Jeannie had started earlier than I did, but we had agreed to meet 'somewhere' on the way to Roncesvalles, the first place to stay in Spain.

As I trudged upwards, kicking at the damp leaves, St Jean melted into green, lush fields. The sun had broken through and bitumen on the road I was following blazed and glistened, making me squint. Ahead, coloured ponchos curled ever up, looking like twinkling Christmas lights. My mental juke box settled on 'Viva España' as song of the day.

Fourteen years previously, I had driven down from

England with a Spanish friend to the north coast of Spain. Those distant memories needed re-kindling. France was beautiful, no question about that, but I was eager to experience a different country, and my appetite for new sights, new traditions and new spectacles was ravenous. I had imagined dusty landscapes and blistered earth. Sitting at bars nursing a Spanish beer and being plied with various tapas. Tomatoes and pimientos drying on rooftops. Smiling Latin woman with black hair. Olive trees and old, earth-coloured villages.

I walked without stopping to the half way point of the pass, the Vierge d'Orisson. A small statue of the Virgin Mary stood by the side of the road and it was there that I looked over and saw Jeannie, who waved. She had taken the opportunity to rest with Sean, Roberta, a Korean girl called Yoko and a Spanish guy called Antonio. We were joined by a French Canadian woman called Pascal. We sat on the damp grass taking in the view and munching on snacks. Hills and peaks rollercoastered before us. The high of the previous evening still lingered, and everyone seemed happy and relaxed. The steady procession of walkers crept past us towards the summit, where the way toppled down again.

At half past two in the afternoon, we rounded a corner and saw the border crossing. I don't know what I was expecting, really. In the Europe of my younger days, border crossings were places that were stringently policed and held in wary respect. Unable to shake off that image, I imagined a Spanish border guard who sported a huge, black moustache and had a cigarette dangling on his lower lip. His feet would be propped up on a chair, his arms folded over a bulbous stomach, snoring with the odd grunt as he shifted his position, just like in the movies. The reality was quite different: just a cattle grid and gate. I admit to having been a little disappointed. I half wanted to be asked to step to one side while they went through my bag and looked at me suspiciously. I wanted that overweight security guard to scan the pages of my passport and ask me ridiculous questions, questions so irrelevant and useless that they could be asked only at those forbidding border crossings of the eighties. I demanded hassle. I wanted those memories rekindled.

While waiting for the others to come, I took photos of Pascal, then Antonio, Sean and Roberta, with Yoko and Jeannie bringing up the rear. We told silly frontier jokes. Someone ran over the cattle grid and back several times, shouting, "Should I stay or should I go?" and we all rolled about giggling.

We continued up to the summit. As we separated out again, finding our own pace, we entered the clouds that had been threatening all day and I donned my waterproofs. Through the clouds that occasionally broke up at the top, I glimpsed the rooftops of the monastery at Roncesvalles, set among trees below me. We all walked down together, the drizzle clearing as we came out of the clouds once more. Steaming hoods and ponchos were removed, jackets peeled off.

Some local people were searching for fungi among the grasses on the slopes around us, occasionally bending over, pointing and gesticulating, beckoning others over for verification, and filling up their wooden baskets with edibles.

As we arrived alongside the monastery, a woman opened one of the countless windows and beckoned us down a short cut to the rear. This was to be our first refugio. More common in Spain than the French *gîtes*, they were a whole new experience and proved to be good and bad, some so comfortable that they were like hotels, others just grubby, dilapidated buildings. Some wardens were helpful and friendly, others would have done an admirable job in charge of a prison.

The monastery was certainly an impressive baptism. It was Augustinian, founded in the early twelfth century and was huge; even the hospital building, which housed pilgrims, was a maze of rooms and corridors. We didn't know where to bed down or whom to see. In the end we dumped our packs in an empty room with a few bunk beds scattered around and Jeannie found the office where we were required to sign in.

At the end of a long, stone office stood a desk, dwarfed by the size of the room, and seemingly an eternal distance away from the door. A woman was perched behind it and a gentleman stood by her shoulder with an air of authority. I took an instant dislike to him. We produced our pilgrims' passports, which she duly stamped, and then logged our details in a huge, leather-bound book that appeared older than the monastery. When we had made our donation, the man instructed us to collect our bags and follow him. No one dared argue.

He led us down steps and through passageways to a smaller room, already crammed with damp pilgrims. I grabbed the first available bottom bunk. He spewed out a list of regulations in Spanish, and then broken English. He told us that there was no food available except in the small restaurant across the square. We must respect the values of the monastery; everyone must be in bed by 22:00 and leave by 08:00 in the morning.

I was still not sleeping well, but the later I stayed up, the more tired I was, and the more chance I had of beating my insomnia. I was not looking forward to the restless night that was bound to follow an early bedtime. As he left the room, some people stood up and saluted, some bowed. At first we looked at each other in silence, taking it all in. Then someone giggled, and soon we were all laughing and joking at being incarcerated.

Curfews and strict rules, we were to discover, were commonplace at the refugios. In some places we felt as if we were literally being locked up. In others the regime was a lot more relaxed. However, they were a godsend, whichever way you looked at them, regardless of our complaints. Providing the rudimentary basics for the pilgrim, they were perfect: a roof over your head, occasionally somewhere to cook, sometimes a hot meal, showers, a haven to be with others and all in return for a mere donation. I would not have been without them for a second and I take my hat off to the people who give up their time to become volunteers there.

Some of us went over to the restaurant to eat. I propped up the bar for most of the evening with Christian, a cyclist. We downed San Miguels with gusto, savouring the new taste. Pilgrims mixed with local people. There was a permanent smoke haze, glasses clinked, espresso machines gurgled and spluttered, laughs burst out and the odd cheer erupted as the local football team scored on the TV. I was already being drawn into the Spanish way, and I was loving every second of it.

Over the next few days, I spent a lot of time getting to know new faces and characters. Sean and Roberta were an interesting young couple, aged about nineteen and a constant source of amusement, annoyance and bewilderment. When I had first met them in the refuge in St-Jean-Pied-de-Port, Sean's face shone with an eager look that I have seen before in people who realise that some long-held dream has suddenly come to fruition. Disregarding the fact that he was due to return to Ireland to continue his studies, he often seemed to be straining at the leash. Roberta had apparently just come along for the ride, because her boyfriend was doing it, and most of the time she was the one pulling back on that leash. They were constantly bickering, even on day one, and it wasn't uncommon to round a corner and find Sean being beaten around the head by Roberta's walking stick, sometimes supplemented by a few punches.

Roberta was incredibly immature, and Sean, for some reason that escaped me, doted on her, which she milked mercilessly. He would run around doing her favours, bringing her food and drink, every time she waved her hand. What he saw in her I don't know. She was attractive, there was no denying, but she must have received a privileged upbringing, for she was used to getting what she asked for. Their relationship very nearly came to an abrupt end on day two, after a massive argument and several blows of the walking stick. By evening she had him doing her bidding like a servant.

I had no time for Roberta but I liked Sean. He had a free spirit, which I could imagine him nurturing over the coming years by travelling the world, seeking experiences and answers. He was extremely intelligent and amusing, and had a genuine desire to become a writer. He was the only person I met on the Camino, apart from me, who carried a Dictaphone to make notes at the end of the day. One day, when we were alone, he told me he planned to write a book and wanted to ask me a favour.

"Really?" I said. "I want to write a book too. What's yours going to be about?"

"Well, it's gonna follow the format of *The Canterbury Tales*. I want some short stories from walkers on the Camino. They don't have to be true. They can be experiences, dreams, hopes, anything. They don't even have to be about the Camino."

"Sounds like a great idea," I said. "So, I'm assuming the favour is you're gonna ask me to contribute. I'm very flattered."

"No, I wanted to bum a smoke." We both laughed. "Yeah. I would like you to give me one of the tales. All I need is for you to borrow my Dictaphone one day, and just talk into it. Around fifteen minutes should be fine."

Yoko, the Korean girl, found her own pace and obviously preferred to walk on her own. I took a liking to Pascal, in fact, I had a bit of a crush on her. She was way too tall, her wavy hair was tied back in a bob, and she always seemed to look great, like a genuine traveller. When we joked about and flirted, she would giggle and screw her face up, her eyes reducing to narrow slits as she playfully hit me. I found her French Canadian accent romantic, and I admit to being a little disappointed when she eventually explained she had a boyfriend, and, worse still, he was coming out to walk with her.

Antonios was a battler. He was Spanish, short and built like a tank. He reminded me of a Rottweiler, someone you wouldn't want to get into a fight with. He was obviously struggling with the walk, but whenever I saw him or walked with him, he had such an air of determination about him, I never once doubted that he would succeed. He was usually behind most of us, and he stopped often, but would emerge at the end of the day, sweating, panting and red in the face, but with a cheeky look on his face reflecting pride in his achievement.

This collection of people formed itself loosely into a group. We would usually start the day together and then drift apart to walk alone or with a companion, taking rests with or without the others. No one asked if they could walk with us, and no one assumed we were even a group, but you knew each day that you could round a corner and be met with an Irish guy being beaten up by his girlfriend, a sweaty Rottweiler, a Korean drifting along in her own world, a cute girl scrunching her features up or a mad American woman.

Pamplona was the largest settlement I had encountered so far on the Camino, and the experience of being thrust into a large metropolis caught me unawares. It is home to the tradition of "the running of the bulls" during the first two weeks of July, when hundreds of young Spanish men, with a few tourists, run for their lives through Pamplona's streets while being pursued by a herd of bulls. Unfortunately it was a spectacle I had missed.

I entered the suburbs with Jeannie. For an hour or so we made our way through the ugly outskirts interwoven with quieter, countrified lanes, between non-descript old and modern buildings, failing to discover any real sense of identity in this place, reputed for its beauty and culture. As we crossed the river Arga over the Puente de los Peregrinos, the tall, grey buildings gave way to the old town. The change was instantaneous. We gawped up at the inner set of ramparts towering above us, crossed over the drawbridge on Calle del Carmen, the wooden planks thudding and bouncing under our boots, and wound our way through to the true centre of the city. I am not a fan of cities but I immediately fell in love with Pamplona and if I had to live in a city, this would be top of the list.

Grand, ornate, stone buildings hemmed in wide, pedestrianised streets, full of people bustling about without any sense of urgency. Most were impeccably dressed, the women in autumn fashions, designer sunglasses and long, sepia-toned coats. Tapas bars abounded, along with a thousand pavement cafés serving good coffee. There were laundries (a rarity in France), several internet establishments and even a condom shop. For me, though a country boy at heart, it was heaven.

Somehow we managed to find the refugio, which was situated on the first floor of a tall building. As we climbed what seemed like an endless flight of steps, I had the feeling I wasn't going to like it.

A squat man wearing a look of grim severity sat behind a desk, and behind him stood an older woman peering over the top of half-framed glasses. Having booked us in, he told us we should be back at the refugio by 21:30, lights out was at 22:00 and we had to leave by 08:00. I was furious. I walked off before they got the full brunt of my attack, and tried to avoid the others, to give myself time to calm down.

"Fozzie, whoa! You look pissed! What's up?" said Sean.

I let it all out. I think he was sorry he asked.

"It's these fucking refugios. They're driving me insane!" I spat. "In bed by such and such a time, leave by this time, don't do this, don't do that! What is it with the bloody Spanish that makes them think pilgrims must suffer? Why do we have to learn to accept hardship, just to be 'true' pilgrims! It's all bullshit!"

He looked at me in silence.

"All I want to do," I continued, "is to be able to go out once in a while, just once, and have a few drinks with my friends, or have a leisurely meal with good conversation and not have to worry about getting back to a refugio by half past bloody nine. I feel like I'm seven years old!" I looked at Jeannie. "If you wanna share a hotel tomorrow night then I'll go halves with you. In fact, I'll bloody pay for it! How's that?"

"Sure," she grinned, which is probably all she wanted to risk saying.

"I'm going to have a shower, put on some clean clothes, and then I'm going out to get pissed, you know, not drunk, really, really trolleyed. You're welcome to join me."

"Sure," she grinned again.

Sean had retreated to the security of his bunk, as half of the dormitory looked at me as if I had lost it. I sheepishly averted my gaze and began sorting out some gear.

By the time I had showered and left Colditz I had calmed down a little. The streets were just starting to fill up with people looking for food, fluid and fun. We checked out a couple of places and decided on a tapas bar with some cheap, tasty-looking offerings. Two American guys whom Jeannie knew joined us at the table, and we all started laying into the whisky. My worries melted away amid a blurred fusion of scotch, animated conversation, laughter and good food. Pretty soon we were a raucous bunch of drunken idiots. Everyone was slurring, laughing uncontrollably, walking sideways to the bar and trying to focus on anything that was relatively stationary and offered a secure bearing. We wolfed down octopus, chips, tortilla, salads and various other delicious dishes before grudgingly heading back just before 22:00.

The others went to bed. I tried to sober up a little, and retreated to the kitchen where I hoped the warden wouldn't check for stragglers. At 21.55 (I know this because I looked at the clock on the wall), the warden opened the door, looked at me, held out his watch and tapped the face. "Doce minutes," he said. "Si," I muttered, returning to my book.

A few minutes later Jeannie and the two Americans came in. They couldn't sleep, they said, and we started to joke around, though trying to keep quiet. We could hardly have known what deep trouble we were in. The door flew open and there stood the squat warden, shaking with rage, legs apart, clearly trying his utmost to look threatening. One hand gripped a cordless phone as if he were trying to throttle it, while the other forced the door back. His face was so red with fury that it looked like a balloon at stretching point. If it hadn't been for his pink striped pyjama bottoms, I might have been a little scared. I couldn't decide whether we were in a horror movie or a comedy.

"Usted vallase a dormir o si no llamare a la policia!" he screamed. We all looked at each other. No translation was needed: the phone in his hand and the words "policia" and "dormir" told us all we wanted to know.

"He's gonna call the police?" I asked, gobsmacked.

"Actually," said one of the Americans, "I'm not sure of the exact translation, but basically he says that if we don't go to sleep, he will call the police." We were all desperately trying to stifle giggles, hands clasped over mouths, avoiding eye contact in case it set one of us off.

"What's he gonna do?" I said. "Arrest us for not sleeping?"

That was the spark for the flame. Jeannie drunkenly collapsed on the table, giggling so uncontrollably that she looked as though she was having spasms. The two Americans rocked back on their chairs in hysterics, holding their stomachs.

"Usted vallase a dormir o si no llamare a policia!" he screamed again, brandishing the phone like a dagger. Jeannie and the other two ran out laughing and went to bed. For some reason he seemed to forget about me, and by some miracle I stayed in there for another hour or so, reading. I deeply hoped he would come back in, as I would have loved to make him call the police, just for the hell of it. He never came back – nor did the police show up.

When I did eventually climb up to my bunk, the snoring in the room had reached epic volume. I lay there for what seemed like an eternity, staring at the ceiling and following lines of cracks. I turned to my right so I could see one of the offenders, separated from me by an aisle. I crept out of bed and retrieved my trekking pole, then returned to my bunk, extended it to full length, gingerly manoeuvred it to above the guy's leg and smacked him just above the knees. He gurgled a little, twitched his nose and swung his palm in front of his face as if swatting a fly. He stopped snoring for a few seconds, gurgled some more and fired up again. I must have hit him five or six times, with more frustration in each blow. Another pilgrim was observing and chuckling at my antics. I decided a new approach was called for. Again I steered the pole over towards the guy opposite, but this time I positioned the end directly over his nose, made delicate contact and pushed down. He snorted, grumbled, turned over while muttering something about carrots and stopped snoring. Amazingly, at that precise moment, the pilgrim below stopped also. The guy who was watching mimed a round of applause and shortly after, about forty-two pilgrims managed to get some shut-eye.

All we heard of the warden in the morning was the dormitory door being opened, the light clicking on and the door being closed again. It was 06:45.

Jeannie and I gingerly emerged on to the streets of a city still immersed in darkness. As I squinted around for a café with lights on, Jeannie grabbed my arm and pulled me in the opposite direction, pointing to the faint glow of a pastry and coffee shop. As we drank and munched, we laughed at the previous night's events.

It was time for a rest day and, having no schedule, I was free to explore this fantastic city and do all kinds of things I hadn't been able to do on this walk so far: sleep in a decent bed, with crisply laundered linen, experience the wonders of tapas bars, drink red wine, sample a good Spanish café au lait, eat sweet pastries, amble around and check out the shops, buy something I didn't need just for the sake of it, take some photos and generally indulge myself.

When the daylight became reasonable we headed off to what looked like a promising hotel that the tourist office had inked on a map for us. As we walked past a bar, our two American friends called to us and we joined them for more coffee and laughter. They were off to hike around the Picos de Europa, a range of mountains to the north, and we shook hands and wished them well. We also bumped into Monica, a Swiss pilgrim, who led us to the fantastic hotel she had found. Before long we had checked in and were making full use of our newfound freedom, strewing gear randomly around the room just for the hell of it. We watched some TV, and I dived into a hot bath. It was total luxury.

Smelling of hotel soap, we forayed out again into Pamplona. We pigged out on croissants and omelet wedged into warm baguette. Sitting on chairs on the pavement, we sipped coffees, and I gave into the temptation of reading a newspaper, looking up every now and then to watch the world walk past. It was nearly October but the sky was blue and I lapped up the heat, wearing just shorts and a shirt. Having finished breakfast and brunch, we moved rapidly into lunch, which included red wine and portions of the tastiest-looking offerings I had yet seen. Glass cabinets lined the bars filled to breaking point. I didn't even have to speak Spanish. I would just catch the barman's eye, point to a dish and nod. Bowls of octopus salad squeezed up against small slices of bread decorated with all manner of toppings. Huge, dried hams hung from the ceiling. I had died and gone to food and drink heaven.

I even managed to grab a good night's sleep. A firm mattress, soft sheets, a gentle breeze and the hum of the street below got me slumbering like a baby. I was out for eleven hours straight. The following morning we left late and in no hurry, satisfied but with a heavy heart at leaving Pamplona.

The landscape was quite different from the greens of France. The wind caught dust and sent it spiralling up from the trail in mini whirlwinds. We passed through small, quiet hamlets, their sand-coloured buildings looking as though they had been hewn from the very earth itself. But for a few tumbleweeds blowing around and a sleeping bandit hidden under a sombrero, we could have been in a Mexican movie scene.

The Monte del Perdon loomed ahead, dotted with a line of some forty white, glistening windmills. At the top, so the story goes, a pilgrim was accosted by Satan, who promised to show the thirsty man a hidden fountain, but only if he renounced god, the Virgin Mary and St James. The pilgrim refused. St James himself then appeared as a pilgrim and led the man to the fountain, much to the disgust of the devil.

The view from the summit was stunning, and I was to

encounter similar views many times in Spain. From here we could see the way spread out before us, like a three-dimensional map, and the Camino linking three villages, Uterga, Muruzabal and Obanos, like a piece of string.

It was then that I saw a pilgrim I had noticed earlier when she walked past the place where I was having lunch. She was tall, with curves in all the right places, and she glided along effortlessly. Her long, ebony hair hung down her back as though it was wet. She was, quite frankly, beautiful. As I had looked up, I smiled. She had smiled back. I was totally smitten.

"Jeannie, I'll stop in Uterga for you!" I called through the wind.

"What are you doing?" she called back. I nodded towards the pilgrim who had just passed, winked and smiled. She understood and winked back, then, calling "Good luck", she disappeared behind me.

It took me two kilometres to catch up with her. I figured her long legs were giving her an unfair advantage. As I finally pulled alongside her, she smiled again, almost as if she was expecting me.

"What is the problem with your leg?" I asked. She was wincing with each step. She spoke little English, but somehow we managed to string a conversation together. It was an old injury that had sprung up again, and, as with many walkers, it centred on the knee. I got the impression it was something to do with a past skiing trip. To be honest, I wasn't too concerned: I was just glad to be talking to her. She told me her name was Tamar.

We talked for fifteen minutes or so until we arrived at Uterga It was deathly quiet, an elderly couple sitting outside their house offering the only signs of life. The woman gave me a toothless grin. Her husband sat in a wheelchair next to her. Tamar told me that there was a refugio in the village somewhere, but it was not marked in any of the guidebooks. She decided to walk on to the next town and as she strode off, I stood there, eyes wide, looking like a puppy that had mislaid its bone.

Jeannie arrived shortly after.

"Any luck?" she said, smiling and winking again.

"I'm working on it. Tamar was saying there's a refugio here somewhere, it's not in any of the books, some sort of a mysterious, local secret."

I was in one of those moods where I couldn't be bothered to apply even a modicum of effort to anything. Jeannie soon noticed and kindly offered to ask around.

"Yeah," I said. "Sorry, want to sit down. Just feeling like a lazy bastard."

Jeannie went about the task with gusto and walked up to the old couple near us. After a few bits of murmured conversation, she called to me triumphantly. "It's in here!"

"What?" I questioned.

"This woman looks after it! We were sitting looking at it!"

It seemed a doctor had reserved one room in his building for pilgrims. It had one bunk bed and a shower room. I couldn't believe it.

"I wonder why she didn't say anything?" I said.

"Perhaps she just thought we were resting before carrying on," said Jeannie.

I came across similar scenarios a few times in Spain. The guidebook might say there was a shop in a particular village, but then in brackets note, "It is unmarked. Ask for it." These secret shops, bars and refugios were everywhere, but were kept quiet. I never did figure out why. Normally, if you are running a business, you want to advertise it. But I guess that if you live on the Camino and have a few thousand foreigners walking past every summer, asking stupid questions in strange languages, you might just want to keep what you have to yourself.

Chapter Nine

Roasting Peppers

The further I walked into Spain the more it affected me. Except for a package holiday to Salou one year, I had affectionate memories of this country. Now, though, I felt I was out there in the thick of it. I saw fields still being ploughed by man and horse. Onions were hung out to dry. People still roasted all their peppers, peeled the skin off, and preserved them for the winter. They ate what was grown in the back yard. Supermarkets hadn't really made their mark out in the countryside, where there was no real need for them. I saw old women making cheeses by hand, they were pleased to let me taste when I asked. Families would want to make conversation when I went over to them. They would give me a bunch of grapes that had literally just been pulled off the vine. They would offer me a slug from the bottle of wine they had, and tempt me with meat crackling over a lunchtime fire. All I had to do was cast envious eyes at picnickers' food and they would obligingly call me over.

On the approach to Ciraqui the rain I had been avoiding for so long caught me up. For three hours Jeannie and I walked along tracks transformed into torrents of water and mud. The elements pounded us relentlessly. Strangely, I was enjoying it. First, it was a new experience, one I had not encountered so far on the Camino and, as much as I normally hated rain, I realised that I had sorely missed it. Second, the waterproofs were doing me proud. After I had cocooned myself in, the feeling that I was dry, and, despite the efforts of Mother Nature, would remain that way, gave me a feeling of security. Jeannie was faring a little worse. She had no pack cover and tried unsuccessfully to strap a space blanket over the whole thing. What is basically a sheet of aluminium foil wriggled and writhed in the gusts as we struggled to tie it on.

We found shelter in a pedestrian tunnel under the road, and sat there reading messages on the walls left by pilgrims stretching back years. We kidded ourselves that we were drying off, and smoked a couple of cigarettes. We splashed onto Ciraqui which offered nothing in the way of overnight shelter; even the church was locked.

Under the thick, dark clouds, we trudged on for another seven kilometres, skirting around freshly ploughed fields, making slow headway as thick, red mud clung in huge lumps to the tread of our boots. It felt like autumn. Lorca loomed above us like a garrison perched on an impregnable hill, I felt I was a medieval soldier planning the best line of attack. We pushed up to the top, through stone streets glinting in the evening sun. The air was ripe with the sweet smell of peppers and charcoal, and we passed people with sooty hands peeling off the pepper skins next to orange and red embers that glowed and faded with the fluctuating breezes.

Two men were working on a car.

"Ola!" I called. "Donde esta el refugio?"

Jeannie did her best to translate as the younger man explained that there was nowhere to stay in the town.

"Shit, Fozzie! I dunno if I can go any further! I'm finished!" She dropped her head and let her eyes roll up at me like a child who had been caught doing wrong.

"OK, I don't need the puppy-eyed routine," I said. "I owe you one for the other day anyway, so I will secure lodgings!"

Again the church was shut; in fact, everything seemed firmly fastened as if another storm was expected. The village had an air of abandonment and decay about it, as if the residents had moved on and let it rot. The occasional drop from a gutter would slap the top of my head and send a trickle down my neck that made me twitch with a shiver. To my surprise, I noted that the guidebook mentioned "Rooms". I walked back to the mechanic.

"Habitaciones?" I said.

"Si." He pointed across the street about twenty metres to a little house. Jeannie and I looked at each other and then at him, with palms up and raised eyebrows.

"Why didn't he tell us that when we asked him?" I wondered.

She shrugged her shoulders and gave me a cheeky grin, as though she was the same kid who had just been given some sweets.

When I knocked at the door, a woman eventually appeared with a face of total kindness. She took one look at our sopping hair and red faces, held her hands up in pity and manhandled us both into the front room. It was like a little Swiss chalet inside, with wooden beams and walls of carved, dark wood. We took our damp gear to the loft, where she showed us lines to dry it on. We delicately stepped around huge piles of nuts being stored on the floor. The bedroom was like something out of Moulin Rouge: vibrant red and gold wall coverings reflected in glass-covered tables, and an elaborate chandelier reflecting the last of the sun's rays around the room.

After a bath, I wandered back out on to the streets, zipping my fleece tighter around my chin and trying without much success to stretch it over my ears, stomping my feet and watching my breath rise out of sight. The mechanics had given up for the day, removing the last sign that anyone actually still lived there. Nightfall shrouded everything in shades from a dead fire, blacks, greys and whites. Menacing clouds parted like a theatre curtain to reveal a blazing moon, sending streaks of silver racing through the streets. The whole scene looked like the set for the opening sequence of a fifties horror movie.

"Buenas noches." The speaker startled me. He walked past me, washed his hands in the central fountain and emptied black coloured water from a huge saucepan, then he refilled it.

"Pimientas?" I enquired, the only piece of Spanish I could muster. I assumed the dirty water was from the burnt skins of the peppers.

"Si," he replied. I pointed to my eyes and then to the peppers, suggesting I would like to see him work.

"Si," he said again, smiling, and gently took my arm. He led me to a garage door and pushed it open. An older man, perhaps eighty, and two kids of about fourteen looked up at me and smiled. They beckoned me sit on the floor. For half an hour I watched as they carefully arranged their pickings from the summer and prepared them for preservation over the winter. In one corner was an oil drum cut in half, with a grid resting over it. Halves of the red peppers were sweating, spitting and blistering as they finally surrendered to the heat. One of the boys would occasionally fetch them and put them in the large pan of water the man had collected, and restock the cooker with a new batch. The other boy and the two men sat on old beer crates, pulling out the pepper halves and removing the skin in several peels, occasionally dipping the piece back in the water to rinse off the burnt flakes. The liquid took on a dark hue, with black pieces of skin floating on the surface like dirty oil. Lastly, the old man would take the now juicy, bright red pieces of flesh and bottle them with a preservative of olive oil. Once in a while, they passed me a piece to taste. With the slightest suggestion of a bite, the piece would disintegrate and the flavour burst out. They ate pieces themselves, rolling their eyes upwards and grinning to display their enjoyment.

The following morning I felt the need to be alone. Jeannie, always understanding, walked with me for a short way and then let me go. I walked through Estella and bumped into Tamar stuffing food from a petrol station into her pack. I asked her how her knee was getting on, and she said it seemed to be making progress. We casually agreed that we might see each other in Los Arcos, my destination for the day.

The afternoon walk between Azqueta and Los Arcos was like being on another planet. For three hours I trod smooth, gravelled tracks. I did not need to concentrate on the surface, so let my eyes wander around at the surroundings. Every once in a while the scenery would change dramatically. In the morning I had been walking through damp, green woods and lush grass. Now, I was passing through a shallow valley, dry and desolate, with the small hills curving up either side of me like a cupped hand. Occasionally a ruined stone building would come into view on the hills as the trees parted. I could see for miles, and still make out the worn surface of the Camino, beige against the ochre soil, coiling away to the distant hill. I wrote my name in the soil with my trekking pole, as I had been doing through most of Spain. Other pilgrims often said they liked to see a familiar name etched in the ground.

Los Arcos seemed like an eternity away. The scenery, bare for miles around, offered no clues until the last minute, when the town appeared, just a kilometre before I got there, cresting a hill and protruding from the landscape, the Camino dipping down to meet it. It caught me completely by surprise, a good surprise as I thought I had more walking to get there so it's premature arrival put a smile on my face. As I entered the town, I heard Pascal's familiar laugh from a shop doorway. I peered in and poked her in the back.

"Fozzie! Where you been?" she said, swinging round to see me.

"Walking ... slowly. Did you find the refugio yet?"

"Oui, come, we show you."

It was a modern building on the outskirts and, like many, right on the Camino and hence teeming with pilgrims. It caught me unawares, I had experienced a thoughtful and serene day, I was relaxed and to suddenly be thrown into the hubbub put me on edge. I had to squeeze past people to sign in, squeeze up the stairs and squeeze through the dormitory. I wondered where they had all come from, the Camino had been quiet for a few days and now it seemed as though a coach load of new pilgrims had been emptied. My checking-in time was perfect, as they had just opened a new room, and as I was the last to check in it remained mine for the night, with a door to screen off the snorers.

I had agreed to cook a meal for Monica, who had kindly shared half the shopping bill in return. As I cooked, Tamar and some others seemed to be watching. I was hungry and needed to relax, the ideal environment for me to cook in, and soon the wine began to soothe me. I prepared kedgeree, a rice dish with fish, eggs, onion and curry powder. I tossed sliced potatoes in butter and rosemary, flecked with black pepper. A small salad completed the meal.

Meanwhile, Tamar, who, when I had first met her, had seemed a loner, quiet and reserved, was eating water melon with parma ham and suggestively kept feeding me pieces. She seemed carefree, happy, as if some problem had been resolved, and could scarcely string a sentence together for giggling. Whenever our eyes met, we would hold each other's gaze for a few seconds, and then laugh. I had a funny feeling in the pit of my stomach, the sort where you are excited about something, enjoying the anticipation. I realized I was seriously smitten.

There were few things about the Camino that annoyed me: the wardens and rules in some of the refugios, inability to find a meal when everyone was having a siesta – mundane things that I had to learn to deal with. Snoring, on the other hand, was really starting to get to me. Having had ample opportunity to study the practice I decided an in depth analysis was in order.

There was a definite pattern emerging and amongst the carnage that was a dormitory in the middle of a night with snorers going at it like their life depended on it, I began to figure out that there were essentially, only four types of snorers. I can therefore conclude my studies as follows.

The Back Snorer

The most common type. This person snores only while lying on his or her back. Some people believe, falsely, that this is the only position that people snore in.

The Side Snorer

Slightly less common than the back snorer, this person snores while sleeping on his or her side.

The Front Snorer

A difficult one to spot but not uncommon, this person is responsible for other innocent sleepers being accused of snoring.

The All-Positions Snorer

A rare breed, this person is accomplished in the art of sleeping and snoring in any position and for extended periods; and is to be avoided at all costs if possible.

Unfortunately, there is little one can do to stop a snorer. The only polite remedy is earplugs, which were a common sight in the refugios. I never bothered getting any, and suffered as a result.

You can try the aggressive approach, which worked for me a couple of times. A carefully aimed, quick and precise swing of a pillow to somewhere around the head area may result in a temporary respite. To avoid being discovered, lean over, aim, swing, make contact and immediately feign sleep. Trekking poles are useful, as I have already explained, and more precise. One remarkable method which I did not employ, but saw used on one occasion, was highly successful. After I had tried the pillow method unsuccessfully and several pilgrims had even thrown objects at the offender, two pilgrims got up, came over, politely shook the guy awake, turned on his torch, apologised for waking him and explained he was snoring, keeping the whole dormitory awake. They finished off by apologising again, and requesting he sleep on his stomach to reduce any possible risk. It worked – but because he was, luckily for us, only a back snorer.

Still worse were the rare occasions when several snorers were going at in harmony, one person snoring as he exhaled while another filled in the quiet spaces with his own variation on the theme. The last resort, if faced with this situation, is to pick up your mattress and bedding and get the hell out of it. Many a morning I would wake up in reception area or in the common room and then realise why. Of course nobody wants to up sticks in the middle of the night but it is pretty much the only wholly reliable method to beat the snorers.

I had lost contact with Jeannie. She had not arrived in Los Arcos the night before. It wasn't a big deal: we had not bound ourselves into being at any place at a certain time, nor were we walking "companions". By this stage, we walked together often but never felt obliged to. I knew I would see her before the Camino ended.

I set off that day with Monica, who kindly asked if she could walk with me as opposed to presuming that it would be all right. We found a great café in Torres del Rio and tucked into bacon and eggs, endless coffees and orange juice, not exactly authentic local cuisine but it hit the spot.

For the rest of the day I walked sometimes with Monica, sometimes with Tamar and sometimes with an Australian girl called Fiona, although she preferred everyone to use her surname of Breeder. I was scared to ask her why! I stopped in vineyards taking photos of local people. Often I would be invited to sit among the grapes with them and share their lunch of steak cooked over an open fire, washed down with wine. They were a joy to be with, for they were always laughing and joking around. The route dipped and dived into mini canyons raging from fifteen to maybe sixty metres deep. Cracks appeared on the soil crust like crazy paving and olive trees appeared, back from the trail, their silver leaves shyly peering over shrubs and small trees.

By this stage of the Camino I was completely at ease and at one with the walk. My rush to get to Greece had been cancelled so I had all the time in the world. I had blended in with a great group of perhaps thirty or so friends with whom

I was sharing and enjoying the experience. No one in this informal group had a particular companion. Some days I would be alone, some days I would be with one pilgrim, other days I would walk with five others. Some evenings there may be a couple of familiar faces dotted around a refuge and other days I would go to a local bar for a beer and end up laughing and shouting with fifteen others who had made the same plan. By this time, walking had become a way of life for us. We were nonchalant about it, feeling that whatever was thrown at us we could take in our stride. It was as though we had accepted that it was our destiny to be on the Camino for the rest of out lives. No one thought of the end. We just got up each morning and did what came naturally, walk.

It was now October. The sun was still out every day, and the temperature hovered around twenty degrees. A pollution cloud hovered in the skies over the city of Logrono as I made my way down the quiet track that would eventually merge into busy streets and roads. I stopped by an old lady at the side of the road and bought a scallop shell, the symbol of the Camino, which she tied on to my pack so that I wouldn't need to take it off. I left a message in her book, scanning the pages to see who was ahead of me. Breeder had passed the day before, and I recognised the shooting star symbol that Val, Jeannie's friend, had left. I regularly saw it on the Camino as well. Although they had parted, she was still leaving her sign for Jeannie.

The refugio was not open until three thirty, so I had a cappuccino at a bar, whose owner kindly agreed to let me leave my bag there so I could go and explore the town freely. I found the 'T' (tourist information) office and subsequently the internet café, where Tamar's shining deep black hair caught my eye and I gave her head a playful tickle as I walked past. She smiled at me from over the top of her monitor. It was all I could do to concentrate on fiddling with my keyboard. When she had finished, she walked over and said she would wait for me outside so we could go and get a drink somewhere. It took me about forty seconds to finish the rest of my emails.

We sat under a covered walkway with people milling about and waiters trying to dart through them. Her English was better than I had originally thought and with a little imagination we got by pretty well. She even read my palm, told me that the back pain I occasionally suffered was due to worrying about money too much, and told me to give up smoking. Whether there was any truth in what she said I didn't know, but it didn't seem to matter. I was surprised to learn that she was married, with a young daughter. I don't know why I was surprised; I just didn't picture her with a husband or a child – or perhaps it was truer to say I had hoped she didn't have a family. My spirits lifted a bit when she said she was getting divorced. She seemed to be plying me with all this information to test the water and see how I would respond. I don't know or much care how she interpreted my reaction. I had become infatuated with her. She walked back with me to the centre of town.

"Fozzie, do you want to walk with me?" she asked.

"I can't," I said. "I'd love to and I will – soon – but today I have walked all I planned to and now I want to rest. I hope you understand."

We hugged, and as she walked off out of Logrono, leaving me in the middle of the city, I wondered what it would be like to kiss her. I tried to figure out why I had refused her offer and rapidly came to the conclusion that I was a complete bloody idiot.

Some roads on the Camino entail taking your life into your own hands. The French appear to have taken this problem seriously. Most of the roads I walked on in France were quiet, country back roads with little or no traffic. The Spanish were aware of the problem and were taking measures, but some sections were appalling.

I had just left Navarette and was forced to walk on the road. This, unfortunately, was not a pleasant little country side road, more a main artery route with lorries and trucks hurtling towards me at a hundred kilometres an hour or racing past me perhaps two metres away, creating a dust-

and grit-filled slipstream that made me turn my head away and stop in my tracks, eyes tightly shut and breathing paused. I walked on the hard shoulder, leaving it whenever possible for a thin slice of gravel running alongside. Occasionally a welcome stretch of white shingle sloped away from the road where the Camino ran parallel for a while, but it would always eventually slope up again to throw me back into the battle.

My guidebook was pretty accurate and the direction signs were always there, somewhere. But now I wanted a map so I could see if there were any other alternatives to walking on the road. I abandoned the idea because I wanted to walk on the Camino regardless, and it had always followed these roads, from the time when they were just dirt tracks. I wanted to walk the same way as pilgrims had always done, see what they had seen and experience the same adventure. I followed pretty much its every whim and wish. If it detoured through a wood for a kilometre, even though I knew where it reappeared, I would follow it slavishly, resigned to its demands, even taking the longer of two possible variants when they came up. I needed to make sure I had walked the entire length and not cheated. I had nightmares that I had missed out a section. I even went as far as making sure every morning that I started to walk from the very spot where I had finished the previous day.

Jeannie.

The border between France and Spain. From the left: the author, Yoko, Jeannie, Sean, Roberta, Pascal and Antonios.

Chapter Ten

New Faces

Two days out of Logrono, I caught up with Tamar and we walked together for the day. Arriving in Santa Domingo de la Calzada, we came to one of the town's two refuges and decided to take a look inside.

The dormitory area, housed in a sort of abandoned warehouse, was huge, with a ridiculously high ceiling, so that you had to shout to hold a conversation with someone on the other side. The beds were arranged all around the outside, leaving a huge rectangular space in the middle. A rare luxury in refuges, it had real single beds, not bunk beds. I liked it straight away: it was weird, different, but certainly inviting.

Monica had checked herself into the finest hotel this side of Paris, a plan she had been talking about for days. All she could think about was stuff like wrapping herself up in three immense, fluffy towels after a steaming hot bath, watching a bit of TV, calling room service just for the hell of ordering a coffee and generally revelling in the opulence. She had invited me to a meal in the evening. I took my time wandering through the hotel searching for her room. Tourists were mingling around reception, where one was leaning over the reception desk complaining and demanding a refund. Bell boys were running around as taxis dropped off new clients and picked up those leaving.

"Yes, who is it?" she said as I rapped on the door.

"It's Fozzie."

She opened the door, indeed cocooned in big, fluffy towels.

"You look like you're enjoying yourself," I said.

She smiled and invited me in, disappearing off to the bathroom. I flicked aimlessly through the TV channels just because I could and settled on a 1950s western dubbed into Spanish. It was either that or a 1930s documentary featuring a woman yodelling in the Alps. The choice was a little limited.

"What time is the meal?" I said to Monica when she came back and plopped on to the bed next to me.

"Eight thirty. Have you seen the restaurant?"

"No. I don't know where we are eating. Have you found somewhere?"

She laughed. "Fozzie, I am treating you to a meal here, at the hotel, as my guest!"

"Oh! Wow!" I exclaimed. "I thought you were taking me out on the town to a small bar or something. Look … you don't have to do that, really."

"It's my pleasure. I'll meet you in reception at, say, eight?"

"Yeah, fine. Listen … thanks!"

I went back to the refugio, had a shower, did the laundry and took a siesta. I explained to Tamar about the meal. Then it hit me. The restaurant opened at eight thirty: the refuge shut its doors at nine thirty.

"I don't believe it" I muttered to myself. "Shit!"

Foiled again! The chance of dining in a top-flight restaurant spoilt by a damn refuge restriction. There was no way I could do it, even if we rushed through the meal, but doing that would make a nonsense of the whole experience.

The warden would have none of it. I explained it would just mean staying open a little longer or leaving the back door ajar. Nothing doing. I was tired and didn't want extra hassle, so I plodded dejectedly back to the hotel and explained to Monica. She understood, and even said she we could keep the offer 'in the bag' for another time. I ended up with Tamar in a quaint little bar munching on portions of tapas and sipping red wine. Afterwards we walked back through quiet streets to the refuge, where most of the pilgrims were already asleep and the lights were off. As she cuddled up against me in one bed, I realised I had probably not even put that much thought into how to get around the curfew problem earlier. I could have crashed on Monica's floor, left a window open at the refuge – there were a number of options. I hadn't really tried because I just wanted to spend the time with Tamar instead.

She had to leave the Camino soon for a week to attend a wedding, so we spent two days walking together. I liked to walk in silence most of the time, fully content just taking in my surroundings. She couldn't seem to grasp this idea and was becoming frustrated at not being able to converse constantly. We walked apart for a few kilometres and by the time we reached the disappointing village of Belorado there was an atmosphere. As we ate a picnic lunch on the steps leading down from the church, she called a taxi.

"We won't end up together, Fozzie," she said.

I looked at her a little surprised and then realised she was probably right.

"I know," I said. "It's frustrating sometimes. We go through these times when you are angry with me and I with you, but I still love being with you.

"Email where you are," she continued. "After the wedding, I will come back to the Camino and walk again. Please contact me some time and tell me where you are."

"I will."

The refugio was the worst I had stayed in. There was one shower for the whole place, which yielded a pathetic trickle of water dripping on to dirty, broken tiles. The mattress on the bunk bed sagged alarmingly and the whole dormitory reverberated with rusty springs twanging and pinging. The other room comprised two benches and a table rescued from a skip outside. One camping gas stove had spluttered to death as two pilgrims tried to brew coffee. It was depressing.

I was in a bad mood anyway. The conversation with Tamar and her subsequent departure had made me irritable.

A group of pilgrims I had briefly chatted to in recent days were occupying the other table. One of them, James, an English guy, the first I had met on the Camino, was suffering with blisters. He had started at St Jean and was experiencing the same problem I had after a couple of weeks of walking. At first I was sorry for him at first, but soon he started to annoy me with his constant whining, as if he was the only one suffering. When I returned to the room after going outside for a cigarette, he was lying on the table while two of his pals performed surgery on his ailments. He was milking it for all it was worth. I raised my eyes to the ceiling and one of his friends smiled in agreement.

I went over and introduced myself to a middle-aged man lying on his sleeping mat in the corner. Sleeping next to him was his dog, which opened one eye when I approached, gave a sigh and fell asleep again. A mountain bike was propped up against the wall with a trailer bolted behind it.

"Great dog. What's his name?" I asked.

"Boom," said the man. "After a book I read once called *Me* and a dog named Boom, or something like that anyway."

He spoke with a hint of Scottish accent. His hair was short and grey, he was well built and, to judge from his equipment, he might have cycled from Nepal. Everything was scuffed and dusty. An odd piece of tape held battered bags and straps. In fact, he looked as though he had spent his whole life travelling.

"Two German guys just left him at one of the refuges," he continued, scratching Boom's head as if to let him know he was the subject of conversation. "I couldn't leave him there, so brought him along. I can't figure out why they left him, he's such a great dog. I set off in the morning on the bike, and he just runs alongside me. Eats anything I give him, treats me like a best friend, he's great. I'm Ian, by the way."

"Sorry," I replied. "I have a bat habit of asking dogs' names and never asking the owners'." He laughed.

"At least you show a genuine interest," he said. "I can tell just from the attention you pay him that you love dogs. Do you have one?"

"No, although I've lost count of the number of times I have been down the rescue centre and nearly brought one back with me. But I travel too much anyway. And there are all those quarantine restrictions. I have a cat, but a dog would probably end up residing at my parents' place for the summer and coming back with me for the winter – if I ever go home, that is. I hope to get one when I am settled in one place. Interesting method of travelling," I said, nodding towards his bike. "You Santiago bound?"

"Probably. I have to go to Germany to get married in a week or so, a lady I met at one of the refuges. She was a warden. I'll take it as it comes."

He declined my offer of a beer, saying he needed to make an early start and get some sleep. Outside, drizzle was making waves in the air as it swept past the street light. A constant stream of lorries made the two hundred-metre dash to the bar a death zone, and a wet one at that. I sat at the counter at El Pajero and ordered a beer. Munching on pistachios and smoking an endless stream of cigarettes, I tried to be interested in a Spanish soap on the TV. For the first time in several weeks I was properly depressed.

I awoke to rain pounding on the windows. I wiped a circle in the condensation on the glass and peered out. The sun had yet to come up, darkness covered everything and the occasional car sent up a cloud of spray. I could just make out the moon, trying desperately to peer through racing dark clouds. I dived back into my sleeping bag and waited, snoozing, until most of the other pilgrims had got up and filed out.

When I eventually got going after endless coffees and omelettes at the El Pajero, the rain had given up, but grey clouds streamed overhead, blocking out the blue, and the way was damp, the soil reduced to a sticky mix of clay and rotting leaves. I walked on fire tracks through forest for most of the day, dodging the puddles and kicking imaginary footballs to send up huge clods of earth that had stuck to my boots. I could see Ian's tracks, three lines representing his machine, and the odd set of paw prints to one side. "He must have struggled through this shit," I thought.

After twelve kilometres I came to San Juan de Ortega, a cluster of old buildings huddled in the drizzle. The church of San Nicolas de Bari stood proudly at the head of the small street. It was constructed in such a way that on the spring and autumn equinoxes at five in the evening, the setting sun would illuminate the capital depicting the Annunciation. I went inside to check it out, imagining the rays streaming in like something out of *Raiders of the Lost Ark*. Apart from the fact I had missed the equinox, it was still raining and there was no sun. I comforted myself with the fact that I could at least add one more "church visited" tick to my list. The fake-pilgrim spotter in Santiago would surely be impressed now.

I carried on along freshly tarred, jet-black roads that wound through ancient hamlets. At the end of a long stretch of tarmac that never seemed to end, I came to Atapuerca. After the miseries of the previous night, this small village seemed like some sort of peace offering. Its damp empty streets reminded me of Damascus, where I had spent some time a few years earlier. It was pleasant enough, but the true reward was the refugio. As I gripped the round iron latch, opened the door and stepped inside, faces peered back at me through the darkness. I made out about ten pilgrims huddled around a table and occupying themselves swatting a huge resident fly population. Blister-ridden James was reciting the wincing script again, and there was that same exasperated look on his friends' faces.

It was one of the best refuges I had stayed at. Recently restored, it reminded me of a Stone Age hut with a few mod cons. The ceiling was high, wooden beams spraying off in a haphazard fashion, with what looked like mud plaster clinging on for dear life in between them. The walls had been distressed with a thin terracotta wash. There were nooks and crannies in the dormitory to rest books, torches and anything else one might need in the middle of the night. A separate bathroom housed three showers with an endless supply of steaming water. The kitchen area and table where the others were recuperating sported a wood-burning stove.

We wrote our diaries in relative silence, except for the odd moan from James, and set about lighting the stove.

Fire wood was limited. Plucking a beam from the wall was ruled out, even though a few of us argued they may not be missed, but for one thing it was vandalism, and for another, any one of them may have been supporting the whole structure. So, three of us were sent out into the elements on fuel-securing missions.

The rain was intermittent, but now it was windy and the temperature had plummeted. I began to wonder if I would make it over El Cebreiro, three hundred and fifty kilometres away before the first snows fell. We stripped an area six metres in circumference around the refugio of anything that looked vaguely combustible and retreated back inside. A German woman was struggling with a pile of ashes in the stove, which sent up the occasional pathetic puff of damp smoke, like a dragon coughing on its death bed. We would keep stuffing in toilet roll, one would hold the lighter, one would throw in the odd piece of kindling, and two of us would blow and make comments such as "Nearly … nearly … ooooh!" or "The wood's too damp" or "Open the air vent, it needs more air". This usually culminated in the orange glow behind the glass receding dangerously low as the vent was accidentally shut instead. I dreamt that night of walking through snow up to my genitals, homing in on an orange glow that never got any nearer. I deliberately didn't analyse it in the morning: it seemed bad whichever way I looked at it.

The wind did its best to blow me off the road in the morning as I scampered from the refugio to a nearby bar for breakfast. At this stage of the Camino I was struggling to get going without at least three coffees, a Spanish omelette and several cigarettes. I had worked my way through enough eggs in the previous couple of weeks to be contemplating a cholesterol test. I asked for an espresso and watched as the waitress expertly operated the coffee machine. I love those things, ridiculously wide, dials and handles sprouting all over the front, warm cups stacked on top, steam rising up, leaving moisture on the chrome, with stainless steel nozzles pointing in all directions. Underneath there would be a wooden drawer, battered and worn at the top by the constant smack of the grounds holder. There's nothing like real coffee. The flip of the grinder depositing the ground beans into the holder, its compression compacting the powder, the sound of the holder being thrust and turned in the receptacle and the sight of that rich, deep brown treacle dripping out bring a smile to my face every time. I know then it is only a short wait before I get my hit.

I sat in the corner watching the weather report on the TV, which promised great things. The silence was shattered abruptly as the door burst open and a seemingly never-ending stream of pilgrims filed in rubbing their hands. The bar was transformed from a silent haven to a bustling rabble of walkers gossiping and overjoyed at having found somewhere that was open. Damp waterproofs were pulled off, hats and gloves removed to reveal faces red and raw from the wind.

Among them was France, whom I hadn't seen since Lectoure, six hundred kilometres back.

"France!" I shouted. "Bloody hell! How are you?! I thought you were way ahead of me."

"Fozzie! Hey, how are you? I thought you were way ahead of *me*!" His face lit up with surprise.

He came and sat with me, turning around, tapping everyone on the shoulder and saying, "Hey, THIS is Fozzie!"

One guy saw the confused look on my face.

"Oh! You're Fozzie!" he said.

"Er ... yes."

"I've been seeing your name carved into the dirt since St Jean! It's great to finally meet you!"

France and I looked at each other and laughed hard.

"Have you seen Jeannie?" I asked.

"The American woman who stays on the public phones for an hour at a time?"

I laughed again. "Yeah, that's Jeannie."

"She's about two, maybe three days back."

We caught up on everything that had happened since Moissac: where everybody was, who was ahead, who was behind. He left shortly before me and said he would see me that night in Burgos.

As I ventured back outside, the wind had intensified. It was by far the coldest day on the Camino I had experienced. I began to worry that the Spanish hills in Galicia were going to be more in the grip of winter than I had thought. I had completed two thirds of the Camino but still had five hundred kilometres left to walk

My poles dug into the chalky soil on the hill out of Atapuerca, walking past pilgrims as I found my pace and everyone spaced out to their own speed. I passed a young woman to my right.

"Ola!" she said.

"Hi," I nodded. I was walking faster than she was and carried on past, not in the mood for a day's company, but she merely increased her speed to stay with me. I relented, thinking some company might do me good after all.

Tania was Mexican, and hovered around twenty years old, maybe a little younger. She was a strong walker, and had been clocking up thirty to thirty-five kilometres a day since St Jean. We smoked and walked. She had shiny hair arranged in a sort of braided fashion framing an attractive face. She smiled a lot and made eye contact often. Her English was excellent with just a hint of Spanish, and she had an infectious humour about her that was just what I needed. After ten minutes I decided I liked her.

We talked away the eighteen or so kilometres to Burgos, a city I was looking forward to as I had planned a rest day and a night in a hotel. We depleted such topics as spirituality, photography, travel and cooking.

France walked with us on and off for the day. As we went through small villages, each one promising the outskirts of the city but not delivering, we reached a motorway. I looked up in astonishment at the Camino sign, which pointed to the other side.

"We gotta cross this!" I exclaimed, laughing.

"No way," Tania replied, in a disbelieving tone.

"Well, that's where the sign is suggesting." We walked for a short way, thinking there was a tunnel underneath. We were disappointed. I looked in my guidebook.

"Uh-oh," I said.

"What?" Tania was peering over my shoulder trying to read as well.

"Well, I'm quoting from the book. It says 'Cross motorway'." We looked at each other and then at the road. France joined us and we explained the situation. Streams of cars were whizzing past, interspersed with the occasional lorry and the odd motorbike for good measure. I was reminded of something my Dad had said to me years earlier when I set off to walk the hundred or so miles that comprises the South Downs Way in Sussex.

"Remember, when you get to a road, be careful. For one, you will probably be tired. For another, that pack on your back has a funny habit of making you think it's not actually there. The end result is a mad dash through a hole in the traffic and you suddenly realise you're making no headway and there are two cars bearing down on you."

The words repeated in my head. In the end, we ran like pilgrims possessed to a small strip of concrete in the middle, an island, a safe haven, where we could launch the next attack. As we caught our breath on the other side, France said that the law of averages would suggest that, with several thousand pilgrims walking here every year, a few probably ended up in Burgos accident and emergency.

The three of us made our way into Burgos, which presented the familiar pattern of uninspiring outskirts gradually giving way to the older buildings nearer the centre. It struck me as another pleasant city, with plenty of green spaces, wide walkways and original architecture. It bustled but in a friendly way.

The refuge nestled in an expanse of grass a short walk from the Arco de Santa Maria, a fortified gateway taking the pedestrian into the old city. Bunk beds were crammed alarmingly into a couple of rooms, and the buildings themselves reminded me of the temporary huts I was schooled in, designed to last for five years but still going strong at thirty. There were plenty of pilgrims claiming their preference of bunk position, going to or returning from showers or blistering. My assumption that any hot water was long gone was confirmed when I entered the shower area to hear cries of pain from the cubicles as the water was turned on. I decided something to eat would be a better idea. I could come back for a shower later.

A short distance from the refuge was a small restaurant advertising a "pilgrims' menu", so Tania and I took a table and, as space was limited, invited some camp Australian guys to join us.

"Oh, you're Fozzie," said Steve, who sported a white trilby and lilac T-shirt printed with the slogan "In your dreams, sugar puff".

"I am," I said, putting my arm around Tania just to confirm my sexual orientation.

"I thought so. I was walking with a woman called Monica and she said you were attractive. She also advised me not to eat with you."

"Not to eat with me?"

"Yes. She said you eat like a horse. She said you'll eat any tapas within your reach, regardless of whom they belong to."

"Thanks," I replied. "I had no idea my eating habits were held in such high regard. I'll have words when I see her. Well, anyway, I'm not mad on onion soup but you'd better guard your fries with your life."

The food, as in most establishments with pilgrims' menus, was good. Walkers filled the place and many, like us, stayed after we had eaten. Waiters whisked around with coffees, beers and spirits. Glasses were raised, conversation wafted around, people laughed and leant back in their chairs with their tired legs outstretched. I would occasionally catch a glimpse of someone I recognised and hold up a glass or nod my head in their direction. Somehow we managed to find our way back to the refuge and I sat down by Boom, who was sleeping outside, scratching his head for what must have been fifteen minutes. I slept well, dreaming of walking a route that took the rest of my life to finish, with a dog running alongside.

Chapter 11

Dreams of Home

I headed off in the morning to find a good hotel for a day's rest and to make up for a missed shower. Stopping en route at the post office, I picked up a parcel that a friend had sent out and sat down at a café to open it. Inside was a large tub of peanut butter, a delicacy in short supply in Spain. I asked the waiter for some fresh baguette and spent several minutes reacquainting myself with my favourite spread, even going so far as hiding it under the table when some American pilgrims sat a few tables away.

After trying two hotels, which were full because it was the last public holiday of the year, I eventually found a cracker a few minutes' walk from the centre. Damp laundry spread around the room, rucksack contents deposited everywhere, I dozed off into a premature siesta and dreamt that I was in my parents' back garden with a storm raging all around me. The base of a tree trunk was swinging violently as the wind tore at it. The wet soil was giving way as each gust pushed and pulled it further back and forth, as though it were being tugged from either side. Eventually it fell over. I woke up and shortly afterwards I called my mum, not because of the dream, just to catch up and report on my progress.

"How's the weather doing?" I asked.

"Oh, Keith, we had a storm last night. Really strong winds and heavy rain. It pushed over a tree in the back garden."

Perhaps the Camino was nurturing my spiritual side after all.

Pamplona was still sitting pretty at the number one spot among Spanish cities. Burgos made a valiant and worthwhile attempt at nudging it into the number two spot. It was pretty close but Pamplona held on by a whisker. A number of ornate bridges span the chasm of the river Arlanzon, whose waters gush and fall over stones, the banks are coated in rich, green grass and a few trees and bushes. Lovers walked along the banks, dogs charged and swerved, glad to be unleashed. People strolled down tree-fringed avenues. There was a hum of small engines as workers blew up great swirls of leaves into pyramid-shaped piles.

Tamar sounded reluctant to speak on the phone. She was due in Burgos that evening, and I said she should come to the hotel.

"Ok, fine, do whatever," I said, and slammed down the receiver. I couldn't figure out her mood swings: one minute she was attentive and tender, the next she acted as though she had just met me.

I hung around with Tania. We cordoned off a table in one of the numerous cafes, and went back to our discussions, mainly on books again. I ordered food far too expensive for my budget, sipped wine and relaxed. It was that Sunday feeling. I swear someone could pick me up and dump me anywhere in the world, without telling me what day of the week it was, and sure enough, I would know instantly when Sunday arrived. My body would feel relaxed: all I would want to do was read and drink coffee and generally do all the things I didn't have time for in the week. I made the most of it.

That evening Tamar and I met at a bar resembling something from Ireland, and while I sipped on Johnnie Walker Black swimming in ice, she told me she had been unable to talk earlier as her husband was in the room with her. Everything, it appeared, was back to sweetness and light as we returned to my hotel. She was due to meet a friend of hers called Espe who was to share her room and walk the rest of the Camino with her. She left my room late in the evening to meet her.

I left Burgos the following morning on my own, knowing that Tamar and Espe would catch me up. I waved and giggled as Ian sped past on his bike with Boom scampering alongside. Before long Burgos was behind and I was engulfed by the welcoming Spanish countryside. I felt calm again, the late autumn sun warming my back as I slowed my pace to take in my surroundings.

In Tardajos, I stopped at a bar where people were staring into their drinks as if someone had just died. The whole place had the atmosphere of a morgue. The saving grace was the TV showing 'Big' and the scene where Tom Hanks is in the toyshop playing the keyboard with his feet. I was humming the tune for the rest of the day. Before leaving town, I loaded up my pack with bananas and oranges from a truck selling fruit and vegetables on the roadside.

The Camino was filtering out into vast, open spaces with little more than scrub and dust for company. I could see for miles. Hornillos del Camino appeared in the distance two hours before I actually arrived there. As I was unpacking in the refuge there was a tap on my shoulder and I turned around to see Pierre.

"Pierre! Holy crap!" I said. "Long time no see! Where you been?"

"Taking my time," he replied. "Lots to see, take more in when I walk slowly."

"I agree, I am getting to the stage now where Santiago is actually becoming a reality, and I feel myself slowing down each day."

It was true. I had about four hundred and fifty kilometres left. After the initial doubts, the long days where nothing was going right for me, Santiago de Compostela now seemed within reach. Everyone was in a similar mood. It was as though the end of the walk was starting to rear up, to creep a little closer each day, like a cat prowling through long grass, and we all knew that there would be a massive moral crash when we had all finished. We would wake up at the refugio in Santiago or Cape Finisterre for those who continued to the coast, to realise it had all finished. There would be no more walking to do. Decisions would have to be made about the next step. Back home? Stay in Spain to wind down? At times, when I imagined how my spirits would be at the end, I almost saw myself turning around to start to walk back to Le Puy again. I didn't want it all to end.

To my surprise, the French Canadians were in the village as well. People I hadn't seen for weeks had somehow concentrated into this small, dusty place out in the middle of nowhere. I entered the only bar, where Gérard looked up from his packet of peanuts.

"Fozzie! Hey, man! What you doing!"

His familiar hippy tones resonated around the place. The others looked up and smiled. I hadn't seen them since Conques, which seemed an eternity ago. We all shook hands, pecked cheeks, patted each other on the back. Although I knew them, it felt as if we were at the stage where a kiss or a handshake wasn't quite cutting it. We would soon be on the rostrum where hugs were the norm. These people, friends, pilgrims whom I had known for a few weeks, would be going their separate ways and we sort of knew we had to make the most of the time we had left on the walk. I was back among friends, happy, and walked around for the rest of the day with a huge grin.

When the warden tapped me on the shoulder the following morning and pointed to his watch, which displayed a time of eight fifteen, I just glared at him. The refuges weren't bothering me any more. In fact, the whole rules and regulations crap was starting to amuse to me. I would get up around eight o'clock, the time by which you should have left, and pack at my own speed, ignoring any reproving looks. At this stage of the Camino, approaching mid-October, pilgrim numbers were dwindling. There were no queues of tired walkers waiting to get a bed for the night. We didn't have to leave early to provide bed space; there was plenty. Everyone was aware of this, so we took our time and generally bypassed the restrictions.

I walked with Espe and Tamar, who had arrived later the previous evening, for part of the morning, but then let them go ahead. I wanted to come to terms with this new part of Spain. I rested more often, content with just sitting at the side of the track, listening to only the birds, insects and the rustle of the grass as the wind whipped through it. Everything seemed intensified. Sounds were amplified, demanding that I stop and listen. I felt as though I could hear things that I normally would miss. My senses were becoming more acute, refined. I took an endless stream of photos to try and capture it all, knowing the real experience, the sounds, could never be taken back with me.

A group of pilgrims had stopped at the only bar for twenty kilometres. If it had received a visit from a health inspector, it would have been closed down long since. As I went up to the bar, I could smell the owner before he appeared from an adjoining room. He looked as if he hadn't washed in a month. Filth and grime made patterns on his clothing. Dirt lined his cracked fingernails and his hands looked as though he had just completed an oil change on a tractor, and then used the old lubricant to slick back his receding hair over a shiny bald patch. His establishment fared little better. Food scraps littered the bar. Flies buzzed around as though they were on vacation. Cured ham rested on an ancient slicing machine that was caked in dust and filth. A sack was propped up in the corner, the bread spilling out on to the floor. As I ordered coffees for me, Tamar and Espe, he dipped three glass cups into a sink full of murky grey water, wiped them on his shirt, and placed them under a coffee machine, which spluttered into life as if it was overdue a service.

I retreated to the warmth outside. Tamar followed me out and we started an argument that eventually had me donning my pack and walking off at such a speed that I knew she had little chance of catching me up. It centred on something so trivial that later the same day I had trouble recollecting what it actually was.

I stopped at Hospital San Anton, where an imposing archway stretched across the road. Pilgrims had left scribbled notes on pieces of paper, weighed down by small stones in niches on the wall – messages to friends yet to pass, poems and tales, or simply a few words to brighten up someone's day.

"11th November. Jeannie, keep going, girl! Love, Fozzie," I wrote, and placed it near the front under a scrap of stone that had once been part of the structure of the arch.

I walked on down the road, as straight as a datum line, leading to Castrojeriz. An ancient fort looked down from a hill. Spotting a rosemary bush climbing the walls of a ruined house, I slid down an embankment and picked a twig to fasten to my shoulder strap. Its scent stayed with me for hours.

Tamar appeared in the evening with Espe. I didn't know whether I wanted to see her or not, but she was affectionate, as if nothing had happened.

"I just don't understand her sometimes," I said to Espe.

"She is walking the Camino to sort out a lot of problems in her head," she replied.

"Yeah," I thought to myself, "aren't we all?"

"And," she continued, "she said the very same thing today about you."

Chapter Twelve

Into Autumn

The sun was making an appearance a little later every day and leaving me a little earlier. It wasn't really light until eight thirty. Sunny days were getting fewer and carrying a chill in the air. Most of the time it was overcast but, thankfully, rain was still rare. Laying claim to being the wettest area of Spain, Galicia was sure to give me a pounding this time of year. I thought the weather reports in England were unreliable; in Spain, when I caught what I could of reports on the TV, I would see those familiar black cloud symbols, but the forecast rain just never seemed to arrive.

The leaves were in classic autumn colours, like the tones of a Turkish rug: reds, yellows, dark and light browns all ducked and weaved in the breeze. The Camino was drenched in a new carpet of colour that comforted the feet. I would kick up leaves and watch them fall back again into the camouflage. Trees arched over in the wind like ballet dancers warming up and stretching to one side, the trunks groaning, the leaves whistling and whispering over my head, caught in wind eddies, twirling, spiralling and plummeting. Soon those coats of trees would reveal the dark skeletons beneath.

It was the perfect time of year to walk. Although I loved the feeling of the sun burning into my back, autumn is designed to be hiked in. On some mornings, for the first few minutes my breath would emerge as a cloud of mist. The cold would snap at any exposed skin. It was a weird sensation, feeling snug, when my face and hands tingled with the frost.

The hills at the latter end of the Spanish section would be even colder. Snow was becoming a real threat and I hoped I could make it over the hills of El Cebrero before they turned white. I must have been one of the last pilgrims to walk the Camino that year, even though there were still probably a few behind me. I was playing a cat and mouse game with the elements, having left my departure later than considered normal. The wet season was due now as well the snow, but my luck was holding and rain was still rare.

After Ledigos, the meseta started to undulate gently and the way started to weave. I walked through a couple of hamlets, unfortunately neither of them with bars, and trees and rivers began to appear. After what seemed like an eternity on the mundane meseta, my morale started to lift.

In my haste to maintain a brisk pace to keep warm, I had completely missed the town centre at Sahagun and had to backtrack, walking under the Portada del Templo Abacial, a big stone arch over the road.

I was ravenous and also in the mood for blowing the financial budget for the day. I craved sugar, coffee, tapas and something cocooned in puff pastry. There were three bars in the centre square, from which I chose a very upmarket-looking one, which by a minor miracle had something made from puff pastry in the window.

Inside, light bounced off endless glass and polished brass. Copious quantities of tapas attracted my attention from every angle, and an interesting choice of 'She's a Model' by Kraftwerk piped though somewhere above my left ear. The place even boasted lights in the toilet that came on by movement sensors. The clientele were posh-looking, all done up in their Sunday best (well, Monday best actually), the women sitting with their legs crossed and twiddling with model-perfect hair while throwing their head back in mock laughter at bad jokes. I felt out of place but I didn't care, there was food to devour, and that always had my undivided attention.

Three kilometres out of Sahagun the Camino threw up a choice of routes, two of which ran through an area that I had been reading about for weeks. I had heard pilgrims discussing the area with fear in their voice. It is known as the Calzada de los Peregrinos, or the "carriageway of the pilgrim".

One of the routes was considered drastically worse than the other, with little or nothing to look at. The other offered a slim chance of finding something to eat or drink if such were needed. Both routes were the same distance, thirty kilometres. I needn't have spent that time pondering as the bad option meant I had another thirty kilometres before the next refuge, and I had already walked eighteen that day. The days when I walked forty kilometres or more were long gone. So I picked way number two, called Camino Real Frances, and hoped it wasn't as bad as I had been led to believe.

After crunching along a gravel track for a while, I lay down in the grass to savour a spectacular storm assaulting the countryside. Clouds loomed up and spread like bacteria seen under a microscope. In the foreground, the church of Ermita de Perales looked like a lost child, crying in the middle of nowhere.

The path dipped and crossed the river Coso, where there was a headstone in memory of a pilgrim who had died there in 1998. Many pilgrims have died over the years on the Camino, most of them as a result of a traffic involvement. However, there was a sad and quiet, almost mysterious air to this location and it made me wonder how the pilgrim had died in such a secluded spot.

The walls of the houses in the next town, Bercianos del Real Camino, were made mainly from a mixture of mud and water, like something out of a Mexican village. It was silent. Leaves and debris flew past me at street corners as though they had been waiting in ambush. Following yellow direction arrows splashed on walls, I soon caught up with two Dutchwomen with whom I had become acquainted, called Helen and Ancha. They told me a friend of theirs had stayed at the refuge a couple of years previously and in the absence of beds had been forced to sleep on the floor. This didn't exactly do my perception of the place any favours. No beds suggested it was lacking in funds and this in turn meant all the other facilities would probably be sparse.

I need not have worried. The arrows led right up to the door and I stepped inside. It was like walking into a small castle. A big wooden door riddled with studs was ajar and led to a porch area with small pebbles set into the floor. It was dark, a little musty and very old, but it enveloped me with a feeling of welcome and friendship. I checked in.

"Leave when you want in the morning," said the middle-aged woman, smiling. "Breakfast and evening meal are included, and any donation is welcomed."

"Thanks," I replied. "Is there a bar in the village? I have a craving for a coffee."

"Please, have a seat in the dining room. I will make one for you. Is espresso OK?"

They couldn't have done more for me, Helen and Ancha if they had tried. OK, so we had to sleep on the floor (albeit with the welcome addition of a mattress) and the facilities were basic, but the refugio at Bercianos del Real Camino squeezed into my top ten favourites. It just goes to show that you should listen to rumours with a dose of scepticism: what travellers experienced in the past may no longer be the case now. The donation I gave was four times more than I would have normally given.

I awoke in the morning after everybody had left and ventured outside to retrieve my laundry, only to be met by an eerie fog that enveloped pretty much everything. I needed a map to find the clothes line. It was dead quiet; I wouldn't have known if someone was standing four paces away. For most of the morning I walked through countryside like the star of The Hound of the Baskervilles or Jack the Ripper. I could barely see ten metres in front of me and half expected to be savaged by a rabid hound any second. It was at this point I realised with horror that I had left my peanut butter at one of the refuges a couple of nights earlier. I cried.

At Burgo Ranero, where I stopped for an early lunch, I pondered the approach to food and eating found in various countries. To me, England seems to charge excessive prices for food, profit taking precedence over everything else. I have no problem with this in theory: after all, making a profit is the fundamental basis of any business. However, in mainland Europe, in particular the Mediterranean, I get the impression that the attitude is different and most places are actually there simply to provide food; if they happen to make a profit, all the better. In Spain and some other countries you often see the inhabitants having a full-blown lunch in the middle of the week, because they can afford to do so. For them, food is a God-given right and most establishments genuinely seem to enjoy feeding the masses.

France appeared from the fog and joined me.

"In France and other Mediterranean countries," he said, when I explained what I had been thinking, "I notice the food is much more reasonable than in England and generally of a higher standard. I don't mean to say that English cuisine is bad, it is not, it just seems of a poorer standard than elsewhere and costs more."

Commercialism plays its part too. To take things a step further, we now have the large companies that care about nothing else except squeezing the maximum amount of coinage from the public, while dishing up crap. They're not there to provide an experience of eating, just to swipe your credit card at the end of the meal. Their ingredients are delivered frozen twice weekly and thrown in the deep-fat fryer by a recycled juvenile delinquent. The chairs are designed to be comfortable for thirty minutes so you don't hang about and then the next lot gets herded in.

I do indulge in the occasional McDonald's and rumour has it I have been spotted in Pizza Hut, but I can honestly count on two hands the number of times I go to those establishments in a year.

"We are what we eat": never a truer word spoken. The more we take a basic food and process it, the worse it becomes. Ingredients are altered genetically, and then sprayed with endless chemicals. Your average hamburger from a fast food chain consists of bread with all the goodness removed, meat derived from poor cuts and trimmings from cows injected with hormones and the like to produce as much beef as possible in the shortest time. A slice of plastic cheese is thrown on top with a generous dollop of cholesterol-filled mayonnaise and a token lettuce leaf for the "healthy" bit. I have walked through cities in Italy and seen babies and children munching on fresh asparagus tips, fruit and water.

Thinking about all this that day, I made a determined decision to eat more healthily and go vegetarian … in the New Year.

France had walked with me for a while but stopped in a supermarket to restock. The fog had cleared and the temperature had risen enough to produce a sweat. A rare sight on the meseta now met my eyes: not a fork in the track, or even a path coming in from one side, but a crossroads. To add to the confusion, a car was stuck behind a tractor. It was gridlock in the middle of nowhere. I had just had to laugh at the preposterousness of it all.

I entered Leon and followed signs to the Youth Hostel, purely because it seemed easier than locating the refuge. The building was huge and resembled a prison block. The thermostat registered 30 degrees, and rising. I bumped into Tamar in the corridor with her daughter. Apparently her husband had driven the little girl down to see her. They left shortly after and we both ventured into Leon for food and wine. Espe very kindly offered to swap her room for mine so Tamar and I could be alone for the night.

My opinion of Tamar plummeted in the morning when she suggested all three of us go to "Cortez del Inglese" for breakfast. For those of you unfamiliar with this Spanish establishment, think of British Home Stores or Debenhams. Not my first choice for a breakfast location but Tamar insisted. They virtually had to drag me into the place as I peered through tapas bars on the way, my pleading look at those inside saying "For God's sake, HELP ME!"

They pulled me in the door and marched me through the underwear section, past the sports department, up some escalators and into an eating hall where instrumental cover versions of crap pop songs were being piped through. It just made me shiver. Needless to say, all I could do was to down an espresso and hope that Tamar and Espe would finish their croissants quickly.

As soon as were out, I went looking for the nearest tapas bar.

"But, Fozzie, you just had ..." protested Tamar.

"Sorry, but I look forward to my coffee and eats in the morning before I start walking, and that place wasn't quite cutting the mustard."

"Cutting? Mustard?" She tilted her head to one side and narrowed her eyes with a puzzled look.

"It doesn't matter," I said. "I mean I wanted to eat in a tapas bar. I like the Spanish food. To 'cut the mustard' is an English expression for being good. I didn't like Cortez del Inglese, and wanted to come here for my breakfast. Understand?"

"Si ... I mean yes. I understand." She sank back into her chair and gave me the odd glance as I munched on my tortilla. I sensed something big was on her mind. Espe had gone off to the toilet, but had been keeping her distance anyway.

"Fozzie?"

"Yes?"

"I lied to you. I told you I wanted fun and that I was not in love with you. I am in love with you."

I stopped chewing and stared at her with raised eyebrows, expecting more information, but knowing she had said the crux of her piece.

"Tamar, oh God, Tamar. I don't know what to say."

The whole place seemed to stop and wait for me.

"You're beautiful, really beautiful, and when we get along, we really get along. But most of the time we argue, and that's when we can understand what we're both saying.

The way you look is more than I could ask for in a woman, but we clash Tamar, we clash big time."

"Clash?"

"Clash, yes," I continued. "Our personalities don't match, we find fault and upset each other, apologise and then do it again. It's a constant circle and I really can't handle it. We can take each other's company in small amounts, but too much is, well, too much."

"So you don't want to know me any more?"

"No, not at all. I just don't think we are going anywhere from a love point of view. I still want to be a friend to you, but a relationship would be a disaster. I'm sorry, Tamar, it just wouldn't work."

"I know, I understand," she said, smiling. "We would kill each other."

She got up and kissed me on the cheek.

"See you on the trail."

"Kato the Faith Healer", now there's a title. Forget Queen of this or Prince of that. "Faith Healer", that's my kind of title. Not sure about the Kato bit, though, which made it sound as if he was straight out of a Pink Panther movie. Nevertheless, I had heard numerous stories about this guy who runs a refuge on the Camino at Villafranca del Bierzo, most of them from Jeannie, who in turn was enlightened by pilgrims she knew from last year. Apparently Kato had the ability to heal using his hands, mind and nothing else. I guessed he couldn't be making much money out of it or he wouldn't be needing the refuge. But, as stories go, it was a good one and I was looking forward to staying with him and seeing what he was all about. My calf was still playing up a little, so at least I was a good test case.

Kato was three or four days away and I had set myself a target of thirty kilometres a day to get there – a bit more than I had been used to walking of late, but hardly breaking any records. I had decided to move to the Leon refuge from the hostel to spend my rest day.

The building was centuries old with a little sprinkling of character to match. It was one of the most cramped I had stayed in but it was nice to see loads of friendly faces. The French Canadians were there, John and Yetty from Canada, as laidback a pair of pilgrims as I had met, and numerous others including Pierre.

Most of them went to a nearby restaurant to eat in the evening but I declined. I wandered the streets for about an hour, just wanting to have my own company, feeling the cobbles through my soles, letting my hands run along cold, damp stone, feeling the indentations, cavities, nicks and dents. Modern lighting recessed in the ground sent shafts of light up against the walls like searchlights, casting eerie shadows. A slight mist hung in the air and created rainbows of light radiating out from the street lamps. And then, suddenly, a side alley would throw me back into one of the main streets, to be engulfed by shoppers, like a leaf floating in a stream entering a powerful river.

As my head hit the pillow, the loudest snorer I encountered on the entire walk made his presence known. As always seemed to be the case, he was sleeping in the bunk under mine. It was frankly unbelievable that the noise he made didn't wake him up.

The room was pretty well lit from outside so when I sat up and looked around the room several pairs of eyes looked back at me with pained and amazed expressions.

"You got to be fuckin' kidding me," said one guy a few bunks away, setting off giggles from around the room.

I had already slapped the guy around the head with my pillow several times, but he didn't even break breath. On other bunks, heads dived under pillows pushed down by hands on either side, and feet kicked up and down in anguish and in the hope it might do the trick and stop him. It didn't.

The solution was remarkable. The crazy thing about a snorer keeping everyone awake is the courtesy his victims accord him. Nobody wants to wake him up. They think it would be rude! I feel the same way myself sometimes. I mean, how crazy is that? One person keeping everyone awake and everybody just lives with it?

This time it was different. A redhead who had up until

now escaped my notice was three bunks away and we were facing each other. She was constantly smiling, and I, naturally, smiled back a lot as well. As it transpired, she was smiling at the guy in the next bed from her, which was rather disappointing, but it did solve the immediate crisis. After a while, during which they had been discussing what to do, they both got out of bed and made their way over to the culprit. The conversation that followed still makes me chuckle now.

The girl proceeded to shake him several times until he came around. In fact, at one point, if she had shaken any harder I think his head would have flown off. He awoke, looking a little dazed.

"Excuse me," whispered the woman ever so gently.

"Huh? What?" came the puzzled reply, as he rubbed his eyes. He then smiled broadly, presumably thinking his luck just might be in as he was being woken by a gorgeous-looking woman in the middle of the night.

"I'm sorry to wake you," she said, "but you're snoring really loudly and keeping everyone awake. Would you please mind turning over on to your side? There's less chance you may snore there. Thanks very much, I'm sure everyone appreciates it." She walked back to her bunk. I peered over the bunk and smiled at the guy, who looked up at me in amazement, raised his eyebrows and went back to sleep.

I awoke in the morning to the usual buzz of pilgrims packing and discussing the day's walk, some holding a mug of coffee, some with toothbrushes hanging out of their mouths, some bouncing about on one foot trying to get the other sock on.

"Hey, Fozzie, make sure you check you have everything this morning. OK?" said Gérard.

"Yeah," I managed, rubbing my eyes and homing in on the coffee machine.

"Morning, Fozzie. Check you pack everything this morning, won't you? Make sure nothing is missing," said John.

"Yeah, will do," I replied, letting some hot, black caffeine slide down my throat.

"Hi Fozzie, good morning," said Pierre, stopping right in front of me and blocking my way.

"Pierre, sorry, I don't wish to be rude but I ain't good at conversation first thing in the morning."

He laughed.

"No problem. Make sure you double check your bag, huh?"

"Yeah, I will," I said, as he started to walk off. "Hey! What? Pierre! Come here a sec. You're the third person this morning who's told me to check my stuff. What the hell is going on, or am I imagining things?"

"Haven't you heard?"

"Heard what?"

Pierre took the chair by me, swung it round and rested his hands on the back rest the way they do in the Westerns. He looked concerned.

"Fozzie, I thought you would have heard. Several people reported items and belongings missing this morning as they packed."

"Right, I'm listening."

He continued. "Well, apparently, someone caught a guy going through their rucksack in the early hours, helping himself to anything he fancied. The victim called the warden and the guy handed over a basic sack full of booty. It was weird. All I heard when I got up was people saying they couldn't find stuff, and where was this, where had they left that? The guy must have been through practically everyone's bags during the night. Do you not have anything missing?"

"Well, yeah, now you mention it, my karabiner has gone." This was a small clip that I used to hang my damp laundry on to my pack so it would dry during the day's walk.

"Well," said Pierre, "go and see the warden, tell him what's missing, and I bet he's got it in the booty bag."

The warden was sitting in the kitchen, and a few pilgrims were queuing up to see him. When I got to him I explained what the karabiner looked like, and to my amazement he pulled it from the bag. Next to him was the thief himself. As I looked at him, his dejected head lifted up and his eyes met mine. If ever I had seen someone looking sorry for himself, this guy got the Oscar. I actually felt pity for him; he looked genuinely remorseful. I thanked the warden and walked back to Pierre.

"He had the karabiner," I stammered. "I couldn't believe it, thought I'd lost it. I mean it's not valuable or anything, but I would have missed it."

"Apparently," Pierre explained, "when the guy caught him going through his stuff, he just held up his hands, admitted to everything, claimed he was a kleptomaniac, and said he deserved everything that was coming to him. The police are coming later, but for sure he'll lose his pilgrim's passport. His days on the Camino are finished."

Leaving Leon was depressing. The sky was thick with ripe clouds, blocking out any light whatsoever. The rain kept stopping and starting. I didn't want it to rain but wished it would just so I would have confirmation of a decision. I observed the elements from a sheltered café on a street corner, watching Leon get to work. Traffic hooted, showers of road spray hung in the air. People dashed across the road bracing their umbrellas against gusts, or stood with their feet in puddles at the kerbside.

At nine I gingerly ventured out of the café and started trying to establish how actually to leave the city. The guidebook was no use; I may as well have been in another country. I guessed that Camino signs were non-existent. I saw the occasional rucksack, so presumed there was a reasonable chance that I was on the right way, although we could all have been having the same problem.

I passed John and Yetty amongst a cacophony of car horns and traffic.

"Morning, John," I said. "Nice, peaceful and tranquil morning!"

"I don't get off on cities," he replied and smirked to show he still had a sense of humour.

Six kilometres out of Leon, I met Pierre and walked with

him for the rest of the day. I had developed a great liking for this man, although on first meeting I hadn't taken to him, maybe because I was at full throttle trying to finish early for Greece and probably not the best company. Then this guy more or less forced me to stop and I felt resentful for it. It pissed me off that I had to struggle with distances and a schedule when he was the exact opposite and could hardly have taken the Camino at a more relaxed pace. Pierre's walking was so laid back that he had passed the horizontal, done a couple of loops and finished back somewhere past horizontal at diagonal. When he walked, he often hummed or sang "Ultreya", the song we had sung at the monastery in Conques. Pierre was sixty-three, tall and lanky, with a slick of silver hair that used to stand erect when a south-easterly caught it.

We arrived at the ghost town that was Villar de Mazarife late afternoon. There wasn't anyone about anywhere. It was way past siesta, and too damn cold and wet for one anyway. We found the refuge up a small side street and peered around the open front door after several knocks had failed to produce a reaction.

An estate agent might describe this house as "in serious need of renovation". Plaster flaked off walls, fading paint clung on wherever it could. It was the sort of place where budget was clearly the primary concern and if something needed to last another year, it damn well better had. I suspected somewhere there was an electric plug with a nail in it because they couldn't afford to buy another fuse when it blew the last time. A pipe would have sprung a leak at some point and insulation tape would have been the answer. When the last building inspector had viewed it, I surmised, he left after five minutes to call for back-up.

But I loved it. It was oozing with character. It knew it was the only place like it in the world and it was going to show it off. There was a courtyard at the rear, and a rickety wooden balcony framed three of the walls above us. Mattresses were spread out so people could sleep out there but the drizzle was working its way under the shelter on to them. I would have killed to have been there in the summer, sitting out in the garden with a late night drink and chatting to other pilgrims, with the laughter echoing off the walls. The showers were outside but hot. My bunk for the night was a bare mattress on a wooden floor, just the way I liked it. Wind whistled through cracks around doors and windows and brushed past my face.

"G'day, mate!"

I swung around to be met by a short, well-built woman of about thirty-five. She was totally out of place, especially as the Australian accent just didn't fit. But it didn't matter: the place kept getting more quirky every minute. It was like something out of Monty Python. I half expected a parrot to appear any second.

Blancetta (pronounced Blanketar, not, as we kept being reminded, Blanchetar) was, well, funny. She had long, dark hair that made her look ten years younger than she was. Her Aztec excuse for a jumper looked as if it had been knitted from a dead yak; fishnet stockings bulged out around her legs and were met at the bottom by a pair of Dr Martens boots. Pierre took a dislike to her and her bubbly manner, and his temper began to fray, which made her bite back.

"So," I interjected, to break off another spitting match, "Blanchetar, what on earth are you doing out in the middle of remotest Spain, running a wreck of a refugio, but a unique wreck at that, with an Australian accent?"

"It's BLANCETTA, not Blanchetar. I'm originally from Spain anyway. My mother is Spanish, Basque, to be precise, and she married an Ozzie. I moved to Australia when I was about five and grew up out there. The other kids used to take the piss because I had a Mediterranean complexion, so I grew up learning how to take care of myself. I completed the Camino a month ago and came straight back to this place because I want to buy it, renovate it and spend the rest of my life here. Look, this is probably the first time you have seen one of these." She handed me an A4 size piece of thin card.

"Oh, my God!" I exclaimed. "Pierre, look at this, it's the certificate we get in Santiago."

We both studied it, poking it, almost to see if it were alive.

"They write your name in Latin usually," Blancetta explained. "But they couldn't find mine on the list so it stayed the same."

This had totally thrown me. I was holding what was in some weird way a glimpse of the finish line. It was recognition that the end was coming.

"Blancetta, what, I mean why, sorry, how exactly do you get it once you've arrived?"

The fake pilgrim spotter was creeping back into my thoughts. I half expected her to confirm my fears with tales of torture dungeons.

"Well, mate, you just kinda go to this room at the back of the cathedral where two very nice Spanish girls ask you a few questions, check your name in Latin, ask you to fill out a couple of forms and they hand it over. There's no big ceremony or anything."

"Questions? What sort of questions?" My eyes narrowed at hers.

"Just name and address, that sort of thing. You know, tourist information to compile reports and all that."

"Oh ... OK."

I fell asleep with a draught on my face, listening to the floorboards creaking, and wondering if the Camino could throw up any more surreal surprises.

Chapter Thirteen

Villafranca del Bierzo

After spreading out for an eternity, the mundane Meseta at last started to fade out after Leon. Bends and turns became more frequent, rumples and hills appeared, along with a certain randomness which everyone had missed. The occasional stream flirted with the Camino and trees sprouted along its side. After travelling a path that seemed almost obsessively straight, I felt I was in a new playground and gratefully accepted the change. For the first time, I walked with hat, gloves and a neck buff. On the higher elevations a stinging wind whipped my face.

On Sunday 21st October I awoke to accusations that I had been snoring. The refuge in Astorga was a cramped affair. Beds stacked not two, but three to a bunk balanced like uncertain skyscrapers and the narrow space between them lent a certain claustrophobic element to the dormitory. There were a lot of people jammed into a small space, hence there were several witnesses to back up the claim, which came from Chantelle, one of the French Canadians. At first I gave her my best look of horrified innocence, but after several pilgrims nodded in agreement, I backed down and apologised, admitting that I did snore when I slept on my back ... sometimes.

I have a proven and precise method of getting to sleep, which had obviously been disturbed, otherwise I wouldn't have ended up sleeping on my back. Usually I get into bed, lie on my back, tuck my feet under the end of the sheets, roll to the left and tuck in again, and then roll to the right and do the same. The pillow sits under my head and I pull the corners so they sit on top of my shoulders. I cross my left leg over my right, and place both my hands on my heart. I then tense every muscle in my body for about ten seconds and let go, which relaxes me. After about thirteen minutes I roll over to my right side, tuck in again, and place both hands just below my chin. This position suits me for about another twelve minutes, when I complete the falling asleep regime by rolling over to my left side, and assume the same position. I'm usually asleep in this position after a further few minutes. Clearly, on the night of the snoring episode, I had not made positions two and three, and had been so tired that I fell asleep on my back.

I just couldn't understand why no one took my side when I explained all of this.

After a little frustration getting out of Astorga, the day blossomed into one of the best since Le Puy. As it was Sunday, there was little traffic, so even though I walked on the main road for a few kilometres, there was a weird silence. The sun was warm and low, providing the chance to take some good photos of autumnal colours and long shadows. A collection of hot air balloons drifted above and around me, sending out the occasional roar from their burners. It reminded me of the fairground, for some reason, maybe eliciting some forgotten childhood memory. I walked in a T-shirt and shorts and let the sun keep me warm.

Everyone else sensed what a perfect day it was. No one was in a hurry, and they were all smiling, taking their time, apparently putting aside their worries about finishing the walk and what might come after. It was like one of those classic autumn Sundays in the park when people were out strolling, hands in pockets and holding their face to the sun as if to soak up the feeling before winter arrived.

I passed pilgrims on the grass just off the Camino sipping wine and having a picnic. People I knew would acknowledge me and smile or wave and not say a word, because words weren't needed. No one had to focus on the walking: their legs automatically carried them along, leaving them free to look around and experience the day.

There were hills in the distance, the last major hurdle before Santiago. Heathers erupted in greens and purples everywhere. It reminded me of Scotland. After walking with Pierre again for a couple of hours, we pulled off the way, about half an hour short of Rabanal del Camino, to where Ancha and Helen were resting under a magnificent oak tree. The tree and the small clearing underneath lured us in, a place to rest and capture the last of the daylight hours. The two Dutchwomen had sensed it as well. Pierre said he had heard about a large oak tree before the village, which, it was claimed, beckoned people to it.

I climbed a short way up the trunk, like a little kid, and let my legs dangle either side of a thick branch, with my head resting on my hands. I focused my mind on the tree and soon familiar wisps of white energy started to dance around, emanating out and up. None of us spoke, simply absorbing the experience.

The refuge in Rabanal del Camino rounded off a splendid day. It nestled in the corner of a small square, flanked by a church. Everything was hewn out of stone or carved from deep brown wood. Smoked wafted out of chimneys, reminding me the nights were colder now.

The refuge had recently been restored beautifully and was being run by two Englishwomen from the St James Society back home. They were motherly figures, old and grey, with kind features. Tea and cakes adorned the kitchen like a patisserie shop. The rooms, indeed the whole place was immaculate. They even had a spin dryer, which took me back a few years to my mother's kitchen, where she would sit on the dryer to prevent it from taking off after ignition, and then from bouncing down the hall and ending up in the garden. A deep orange fire roared in the common room, where pretty much everyone ended up reading or writing diaries, talking little and savouring the perfect day they too had experienced.

The morning could not have produced a more dramatic

change. By eight o'clock I was walking in what felt like a horror movie. Intermittent rain slapped haphazardly against me, whipped up into a frenzy by gusts of wind. The sun had not risen, but I doubt if it would have had any effect. The sky, barely discernible in the low light, looked menacing, to say the least. Soot-black clouds sped over me, barely seeming an arm's length away. The road snaking up over the hills shimmered from the night's rain. Huge dead, black trees loomed over the road like terrifying giant hands.

It was the road to the Cruz de Ferro. At an altitude of 1,504 metres, this large iron cross is perched on top of a huge cairn of stones left by pilgrims over the years as a representation of their worries. The tradition goes that you start the walk with a stone from your home and deposit it at the cross so that you leave your worries behind. I had decided at the start to leave my neck pendant from the church at Le Puy here. It was lucky I had been unaware of the tradition when I left home. If my stone had signified my worries at the start of the walk, it would have had to accompany me strapped to a lorry.

Numerous other artifacts adorned the site: photos pinned to the cross, messages scrawled on scraps of paper, underpants, glasses, you name it. If some archaeologist happened on this site in ten thousand years' time, it would be the find of a lifetime.

A long procession of sodden pilgrims wiggled down to the tiny hamlet of Mandarin, famous for being the home of a Camino legend. It was tiny, a few stone houses limply scattered along the road, all of them abandoned years before except for one. It had been rudely made inhabitable by whatever material was available: plastic sheets, corrugated tin, wood. It looked like a salvage yard. I was drawn up its path by medieval-type music wafting out of a vintage stereo. Two or three pilgrims were reading an article in the window about the guy who lives there. I realised it was a man Jeannie had told me about a few weeks earlier.

The Knights of the Templar, guardians of the Camino, were entrusted centuries ago with ensuring the safe passage of pilgrims. The occupier of this run-down shack way up in the mountains was referred to as Thomas the Knight. He claimed he was a true Templar Knight and had left his middle-class existence to come to Mandarin, set up his home and provide shelter and food for the walkers.

I peered inside the mess that was the refuge, to be met with the sight of two puppies climbing over each other in squalor. It was disgusting, not to mention cruel. The decision not to stay there, despite Jeannie's recommendation, was pretty easy. All credit to the guy for setting up the place, but it wasn't for me.

From the village of El Acebo to Ponferrada the going was all downhill. The rain that had been trying to make up its mind finally gave up mid-afternoon. I made my way down to the town through sodden vegetation. Everything shone in the sunlight and water droplets glinted as they fell to earth from glistening leaves. Grass seemed twice as green as usual and streams gushed over boulders and stones. An aroma like incense assailed me and I looked around, expecting to see someone burning a fragrance stick somewhere. Eventually I fathomed the source. Small brown seed pods in the small bushes that lined the path had burst open and were releasing this fantastic perfume. I later found out they were called Cistus bushes and the smell is indeed likened to incense.

I walked through the charming village of Molinaseca, dodging streams of water from overhangs and gutters. The narrow streets made dusk seem more severe and slimy cobbles reflected the moon like a thousand cats' eyes. Black clouds whisked past, occasionally clearing to reveal a vividly blue night sky.

I had walked about one kilometre out of town and was about to turn back because I thought I must have missed the refuge, when a giggle from one of the French Canadians made me execute a sharp left to an old church. It had been completely refurbished with pilgrims in mind, and the warden proudly boasted that Shirley MacLaine had stayed there on her pilgrimage.

Downstairs had the feel of a Middle Eastern room, even if

the décor didn't match. A log fire was crackling right in the centre and the walls were lined with cushioned benches close to the ground. All that was missing was a Turkish carpet.

Hearing a constant squealing and whimpering from outside, I went to investigate. The warden's dog had given birth to a pup whose rear leg was deformed and useless. The bitch, unable to accept it, was picking it up with her teeth and literally flinging it against the wall. If it hadn't been for the noise, I might have let Mother Nature take her course, but my conscience took over and I brought the pup inside by the fire. I imagine it was probably the best night of her life. Practically everybody gave her a bit of love, not to mention numerous food scraps. She was running around, ears pricked up, and playfully nipping at people's legs. I didn't have the heart to send her back outside to be beaten up again, so she spent the night curled up against my leg in bed. She never stirred once.

In the morning fat clouds still threatened, their bellies glowing orange from the sunrise. One particular cloud seemed to be winning the daily beauty contest, and when a rainbow joined the scene, I knew it was one of those once-in-a-lifetime photo opportunities. By the time I located my trusty SLR from the rucksack, however, the cloud had pissed off somewhere and the rainbow had faded. I had to settle for taking a shot of the road winding down to Ponferrada.

I found the town disappointing. I tried to picture the place in summer, which didn't help. Modern concrete blocks looked dirty from traffic pollution. Uninspiring architecture just inflamed the ugliness, and there was the constant smell of industry. To be fair, I should say that I entered the town on the west side, which was built more recently. Another branch of the Camino brings you through the prettier and culturally richer east side, which slopes down from the hill where the thirteenth-century castle built by the Knights Templar perches. This part of the town is well worth seeking out if you want a historical detour.

A huge slag heap on the way out of Ponferrada seemed to be summing up a depressing day, but the afternoon couldn't have been more different. The town filtered out to countryside that seemed to be throwing an autumnal party. The sun kept appearing through huge breaks in the clouds, illuminating everything like a lightning strike. Distant hills and mountains flashed and changed as shadows and rays swept over them. The changing light was astonishing. Colours seemed more intense and vivid, even blinding. The vineyards mutated from one colour to another as their lines of perspective merged and ran on a rollercoaster up to the horizon. It was extraordinary, a visually magical afternoon.

Little did I know that when I came into the beautiful town of Villafranca del Bierzo I wouldn't be leaving for ten days. I had every intention of spending the night and leaving in the morning. By the time I did actually leave, nearly two weeks later, I could spell its name without checking the handbook, and give directions to the post office. I even knew what evenings the bar was showing the European football matches.

Jeannie told me to stay at one of the two refuges in town because the owner claimed to be a faith healer. Jato the Faith Healer's refuge was shadowed by the church and immediately I could tell it was going to be special. Jato built the place with his bare hands, and it just sweated character. It had been constructed in stone and wood, made to look as old as the church, and it worked.

Upstairs in the dormitory, I shunned a bunk bed for a mattress on the floor in order to be blessed with some good sleep on the firm surface, even if I only had thirty centimetres of head room, as the roof slanted down steeply. Everywhere you went, it seemed, you either had to duck under a low beam or walk up little stairs. One dormitory had a sign pinned to the door saying 'Over 40s only'. I peered in to check that didn't entitle them to any perks we didn't have. What was worrying was the woman I passed coming out nodded and smiled at me as if I was in that age bracket.

The dining area was the main focal point, where people gathered to eat, drink, write, read or sit by the stove. Food was included each night for a small fee, and I took full advantage after seeing the huge portions of Spanish dishes on offer.

On the first evening I got talking to Kylie, a Canadian guy, whose favourite phrase was "Yeah, but I'd have some issues with that". He was about twenty-two, but looked seventeen. He was short, with ruffled hair, a beard and looked a bit like Kevin from Coronation Street. I asked if he knew Jeannie and it turned out he had walked with her for a while.

"Me too," I said. "We were together for a couple of weeks coming over the border."

"Wait a minute, are you Foz?"

The accusation made me feel mildly famous.

"Yep, that's me."

"Jesus, I've heard about you from loads of people. Jeannie, Barry the Irish guy and someone else."

I was just about to say that I didn't class four as 'loads' when he continued.

"I've been seeing your name etched on the Camino for weeks!"

I laughed. It seemed my name in the mud was sticking in loads of people's minds - well, at least two to date.

Together with an American called Warren, they were helping Jato build an extension on to the existing property. Jato's own inimitable style of building meant it was kind of thrown together with whatever materials were available on a given day. I watched him often and he would stop every once in a while, scratch his stubble, cock his head for a closer look at something, then seem to decide that although it probably didn't meet building regulations, if indeed there were any, no one would ever know.

When he was doing some groundwork, he had found what he thought was an old pilgrim bath. There had apparently always been a refuge on the site, and the bath was centuries old. It was made of stone and about six times the size of a normal bath. It would make a great attraction to the place, especially if it was in full working order. You could tell from the way he looked at it that he was trying to work out the plumbing plans.

The first morning I awoke to the usual bustle and rustle of pilgrims preparing for the day's march. The sun didn't penetrate our room, as there were no windows, but I knew roughly it must be eight o'clock. I was tired, Villafranca seemed like a pleasant enough place, and I was due a rest day. Then I thought, "Fuck it! Why do I have to be DUE a rest day? Why can't I have a day off whenever I feel like it? Why do I have to be owed one?" So, I took a rest day.

I wandered bleary-eyed down to the common room. Warren and Kylie were having the last mouthfuls of breakfast before another day of mixing mortar and throwing bricks around under Jato's watchful eye. I did manage a brief bit of faith healing with the man himself, though. My toes occasionally suffer from loss of feeling. He removed my sock, placed my outstretched leg on his knee and began rubbing the area while his face went into contortions like those of someone with his eyes shut trying to locate a fly buzzing around his head. He seemed to get fed up after a while, patted my foot and went off to do some building. I decided the village might be more interesting.

I walked down the steep streets to the central square, built in the architectural style I had become accustomed to, with a church commanding the scene and a smattering of bars and restaurants around the edge.

It was a good place to rest. Villafranca had all the usual amenities, plus a few interesting diversions as well. The first was the photographic shop. I had to go in to get film anyway, but ended up spending a good hour in there. The owner, who had walked the Camino, had displayed on the walls several of his excellent black and white prints of life on the trail.

At a café I treated myself to a good old greasy fry–up, which made me feel like a stuffed walrus, although I found room for a dessert.

A hair trim was also in order. My hair was long, so all I needed was a shave on the back of my neck under the hairline to get rid of that fluffy stuff and a sideburn tidy up.

Trouble was, as my Spanish was non-existent, and I was always terrified of going into the barbers in case they misunderstood me and cut the whole lot off. There were four women inside, one of whom, I deduced, must be the stylist and another, with blue hair, her current customer. The stylist sat me down on an ageing chair and after a lot of pointing and gesturing and saying "per favor" and "no" and "si", I finally got the trim I wanted. This was the limit of our conversation until she had finished, when she asked "Pilgrim?"

"Si," I replied, reaching for my wallet.

"No, no. Pilgrim. OK?" Gesturing no money was required.

"OK, gracias. Muchas gracias."

I called Trish as her job in Greece was due to end soon, and I wanted to discover what her plans were.

"How are you?" I said.

"Erm, I'm a bit wobbly, really, Fozzie. Season's finished and I'm at that 'what to do next' stage." She sounded tired of making decisions and considering her options.

"Trish, listen," I said. "Why don't you come out and walk the last two weeks with me? I know the impression you got last time was that I wanted to walk this thing on my own, and I did, but the end is in sight now and it would be great to see you and have some company. It's apparently the best two weeks of the whole walk, at least in terms of scenery. I'm in no rush and I can hang somewhere while you get yourself sorted. Plus, you get to walk into Santiago de Compostela! What do you think?"

"I'd love to, Fozzie."

We discussed a rough itinerary and I said I'd call again in a few days. It would be great to walk with her, and enter the square at Santiago with a companion. I couldn't wait.

The problem now was how to kill a week. I didn't want to carry on walking because Trish wanted to see the mountains and they started after Villafranca. It was pointless backtracking, so I decided to chill where I was. Then I had an idea. If Jato wanted someone else on the construction site,

I could do that and at worst, get my food and board thrown in. He scratched his stubble briefly when I asked him and then said yes.

On the first day I was helping myself to breakfast with Kylie and Warren in the common room, expecting to spend the day shaping some stone bricks, mixing a bit of cement and sitting on my arse when Jato wasn't looking. He came in, muttered a few words and beckoned us to follow him. Carrying spades and shovels, we walked in thick fog up the hill at the back of the refuge and stopped by a pile of dirt and rubble about two metres high. Kylie and Warren, both of whom spoke good Spanish, listened as Jato instructed them before he walked off back down the hill.

"What's the deal?" I asked.

"We sit down, have a smoke, admire the fog, talk for a bit, then do a few minutes' work. Then we repeat again," Warren advised with a smirk on his face.

"What's going on with all this dirt?" I wanted to know.

"We prop this old bed frame up and then take shovels of dirt and throw them at the springs," said Kylie. "It sieves out all the crap and we're left with a nice, fine dirt to mix with water and use as a finish over the cement so it looks as if the stones are held together in the old-fashioned way. Basically, we're gonna be his sieve bitches."

And there it was. We spent most of the day talking, smoking, eating grapes, and every once in a while, we would all get up, go crazy throwing dirt at an old bed so that it looked as though we had done some work. At two thirty we took a break and walked back down the hill to lunch prepared by Jato's wife. She was a woman of few words. Of short stature, with a crop of dyed black hair not quite covering the grey roots, she spent most of the day preparing food and throwing abuse at Jato. But she was a damn fine cook. She would poke her little head out of the kitchen door, do a quick squint around the tables, then scuttle back in and out again with a top-up of whatever dish had been finished. Occasionally she would sit down, grab a few swigs of vino, eat a couple of mouthfuls, throw some smiles and make some conversation. Then she would go back to the kitchen.

I was sleeping well after the work and food but had developed an annoying habit of getting up in the night to go for a wee. I always thought that was something I would experience in later life, but the problem had started, it seemed, earlier than I had expected. A woman I knew once told me how, regular as clockwork at three am, she would wake up and go to the toilet, then go back to bed again. This happened every night, whatever she had eaten or drunk before going to bed, and she had just come to accept it as a fact of life. Now I found the same thing happening to me, but rather than accept it, I took to going to the toilet for a long leak every night before hitting the sack, in the hope that my head would remind my bladder that it wasn't time to wake up yet. No such luck. It is a major operation getting me out bed at any time, let alone at three in the morning. For an hour or so I would fight the feeling, kidding myself that I could actually go another five hours without giving in, but eventually let out a sigh and cave in. It was of paramount importance to do the job quickly, but it was always bloody freezing and I could never be bothered to get dressed for the sake of five minutes.

I would unzip the sleeping bag and sit up, usually forgetting there was a big rafter just above my head. Next I had to fumble and grope aimlessly around in the dark to find the stairs. I didn't want to turn on the lights because I was a considerate pilgrim and didn't want to wake anyone. Think of the last part of the film "The Silence of the Lambs". Clarice Starling has found the killer's house and he has just done a runner and turned off all the lights. Switch to what the suspect is seeing through his night vision goggles. Our heroine's arms are outstretched in front of her, waving helplessly from side to side. Her face is green except for these two big golf balls as eyes, staring blankly at nothing. She touches something and then jumps because she doesn't know what it is. Well, that was me. First I had to find the banister so I knew where the stairs would start, down three steps and then turn right and get the other banister for the second flight. Once I was at the bottom I turned on the outside lights so I could see better. At this point I was shivering and stood at the urinal shaking, impatiently waiting for my bladder to empty. I usually turned on the lights to get back in bed because I was in such a hurry to be warm again.

One day a local guy called Jose turned up and he helped with the building for the rest of my time there. He was in his mid-thirties with a short, tight perm. His skin was Spanish olive and he wore the same pair of jeans and white T-shirt every day. His favourite word was undoubtedly 'tranquil'. Jose liked to take regular breaks and do little work, so he fitted right in immediately. Cigarette breaks, tea breaks, coffee breaks, sit-down breaks, eating breaks, spliff breaks, laughing breaks, talking breaks, you name it. When in full flow, though, we would blitz the work. I remember one day, from eight to four, we must have worked for at least three hours!

I had, by now, been promoted to staff quarters. A door leading from the main dorm led to where Kylie, Warren, Jose and I had our own space to retreat to at night, away from the bag rustlers. In the late evening we enjoyed quality relaxing time. Warren would probably write his diary or draw stupid pictures. Kylie would be trying to decide whether to have a snooze or darn his socks. Jose would be smoking a fat one and I would be probably reading or dreaming about mountains. My new quarters afforded increased head space, although it was in the loft, so there was still some crouching involved. It had bags of character, a couple of dormer windows let in some light and we each had a mattress and some personal space. There was only one light bulb so at night someone usually lit some candles. It was a far cry from luxury but we liked it.

The following day I was getting dressed on my bed when I looked over to see Kylie standing in the doorway with a grin on his face.

"Someone to see you," he smirked and stepped to one side.

In the split second that followed, "someone" came

sprinting towards me, arms outstretched, with a huge smile on her face. It was Jeannie. She hit me head on and the momentum carried us over and we landed in a heap on Warren's mattress, much to his surprise.

"You little fucker! Where the hell you been? You fucking went off and left me, you bastard!" she screamed. We just lay there in a heap, giggling uncontrollably until we hurt.

"I got your note," she cried. "Foz! Where the hell you been?!"

My mouth hurt so much from laughing I couldn't speak.

"Walking!" was all I could muster, and we both collapsed again.

Lunch in Pamplona with Monica and Jeannie.

The Camino winding through the wine region of Rioja.

Typical Spanish direction sign.

Chapter Fourteen

A New Companion

Jeannie could sell anything to anyone. By the time evening had arrived, she had secured a job cleaning for a few days and Virginia the manager was her new best mate. It transpired she had never been much more than two days behind me. That was the thing with the Camino. You could meet someone and then not see them for four weeks and it would turn out they were always just a few kilometres behind you, when you thought they were days ahead. Walkers make friends and then lose them, not realising that they probably pass them a few times a week sitting in a bar or staying at a different refuge.

Pierre had also arrived, looking a little the worse for wear but with a glint in his eye confirming he would make it. Reginald, the only walker whom I had really known since Le Puy, also arrived, sporting the same old pipe held together by the same sticky tape. He was as surprised to see me as I him.

"Fozzie!" he exclaimed, actually removing the pipe from his mouth which I took as a compliment. "Why, I thought you would be finished for sure!"

"I thought the same about you, Reginald."

I got down to the kitchen the following morning to find Jato with his head buried in his hands and snapping at people when they asked him where the food was. Virginia had failed to arrive to cook the breakfast, but she eventually huffed and puffed her way through the door at nine, calmed everyone down and sorted out food. Jato perked up at this and when we left for work he was laying healing hands on a very worried-looking Austrian lady.

He was going off to Madrid for the weekend, so Virginia was left in charge. When we asked her what we were to do, she simply shrugged her shoulders and muttered something about looking busy. So we climbed up the hill one more time on the pretense of being sift bitches, and spent 95% of the day talking - a new record.

"Every man's revolution is a tap on the snooze button," said Kylie at one point. All three of us nodded sagely at this piece of nonsense and muttered a few "Yeah, Man's."

The conversation covered such profound areas as fair trade coffee, organic farms, revolution in Mexico, oh, and the benefits of online gaming on the Internet. Kylie and I shared a passion for medieval warfare games - sad, at my age, I know. Warren was struggling to see the attraction.

"You can learn more from gaming than from history books," I explained. "The gaming is based, more or less, on actual war units, infantry, siege weapons and such. You learn where and when to use a particular unit, what to counter another unit with, war planning, lines of attack, surprise hit and runs. It's cool."

"You sad, English boy."

Virginia took her new role to heart and gave us the afternoon shift off. This would have provided me with an afternoon siesta for once, had Warren not been engaged in throwing wet pieces of bog roll at me and refusing to turn down his radio because the volume button was "wrecked".

To my surprise, I was getting tired of Villafranca. Jato was getting on my nerves and I could see myself getting stuck there like Kylie and Warren, like a fly in treacle. They were happy muddling along but I could see they had lost the spirit of the Camino. Maybe it was because of the fear of finishing, the fear of actually reaching the stage where you don't have to walk any more. Perhaps, I thought, that was why they were there, because they knew if they stayed at Jato's then the finish wasn't getting any closer. I could feel myself starting to stick as well. I had not heard from Trish and it was getting on for a week since I had arrived. The work was getting monotonous, I begged new scenery, my legs were getting restless and I wanted to feel my pack on my back again.

The place did have its advantages, though. It was undeniably a beautiful village, I wasn't spending any money and it was the only place where Trish could get hold of me. She had the number for the refuge and if I moved on she would not be able to contact me.

There was the occasional event that broke the boredom up. Jeannie and Jose had been caught by the police for smoking a spliff in the bushes in the park. Naturally, this worried me when I heard. I mean, what was she doing with Jose in the bushes?

They had been spending a lot of time together and flirting around. A few of us had gone into town one evening for a meal and the two of them had wandered off for a walk. Villafranca park was a maze of short, cropped bushes about waist height, with the occasional bench. As night fell, they had sat down, laughing and joking around, and decided a little harmless substance smoking was called for, for which they obviously had to use a lighter. This proved a very inviting beacon for the local police patrol, who put two and two together and called six colleagues and, before Jeannie and Jose knew what had hit them, eight law enforcement officers jumped over the hedges from various angles, blinded them with torches and held them at gunpoint.

Jose had somehow managed to see all of this coming and tossed the offending substance into the bushes. Jeannie faked her best innocent look whilst holding up her arms, her horrified eyes fixated on the torch beam like an escaped prisoner caught in a spotlight. The police searched everywhere but couldn't find anything, leaving them with the only option of telling Jeannie and Jose off for possession of a small amount of hash. If they had found Jose's larger stash, it would have meant jail for both of them. Jeannie was clearly shaken by the whole event.

"I though I was going to jail, Foz," she said. "The last thing my daughter said to me before I left was not to get into trouble because she couldn't bail me out."

Jeannie's good humour about the refuge lifted my spirits a little. I was still waiting for news from Trish, made all the more frustrating because I had no contact details for her. I found the work a little less monotonous and the conversations with Kylie and Warren always made me giggle. Warren especially was given to spouting stuff quite randomly.

"Did you ever get the feeling your ex is getting laid?" he offered one morning. Kylie looked at me and smiled.

"Yeah, I do," I replied. "It's weird, like you, well, you just know she's having sex with someone else at that precise moment. What's she doing having sex at eleven thirty in the morning anyway?"

"Huh?" Warren looked a little bemused.

"I said, what is she doing have sex at eleven thirty in the morning? You said you knew your ex was getting laid: how does she get sex at eleven thirty am?"

"How should I know? Does it matter?" he said uncomfortably.

"In fact, that's not strictly true," I added. "I take it she lives where you use to in Portland. Therefore, they are around, what, ten hours behind us here. Therefore, she's having sex at roughly ... two ... three thirty am! Did you two normally get it on at irregular hours?"

"Well, no, not really. Sort of normal hours, really, in the evening and stuff."

Kylie had his back to both of us but I could tell by his shaking that he was quietly giggling.

"I think maybe her new man is giving her a rich and varied diet, Warren. Maybe this is why she left you in the first place. Maybe you weren't sugaring her coffee? You know, weren't buttering her baps?"

At this point, Kylie collapsed backwards in a fit of hysterics and promptly fell off the dirt heap, throwing up a cloud of dust.

"Do you think she knows when you're having sex?" I asked.

"Well, if she does, she probably knows I'm celibate right now."

"You two are weird," chipped in Kylie, who stood up looking like someone who had, well, just fallen off a dirt heap.

One day Jato took us to a rectangular, raised tomb in the graveyard right behind the refuge. He gave us each a wire brush, explained to Kylie what he wanted, and walked off.

"What's going on?" I asked.

"Well, he just wants us to clean off this tomb and then give it a couple of coats of emulsion this afternoon."

So we spent the morning rubbing and inhaling a mixture of old paint, cement dust and the occasional bit of dried lichen. There was unusual bustle around the headstones. Half the village seemed to be pruning, placing flowers and doing a spot of DIY on their lost loved ones. There were tubs of white paint everywhere - it was like B&Q on a Sunday morning. The local florists must have done 80% of their yearly trade around that time of year. I never did discover what the occasion was but by the time we had finished and trudged back to the refuge, the whole cemetery had been scrubbed, scraped, cleaned, given a lick of paint and polished. We did find out, however, that the tomb we had worked on was Jato's grandfather's.

One evening the phone rang. Kylie answered it.

"Call for Keith, do we have a Keith?" he shouted around. I was outside, smoking.

"Who the hell's Keith?" asked Jato.

I was just walking back in.

"Last call for Keith, Trisha on the phone, KEITH!"

"Whoa! That's me!" Everyone looked at each other, surprised, and muttered in unison "Keith?"

Trisha had managed to secure a flight for the Saturday morning, so on Friday, needing an excuse to get out for a couple of days, I was heading towards Madrid on the 10.05am from Ponferrada. And what a coach it was! Forget the best of National Express, this thing was like Concorde. There was so much leg room that I had to squint to see the person in front. The seats reclined back so far that if I looked back I could see the woman behind looking at me; she looked a bit funny upside-down. The headrests even had little upturned bits at the edge, so my head wouldn't roll off when we went around a corner. TV, video, radio ... I half expected a flight attendant to announce when we would be landing.

I was looking forward to Madrid. Cities aren't really my thing but after being in Villafranca for an eternity, I was looking forward to a strong dose of the twentieth century. Unfortunately, it proved a little too much. I had inadvertently picked the weekend of the Real Madrid and Barcelona soccer match. The locals, wisely, had moved out and let the hordes in. This included the footie fans, the usual city workforce, some Christmas shoppers and a few general misfits. It was horrible. Oxford Street on Christmas Eve had nothing on this. After walking so far and not having to worry about anything getting in my way, my brain was in turmoil trying to dodge everybody. It was like a human version of bumper cars. People were stressed, tempers were fraying, everyone was constantly saying "Excuse me" or "Pardon". I was completely out of my depth.

Accommodation was proving a problem as well. I would have liked to dump my bag in a room, have a quick shower and then get back into the fray to survey Madrid from the sheltered vantage point of a street-side café, but there were no rooms anywhere. I had never experienced a city or town being "fully booked". Well, I was in the middle of a city well past its population limit, with a tired friend flying in, expecting at least a bed for the night. At this rate we'd be sleeping in a cardboard box with the other homeless.

I used the last available option open to me, the tourist office. I was in a queue of about ten people and as I moved closer, I realised that for once I had picked the correct attendant. Hearing what other people were asking him, I could see that he knew everything, and I mean everything.

Not only could he give you several options for a barber, he could rattle off the opening and closing times and the exact address, all without checking any paperwork. I guessed if had I asked where I could have a pint of Guinness while relaxing in a sauna with a leggy Danish masseuse fondling my steam settings, he could have given me the answer and told me the colour of the towels.

The first of the two room options he gave me were full. The third place I walked into had one room left and I was so tired that I agreed to take it without viewing it. I hoped the owner's appearance wasn't a clue to the condition of the rooms. Greasy black hair hung in his eyes. A week's worth of stubble protruded from his tired face and his eyelids were on the verge of closing. He wore jeans and a white vest with egg stains on the front and kept brushing off ash from his stomach because he couldn't be bothered to use an ashtray.

The room wasn't as bad as I had feared. Two single beds took up most of the space. A forlorn-looking washbasin lurked in one corner, and a frosted window set three metres up the wall provided a little light. The bathroom was a shared affair with a few other rooms, but hey, when you're a budget traveller, you have to take what you can get.

Budget accommodation isn't necessarily shabby, El Camino being a prime advert for that (oocasionally). I generally stay in Youth Hostels when I travel. They are usually basic but at least clean and cheap. I like the atmosphere and you meet like-minded people there. One of the best places I ever stayed was a cave in Cappadocia, Turkey, an area that is littered with caves that the local people have for generations used as homes. The particular one I stayed in was circular in shape with a fireplace, and a helping of rugs to take the coldness off a bare floor. It was unique and bursting with character, and cost the grand sum of £1.00 per night (a gas heater was an extra 20p). These places exist; you just have to know where to look for them.

As Trish was arriving in the evening, I decided to try out Madrid's tube network. There was a direct line straight to the airport but the train driver had other ideas. He stopped a few stations away from the terminal and then walked through the carriages announcing something I didn't understand. All I could get from him was that the train was stopping and another one was not forthcoming. I resorted to the ever-reliable cab for the rest of the journey and sat down in the airport bar waiting for the arrivals. My head was darting from side to side and up and down trying to see over and around people for Trish. She eventually came through and stopped in the terminal to try and fish something out of her bag. I executed my usual welcome by creeping up behind her and poking her hard in the side. She performed a flawless two-metre jump with contributory yelp, maximum scoring from the judges.

"Fozzie! Fuck! Hi, darling!" she squealed.

I can best describe Trish as someone who follows dreams and doesn't conform to society's expectations - like me, really, which is why we got on. She was in her late thirties. Long, curly, rustic-looking brown hair tumbled down her back and got in her eyes. Occasionally she would tie it back with a pink band kept on her wrist. It had been bleached by the Cretan sunshine over the summer, and her skin was tanned. Her dress sense was a little different but, no matter what the occasion, whether it be hiking, swimming, cooking or whatever, there would always be little feminine touches like a small bow here or a flower there. She also loved going clubbing in hiking boots. Try and mock her attire and she would just say, "But I'm a princess, Fozzie. Princesses are beautiful whatever they wear!"

She was a chef by trade, and a damn good one at that. We had spent the summer working at a yoga retreat on Crete and just clicked. She taught me a lot about the catering trade, food and nutrition, as well as how to dye my eyebrows. On our days off, we would go out on what we called our adventures, she riding on the back of my moped. We might climb a mountain, find the most out-of-the-way taverna possible, swim stupid distances or just get pissed in the local bar. Whatever it was, we had a great time. I had left because of a dispute with the owners in which Trish had been heavily involved. She had done the brave thing and seen it through to the end. No matter how bad the situation, that's what she did. She was one of the kindest and most sincere people I had ever met. It was refreshing. People always warmed to her and she never had a problem talking to strangers. She had an uncanny knack of having long conversations with me and sorting out my problems without my even realising what she was doing.

As usual, we ended up going out in the evening to catch up and the wine flowed. My budget was annihilated as glass after glass kept coming, but that was what we were like when we got together. Looking back after the walk I realised that most of the evenings during the last two or three weeks spent with Trish were an alcoholic blur. We must have tried every different type of Rioja available and kept the Spanish wine industry going single-handed.

We were accosted by three girls on a hen night from Manchester. I asked the bride-to-be what her intended was like.

"Oh, he's great, we have a really open relationship. It works because we both allow each other to flirt with other people and we can have sex with them as well, just not penetration," she explained.

"Oh, I see," I replied. "That's all right, then."

We left her trying to explain why they were going to quit their nine-to-five lives in Manchester to take up the same profession in Australia, working nine to five.

The next day we both headed back to Villafranca for one more final night's rest and then the summit push to Santiago de Compostela. I was now looking at the distance in terms of days instead of weeks. I felt happy to be on the crux of walking again but the fear of finishing and what would come after still haunted me.

I was adamant that the final two to three weeks of the walk were going to be the best. I had met a few people who had walked the Camino previously and they all said the same about the last part. Beautiful scenery, a sense of anticipation and, if Galicia's weather held, the best chance to take it all in.

As it turned out, the rest of the Camino was to be the sternest test. The hills weren't enormous, but they certainly weren't small either. The countryside dipped and dived as the foothills warmed themselves in preparation for El Cebreiro, which, at 1,300 metres was neither the highest point on the Camino nor arguably a big mountain, but it did have a reputation.

I always find walking so much better and more rewarding when I am at altitude. It doesn't have to be six thousand metres. My local hills in Sussex are probably only a few hundred metres high but that view from the top down on the rest of the world is enough for me. I feel free in the hills and mountains, where either I forget my problems or the solutions come to hand. For those few hours, I am not part of the world down there among the cars and people. It is an escape that I thrive on. The air is cleaner, the wind fresher and the aromas more intense.

Mountains are pure, sincere and innocent, untouched by anything that might change them. A mountain would not lie to you, it is as it is, it makes no pretence, and you can take it at face value when it proclaims it is a thing of beauty that has been there for thousands of years.

The day we left was perfect. Mist was wafting and streaming around Villafranca like ghosts, dying as the sun lifted. There was the tiniest of breezes which I could just feel on my face like the brush of a feather. The shadows were retreating and cowering.

A smell of damp stonework moved around in the village as we made our way through the rustic streets for possibly the last time. The chill of the damp walls in the tight alleys seemed to be trying to penetrate me. And then I walked with Trish out into the main square. It was different. Certainly more beautiful and charming. It had saved its best until I left.

We passed the bar that had served me with numerous fry-ups, gave one last look at the photographs in the camera shop, took a quick, deep sniff of the bakers as I walked past, and glanced in at the hairdressers and all the usual customers gossiping and giggling. Feeling the delicious pressure of the cobbles on my heels and toes. We were both smiling.

El Cebreiro was thirty kilometres away. Not a huge distance, but in that sort of terrain we could be beat after fifteen. I had said my goodbyes to all the friends I had made at the refuge. Jeannie had left about three days earlier, and we hoped to meet in Santiago. Virginia gave me a pendant for my neck chain, which was touching. Slaps on the back from the chaps, Jose muttered "tranquil" and even Jato touched the peak of his cap and smiled.

It was sixteen kilometres to Vega de Valcarce and the next refuge. Bearing in mind I had not walked for nearly two weeks and Trish needed some gentle breaking in, we agreed it was a reasonable target. We crossed over the river and took the right fork. This was the steeper and harder of the two possible routes, but it was away from the main road. And boy, was it steep! We were both hunched forward, gasping for air and sweating profusely. It smoothed out after about thirty minutes and the climb mellowed out to a good incline. We caught our breath and lay by the trail trying to cool off, laughing and soaking up the sun.

It was now the first week of November but it still felt summery. Insects buzzed around my head, many plants were still green, the earth was dry and the pollen could still be smelt. This was my eightieth day of walking and the total now under my boots was thirteen hundred and seventeen kilometres. However, the signs of autumn were also all around us. Polished horse chestnuts peeked out from their spiky cases, shining like lacquered mahogany. Leaves hung in drifts against stone walls, while others spun and whipped skywards in wind flurries. Golds, reds, browns and greens blurred into nothingness as they flew around us.

Trish asked me how many footsteps I had taken, which we soon agreed would take too much working out. However, I started calculating the number of times I had done certain things. I reckoned I had drunk 300 litres of water. Not surprisingly, taken a pee around five hundred times. Eaten about forty omelettes (even more worrying, that's about a hundred eggs). I must have picked my nose a lot, maybe even three times a day, so that's about two hundred and forty pickings. Lifted my pack on and off (I had to spend a bit of time on this one) about six hundred times. Sung a lot of songs, or at least hummed them and taken around twenty wrong turns.

I was just compiling the options for tracks eleven and twelve for the Song of the Day album when I realised we were lost. Typical, I thought, on the first day of my new guide status and I'd already taken a wrong turn.

"Nice one, Fozzie," commented Trish. "Been reading the book properly, have we? How did you manage up until now, then, Fozzie? Not the best of starts, is it?"

"Yeah, right," I offered. "Come on! It's all part of the adventure! We're still heading vaguely west, I think. We're not that far off. Where's your sense of spontane ... spon ... spontinuit ... spon ... you know, adventure?"

I ignored the heated gabblings of four local people waving us back the other way and then had to eat a serious portion of humble pie when we passed them later after I realised they were right. They shook their heads from side to side and smirked as we passed.

The countryside gave way to a main road and one of the most dangerous stretches of the Camino I had walked on. There was an occasional path on the side of the road, but most of the time we had to walk hemmed between crash barriers and the traffic. We eased into Vega de Valcarce at seven in the evening. It was cold, very dark and we were both tired. The refuge was a lacklustre affair with bunk beds made from wrought iron and mattresses looking as though they were full of potatoes. The shower was a cold trickle but I didn't care any more. My attitude towards these safe houses now was that, no matter how bad some were (and only a minority could be described as bad), I knew I would have a bed with a roof over my head. What more do you want at night?

The local bar provided us with soup, chips, an omelette and some half-decent beer. The food was getting tedious.

Trish was fed up with the same options already. It was invariably chips, "bocadillos" (sandwiches) with either cheese or chorizo (a sort of Spanish sausage) or the ubiquitous Spanish omelette. My cholesterol quota for the year had been exceeded about three weeks before. But most places obliged when we asked for stuff that wasn't on the menu board such as a tuna sandwich, a mixed salad or soup. The only real food to be had was in the larger towns. It seemed an age ago that I was in a tapas bar like the ones in Pamplona. Some days when the culinary offerings were becoming too tedious I would drift off into a daydream about sitting in one of those bars: twelve metres of polished mahogany supporting cabinets teeming with collections of tastebud heaven.

I awoke the following day after little sleep. My tortilla bocadillo the night before had been waging all-out war on my digestive tract. You could have set your watch by the cyclist in the bunk next door and above, who would snore constantly for thirty minutes and then break into a coughing fit, which sounded as if he was trying to hack up a golf ball. Yet he never woke up. The "selective noise recognition while asleep" phenomenon is truly astonishing. Why is it that someone can snore like a road drill and not wake up, yet if they hear a certain sound they come to? An ex-girlfriend used to snore pretty loudly while sleeping like a baby, yet she would reply as soon as I spoke to her.

Trish inadvertently hadn't helped either. I had told her to bring a two or three-season sleeping bag. Some college leaver in the outdoors store had sold her a one–season bag with one of those marvelous cock-ups of design, the space blanket. I understand the theory, but the disadvantages far outweigh the benefit. They may reflect heat back on to your body, but they make a racket similar to several hyperactive chipmunks having a party in a pile of empty crisp packets. The only time I ever used one, all my body moisture collected on the underside of it and I ended up cold because I was so wet.

We casually meandered through a Camino that was

becoming more outstanding every step of the way, it never failed to surprise me no matter how well I thought I knew it. The area approaching the climb to El Cebreiro was in full autumnal display. Grass a vivid shade of green looked almost edible, crisp and glistening with moisture. There always seemed to be the sound of gurgling water near by and occasionally I would catch a glimpse of pure mountain water cascading over rocks and tree roots.

Standing at her front door in one of the many small hamlets we walked through was an old woman, who looked really miserable and ready to snap off the head of any pilgrim who even dared look at her.

"I'm not going to say hello to her," I said. "She looks far too miserable."

Trish, in her usual wise fashion, replied, "Maybe she's miserable because no one ever says hello to her."

I didn't really have an answer to that, but I did promise to try and smile at anyone that looked a little down for the rest of the day.

Trish was good to walk with, but then I wouldn't have asked her along if I didn't think we would get along. Most of the day we would walk together, but occasionally I would get an adrenaline rush and go ahead for a couple of hours, usually checking behind me just to make sure she was following. Sometimes she would walk ahead. It was a great mixture of walking with company but having our own space as well. We got hungry at the same time and after a while started buying more food at shops to carry with us so as not to have to rely on finding a suitable bar. We would get the crispest baguette possible and stuff it with maybe tuna, peppers and a pile of parsley, or cheese, rocket and onion and then sit on a stone wall, legs dangling, and stretch our mouths to cram in this ridiculously tall feast.

Trish sensed that I didn't want to finish and took everything at a sedate pace, which was fine with me. The last thing on my mind now was any form of schedule. I didn't want to be thinking about doing twenty kilometres before lunch or just making the next hamlet by three fifteen so I could push out another ten before dark. We would walk fifteen to twenty-five kilometres a day and take it easy. If we had walked only ten and it was another sixteen to the next accommodation, we always considered that stopping was a viable option and not a cop-out. Never had such a lack of planning worked so well.

"How you feeling, Trixi?" I would enquire at one in the afternoon.

"I'm OK, Fozzie. Little tired, darlin', but OK."

"There's a refuge two klicks away, sounds really nice."

And we would stop early in the afternoon just because we could. We were developing a blasé attitude, as though walking had become random roaming.

The sleepy collection of decaying buildings that was Herrerias signalled the start of the ascent of El Cebreiro. It sat at 680 metres, which reduced the altitude difference to 620 metres. It was reputedly the hardest climb of the whole Camino but it seemed much easier than the Route Napoléon out of St-Jean-Pied-de-Port. To my mind, it was also far superior. Once above the tree line, the hills opened out like a friend with outstretched arms to reveal boulder-shaped hills undulating all around us. We took regular rests, stopped at a couple of cafés and just eased our way up. At one point we felt so nonchalant that we had a cigarette break and lay back in the grass for a siesta. One of the few photos Trish took was of me at that rest stop, with a look on my face of total contentment that summed up the whole day, possibly the whole adventure. I could go back tomorrow and find the exact same spot.

El Cebreiro commanded views in every direction. The assortment of dwellings and a few bars perched on top had entered winter earlier than expected. We booked in at the refuge and, once washed and changed, did our usual search for a couple of bottles of Rioja.

Sitting in the local bar was a serious wind-down that day. We could see orange lights twinkling over the hills around us like candles at a concert. Occasionally the barmaid would come over, check our drinks were OK and carefully place another log on the fire. If this had been a plush ski resort, we would have been paying a small fortune for the privilege. We sank back into our chairs, smoked a lot of roll-ups and drank a lot of wine. Speech slurred, objects on the table doubled up and we giggled a lot at the adventure so far.

Jennifer, a Canadian pilgrim I had got to know since Villafranca del Bierzo, joined us. She had taken a little persuading as she was sober and we clearly were not, but we enticed her over by raising and lowering our eyebrows in temptation and stroking a bottle of delicious '98.

She had been with her boyfriend but they had decided to be apart for a while. He had stayed behind at Jato's, taking advantage of the construction vacancy I left. It seemed a strange thing to agree to. Whether they were planning on meeting up later I never did find out and she seemed content with her own company. She was tall, nearly two metres, but she didn't appear imposing. Short blonde hair was tousled up over her ears and her eyes peered out from behind wiry glasses.

Luckily the bar closed up while she was still able to walk because she had to assist both of us back. Clear stars gazed back at us from a blanket of the darkest black possible. The Milky Way splayed across the sky like a plume of faint mist. The air was biting but marvellously fresh. Winter was definitely arriving. As always, I was afraid of hitting snow before I finished, although, once down from El Cebreiro, the rest of the trail was at low altitude where the risk would be less. Little did I know what the weather had in store overnight.

Chapter Fifteen

Closing in

When I opened the door of the refuge in the morning, I saw a scene transformed. Snow had fallen overnight and the footprints of foraging birds had left arrows in it. Only the black, shiny roads interrupted the vast, white uniformity. As I had thought, the lower altitudes, easily visible, were untouched. I had timed my walk to absolute perfection. A couple of kilometres down the hill and we would be out of the fresh fall and back on firm footings. Fingers crossed, the snow would not fall on the lower levels for our remaining time on the Camino.

We digested El Cebreiro one last time as we sat in the bar and had a leisurely two-hour breakfast, mainly because my diary was seriously behind. After the descent, the temperature soared and we found ourselves taking a warm siesta once again.

Trish had by now developed a pace quicker than mine and she was usually half a kilometre ahead of me, but then slowed down on the hills. At this stage, I was just ambling along, taking it all in. We would meet up at the top of any hills, sit down, maybe have something to eat and just rest. I remembered a message I had read in the visitor's book at El Cebreiro refuge: "I have just begun to realise that Santiago is only the destination."

That pretty much summed it all up for me, as I began to understand its full meaning. I had approached the walk with the idea that there was a beginning and an end. You start at

Le Puy and Santiago is your target. It didn't work like that. The truth was that everything between those two points, the experience in the middle, was the clear meaning. It wasn't about getting from A to B. It was all about experiences that in turn made the memories.

We passed the Alto de San Roque, where a huge bronze statue of St James dominated the road. Sitting on the grass, we made sandwiches from tomatoes and parsley that we had picked from the window sill of a bar, while the owner looked on smilingly and indicated by gestures that it tasted good.

At day's end we found the refuge at Triacastella, which looked like a school building in the middle of a playing field. Jennifer was sitting on the stone wall outside and pointed us in the right direction. Inside too, it seemed like some sort of school building. Polished lino on the floor gave way to bare breeze-block walls. The rooms echoed conversations and there was a strong smell of disinfectant.

The warden checked us in and we made our way to the designated room. As I pushed the swing door, it stopped abruptly and a hand appeared over the top and gently eased the door open. The hand's owner bore a striking resemblance to Christopher Lloyd (the mad professor in the "Back to the Future" movie), only younger. He must have been at least two metres tall. He was bald except for a line of greying hairs clinging to the back of his head as though they had slipped from the top. I'd not seen him before and he didn't look very happy.

"You can't sleep in here, I'm afraid," he said. His voice was soft, an unexpected and striking contrast to his presence.

"Why?"

"Because I am ..." He was cut off by the warden who was behind me and moved me to one side apologetically.

"You have no reason to deny them a room. I have booked them in and I allocated them this room because there are two beds free. I am the warden here, not you. Let them in or I will let you out." He spoke with such authority that no one would have argued with him.

Although I would not have minded finding another room,

I was a little curious as to why he didn't want us in there. It soon became apparent. Jennifer had passed us checking in and was sitting on one of the beds, looking a little sheepish. It would appear that her ex-boyfriend back at Jato's had been well and truly dumped and she had taken up residence in the Mad Prof's bed. I gave her a nod and a wink as I passed.

Later, after we had eaten and were back at the refuge tucked up in our bunk beds, Trish was just kind of staring into space and Jennifer and the Prof were reading, still playing out the "only friends" act by occupying separate beds.

"What you reading, Fozzie?" Trish asked.

"Erm, *The Pilgrimage*, Paulo Coelho."

"Any good?"

"Not bad, I s'pose."

"Read us some, then."

"Yeah, OK. Huh? What you say?"

"Go on, read us all a story so we can get comfy and wind down to sleep."

So I did. I was in the middle of some big hills in north Spain, sleeping in a converted school, reading a story to my best mate, a cute Canadian and a mad Prof.

Jennifer had slipped into the Prof's bed at some point overnight and their heads were romantically nuzzled up together. So close, in fact, that he looked as if he had miraculously sprouted some hair overnight.

I went outside to retrieve my clothes, which had been drying overnight on the washing line. It had been so cold in the night that my T-shirt and other items had frozen solid, so instead of draping them over my arm I carried them under it, as one would a stack of large books.

Trish went on ahead as usual. I always revelled in my own company and Trish, although a sociable person, was using the time to figure out where she was in her life, in the big plan of things. Her job in Crete had proved hard work with long hours, high temperatures and many mouths to feed. It appeared she was taking to her newfound solitude and freedom with relish. Once in a while she would grab her long hair, push it out of the way and turn to check that I was still visible and smile, just as confirmation she was comfortable and to let me know that, although we were walking apart, she was happy and wanted me to be too.

As the day moved on and the sun lifted higher, it warmed. The frost on the ground gradually darkened from whites to vivid greens as the grass broke through. The light from the damp, shiny countryside twinkled back at us from a million different locations. We passed through San Cristobo do Real, a small hamlet forcing the river Oribio to split and flow either side of it, we followed a muddy track through and passed stone dwellings covered in moss. Straw lay here and there, moving slightly in the breeze, and leaves floated down from side to side like someone swaying in a hammock.

The Benedictine monastery in Samos appeared at the end of a leafy lane, an imposing stone masterpiece, which dominated the small village and still housed a few monks, but in its heyday was home to about five hundred of them. We walked around it but all the doors were closed and the windows tiny, leaving the whole place eerily lonely and like a closed book. A fine drizzle engulfed us as we left and the sun disappeared, leaving us pulling on fleeces and waterproofs.

Spain had changed in a matter of days. Winter had sneaked up quickly and caught summer by surprise. It was difficult to get moving in the morning, but after half an hour our bodies had warmed up and we were removing gloves and hats, unzipping jackets and squinting at the low sun with rosy cheeks. We passed through an uninspiring Sarria and looked behind to a backdrop of white where we later learnt it had snowed in Samos also. We felt as though the cold was chasing us.

"Fozzie! Fozzie!" I spun round to see Tamar emerging from a small café in Cortinas.

"Who's that?" Trish enquired. I sighed, asking her how much time she had, so I could explain to her the paradox that was Tamar and me. Espe looked on and watched Tamar approach and hugged me as though her life depended on it.

When Trish saw the resigned look in my eyes, she realised our relationship was not as promising as Tamar's welcome.

We all shared a surprisingly light-hearted coffee and for the rest of the day I walked with Tamar and Trish seemed happy with Espe, who was no doubt filling her in on the previous weeks. Before long we had slipped back into the old routine of trying to hold a conversation, becoming stressed and settling for a language that held no barriers – kissing. When we had originally met it had taken only half a day to realise there was a huge physical attraction and even less time to understand that that was all there was ever going to be. It was all about desire, nothing more; I knew that now.

We reached Morgade, a simple collection of small, old buildings and Trish had found a little place capable of sleeping two pilgrims, with the option of some home cooking. Although we hadn't done much walking that day, it felt right to stay there. Tamar had never asked to stay with me at any of the places where we slept, but had always waited for me to ask her first. This time I didn't. Part of my reason was that I wanted to walk with Trish and if Tamar was with us then I knew she would demand all my time. More importantly, I realised at that point it was time to say goodbye and although I somehow knew I wouldn't see her on the Camino again, something told me our paths would cross at some future date.

I explained as best I could but a resigned look crept over Tamar's face before I had said much. She said she understood and to some extent agreed but had hoped we could have spent more effort working on the bad areas. We hugged and kissed for an eternity and then she turned and left. I watched her slender figure becoming smaller with every step until eventually she vanished.

The rest of the day I was in a sombre mood. Trish sensed this and just did her own thing. I took a siesta and then went for a walk - of all things. It was quiet except for the odd call of a crow and the distant hum of a tractor. There was no wind; water trickled and wove around the stones on the path. A tiny chapel barely big enough for one person sat about fifty metres from where we staying. Some pilgrims had left the usual notes for others, the sort of trail grapevine.

'Hey Foz, steps at two, miss you. Jeannie x.'

It was written on a piece of cloth, like a hanky, and was draped over the table's edge and kept there with a small stone. It was dated ten days earlier. "Steps at two" referred to our agreement that for as long as we stayed in Santiago, every day we would each go to the steps outside the cathedral at two o'clock and wait for ten minutes to see if the other showed up. I smiled, despite my low mood after dealing with Tamar, Jeannie still had an uncanny knack of cheering me up even though she was ten days away.

I returned to find Trish tending a roaring fire that threw moving shadows everywhere and transformed our little hideaway into several shades of orange and red. The owners arrived with several dishes of delicious food and even threw in a bottle of Rioja. We drank toasts to open fires, little hideaways, comfort food, being lucky enough to be doing what we wanted to do, and to finishing the Camino. We went outside to watch a full moon, pulling our jackets tightly around us. Smoke from our cigarettes vanished and reappeared as it rose up and caught the light of the moon through gaps in the buildings. The episode with Tamar notwithstanding, it had turned into a day I knew I would remember with great fondness.

The following morning, as we were thanking the owner for her hospitality, she showed us a pair of huge hiking boots.

"These belonged to Andreas," she explained. "He didn't stay here but just stopped for a drink. We don't know whether he left them here by mistake or intentionally. We presume it was intentionally - either that or he doesn't mind walking in his socks! Do you know him?"

I said we didn't know anyone by that name. "What did he look like?" I asked.

"Oh, he was very tall, all the hair was on the back of his head and he was with a lovely girl. They seemed an odd couple."

I looked at Trish and we said in unison, "It's the Mad Prof!" We then made it our mission for the next few days to return the boots to him. Renaming him Bigfoot, we tied a boot each to our rucksacks and set off to hunt him down.

The truth was at this stage of the walk that Bigfoot was the last thing on my mind. Each time I walked up a hill I half expected to come over the brow and see the spire of Santiago cathedral. We were only about eighty kilometres away now and the end of the walk was consuming most of my thinking time. Of course I wanted to finish, I had to finish. My determination had surprised me over the last few weeks but a lot could happen in eighty kilometres and although I felt confident, I never took it for granted. What I was struggling to deal with was that I had become settled in this way of life. I was comfortable walking twenty-five kilometres a day, in whatever weather. It made no difference if I stopped for lunch at one or two, if at all. I was grateful to have a roof over my head each night for the cost of a cup of coffee. I was completely at one with the trail and to stop what I was now doing was going to leave a very large void in my life.

I had already considered turning round and walking back to Le Puy but knew that delaying the inevitable wasn't going to help. I would be returning home, with little in the way of funds, and that would mean looking for work until such a time as I could head off again somewhere to pick up with this walking thing that was engulfing me. I felt I could be completely happy if I could just carry on walking until I was too old to do it any more. I didn't care about finding a job, looking for somewhere to live, going food shopping, going out on a Friday night. The Camino had taken over my life.

Of course the physical act of "walking" was only 1% of the journey. My legs just did their "thing", which left me free to think about what I was doing and had done, and what the future held in store. I don't mean spending a few minutes on one area or another; I mean taking one aspect of my life and really getting involved in it. We seldom have time these days just to get into our own heads: mostly we're too busy working, looking after children, making a home or whatever.

I always used those few minutes while falling asleep as thinking time, but on the Camino I had the day as well. I was becoming spoilt.

Most of the refuges were manned by part-time volunteers and, although many continued to stay open during the winter, some were shutting up shop. Many had phone numbers pinned to the door, so a quick phone call meant someone would arrive and open up for us, but we were caught out on numerous occasions and had to find lodging somewhere else, which was inconvenient financially. Shops and bars were opening later and closing earlier and we had to rearrange our days to take account of this.

Gonzar appeared to be shutting all its doors like an out-of-season seaside resort. We reached it late one evening after the sun had set, knowing there was a refuge there. We were both cold and hungry and trying to stave off the start of the "winter blues". The school was doubling up as the refuge and there was a good kitchen to get some food going. The sleeping area consisted of several bunk beds crammed into a small and cold room. The place was empty apart from a solitary lady who looked a little depressed. I disappeared off to the local bar for a couple of warming whiskies while Trish tried to cheer her up.

There was a fine mist hanging in the air, refracting and absorbing what little light crept out from windows. I could feel the moisture glance against my face and creep down between my jacket and neck. A couple of cars went past, their tyres hissing against the damp road. I shivered, stuffed my hands deeper into my pockets, tried to lower my head into the collar of my jacket and squinted through the gloom to try and locate the small illuminated beer sign I had seen earlier on our way in.

The place seemed homely enough. A handful of old guys were smoking and drinking an assortment of spirits. There was a small tapas display next to the beer pump and empty sugar sachets and matches littered the floor under the bar's steel foot-rest. A fish was sucking the inside of its bowl in search of some small morsel. I ordered a large whisky and small beer and raised the glass with a nod of my head to the locals, who returned the compliment. The TV flicked into life to show a weather guy getting a bit carried away with a few cloud symbols and some alarming-looking temperatures.

Trish arrived about an hour later with Ulrika from the refuge. Trish's amenable character and infectious playfulness had rubbed off on the German woman and we sat at a corner table, giggling from the alcohol. It transpired that they had bonded over, of all things, face packs. Trish, for some bizarre reason, had thought it prudent to pack a small tub of some concoction to be spread over her face when she felt in need of treatment. I discovered that we no longer needed to pursue Bigfoot. Ulrika had been in Morgade when he was there and witnessed him leaving him boots. Apparently they were simply not comfortable and he could not break them in. We left and made our way back for a cold night's sleep.

Santiago was less than five days away. We walked under canopies of overhanging trees, their branches bent over the trail, forming tunnels, which beckoned us to follow and go deeper. Sunlight filtered through, dappling the path, as we scrunched through piles of leaves. Shadows became longer, bird song less frequent. The evenings and nights gave us opportunities to gaze up at cloudless skies and the Milky Way stretched from horizon to horizon. The good weather was holding and the deep blue above us contrasted beautifully with the mellowing of the foliage.

We arrived in Melida too late for lunch and too early for dinner, so settled into a bar and checked our emails. News was the same from back home. A mate advised me that lots of the women we knew were having babies and his wife was broody. "I don't understand it 'cause I'm a bloke" was his comment.

I had several emails from friends and family spurring me on and congratulating me on my achievement so far. I left with a warm glow as if I had just received a good school report.

Melida is famous for its numerous eateries that serve

pulpo (octopus), cooked the traditional way, that is, boiled with a sprinkling of paprika and served on a wooden board with a little lemon. We had both been salivating at the prospect of a walker's portion (the largest available, twice for each of us) with chips all day. We were spoilt for choice but settled on a rustic bar filled with people laughing, eating and drinking. Although used to the enormous appetites of pilgrims, they watched astonished as we piled through plates of *pulpo*, only coming up for air to point at the next dish we wanted or for wine. We ate and ate without feeling full - although half an hour after finishing we had moved to a couple of chairs and there we sat, legs outstretched, hands on stomach, blowing air through puffed cheeks.

Food is possibly one of the most talked-about topics on the Camino and other long-distance walks. Food gets you going in the morning, carries you to a lunch stop and lures you through the afternoon. I was astonished during the first few weeks by how much I was tucking away and thought I had something wrong with me, until I saw all the other pilgrims consuming vast quantities of food in the evenings. Normally, 2,500 calories a day for a man and 2,000 for a woman is average. It's not unusual on long-distance walks to need double that quantity. In fact, 6,000 calories a day is not unusual for some trails, notably in America, where extreme changes in elevation and temperature force the body to burn fuel at an alarming rate.

It's a great feeling to be able to get through all that food every day and not put on weight or even lose some. It wasn't just a conversation piece, it was an all-consuming fixation and unless you have completed a long-distance walk it's a hard one to explain. We have all had days of physical exercise when we are preoccupied with what and when we are eating, but it goes deeper than that. Thoughts of carbohydrates were my vice. I would be ambling along minding my own business when all of a sudden my head would be full of visions of potatoes or rice. I would see risottos, chips, jacket spuds, and my mouth would quite literally start to drool. Either that or it was a craving for sugar: bottles of cold Coke, ice-cream, pastries, the sicklier and stickier the better.

Many pilgrims mentioned to me that I was grumpy in the evening until I had eaten and then the transformation was immediate, but I had noticed this in others too. After a day's walk, the need to refuel is all that matters and woe betide anyone who comes between a hungry pilgrim and their plate of food. If you love eating but want to watch your waistline, then go on a long walk: you'll have an absolute ball!

In contrast to the previous night, the refuge at Melida was packed. We wondered where everyone had all come from, bearing in mind the refuges of late were either empty or had a couple of pilgrims at best. The washrooms were so filthy that we both decided to forsake a shower. About twenty people were piled into bunk beds in a windowless room. This did not bode well. At two in the morning the lack of air made me feel as though I was being asphyxiated. At two thirty I grabbed my sleeping bag and went to sleep in the common room, after an all sides snorer started cranking up. I awoke on the sofa in the morning to see Trish sitting on the table tennis table with her legs swinging beneath her. She had gone into town and returned with large espressos and an assortment of pastries. We giggled and stuffed our faces, wiping sugar from our mouths and licking our fingers like children.

The following morning we headed off, knowing that we would reach Santiago de Compostela that day. I had mixed emotions. Happiness, reflection, sombreness and expectation. It was a beautiful morning. The sun was rising over the hills trying to break through some low, wispy cloud. There was a silence everywhere like an early Sunday morning, a few birds sang and our boots crunched along quiet gravel roads.

We had walked through Monte del Gozo, where what looked like a collection of army barracks had been built to accommodate the crowds at an open-air mass when the pope visited in 1989. We dropped down to a road and as we walked over a bridge Trish stopped and tugged me back. I looked at her smiling but confused. Her smile became wider and her eyes bigger and she nodded behind me and upwards, beckoning me to look in that direction. A sign read "Santiago de Compostela". At first I just stared at it, disbelieving; it didn't seem the right kind of sign or the right spot to place it. I stupidly expected something twenty metres high with lights, bells, whistles and "Well done, Fozzie" emblazoned across it, but I was disappointed. Trish was all smiles and hugs and we spent half an hour balancing cameras on self-timers to take shots of us doing stupid antics under the sign.

The further we made gains into the city, the more the architecture blended from mundane to inspiring. We entered through the Porto do Camino, the traditional point for the pilgrim, and walked down the Calle Azabacheria. Occasionally someone nodded at us and smiled, presumably in recognition of what we had done. People went about their business, shopping or conversing with others. Car horns beeped, mopeds whizzed by. I was excited but in a restrained way. We walked into the Plaza de Obradoiro, where we were met by Santiago cathedral. Almost as if it knew we had arrived, it tolled its bells to mark midday. It was a grand welcome that bought a tear to my eye.

We knelt down in the middle of the square to touch the single, solitary stone that marks the end of the Camino. I was beaming, for a multitude of reasons. Obviously, because I had reached Santiago. All those weeks of walking were coming to an end; we only had Finisterre to reach now. For once in my life I had battled against elements that conspired to defeat me and I had won. Neither blisters nor boredom had beaten me and I had resisted my tendency to take the easy way out. We hugged and cried, laughed and took it all in. I didn't have a care in the world, as though my life could never falter in the future. I had an overwhelming feeling as though my life was a jigsaw puzzle that had always been missing a piece and I had just found it. I felt complete, satisfied and immensely proud of what I had achieved.

We found a small guesthouse on the edge of the square

and left our bags to find the office where we were officially supposed to check in and make claim to our certificate. I had no desire to take part in the religious practices that many of the pilgrims come here to do. I didn't need to go in the cathedral and kiss the feet of St James and I bypassed the queue winding back and forth. I felt a little different from other pilgrims who made the journey on religious grounds. Religion played no part in my life and although I respect those who have a faith, my faith was in myself.

I leaned across the desk at the bored-looking clerk who processed the completion certificates.

"Hi, I've walked from Le Puy en Velay and have come for my certificate."

She stopped what she was doing and looked at me, smiling.

"Le Puy is a long walk. We do not get many pilgrims who have come from Le Puy. Congratulations. Did you walk all the way?"

I looked at Trish who motioned me to answer, almost as though giving me her blessing.

"Yes," I replied, looking into the clerk's eyes, "I walked every single step."

Chapter Sixteen

Finisterre

We spent a couple of days in Santiago just for the novelty of having two days with no walking and to have a fix of a big city. We hung out in a small bar tucked away down a side street, drinking Rioja, smoking and talking to the local people. I waited on both days at two o'clock on the cathedral steps for Jeannie but she didn't show. She was a woman of her word and if she had been there I knew she would have met me, so it was with a heavy heart that I realised she was probably back in the States.

I had received an English newspaper clipping from my mother containing an article about the Parador hotel on the square in Santiago. Apparently they provided free meals for pilgrims. I made my way over with Trish to get some more information. The five-star hotel was indeed as grand inside as it was out. Polished wood framed sparkling glass, light bounced off immaculate surfaces and carpet cushioned our every step. We responded to a couple of disapproving looks from guests at our hiking gear with smiles and "I don't really care how I look" expressions. There were two gentlemen standing alarmingly erect behind a metre of mahogany on Reception, and both they and their suits appeared to have just been freshly pressed. Their expressions also suggested we should not have been there.

"Ola. We have heard that you offer pilgrims food in the evening," I said, smiling in the hope of deflecting their disapproval.

"Yes, you are correct," one replied. A resigned raise of his eyebrows suggested he had answered the question a thousand times before. "Please, you have to wait by the underground parking place outside down the street at seven o'clock."

We left, wondering how they were going to allow us in the restaurant. Our question was answered as we returned at seven to find a small group of pilgrims waiting by the car park, including Bigfoot and Jennifer who had finished the day earlier. We were led through back passages, through gardens and corridors and every possible route that avoided actually entering any of the hotel areas. A small room, barely big enough for ten people, lay just off the kitchen and we queued while a chef tended a vegetable stew with rice and expertly adjusted several fried eggs spitting on the griddle. The food was good but we left with the feeling that the whole thing was a bit of a publicity stunt for the hotel, especially as they had gone out of their way to ensure none of the guests actually saw us.

We left for Finisterre the following morning and for the first time on the walk I had real difficulty trying to find the route. Although the direction signs continued to the coast, we couldn't find them and ended up a long way off route. By nightfall we couldn't find anywhere to stay and ended up getting a bus back to Santiago to stay at the same place where we had spent the previous two nights. Trish said she knew things weren't auguring well when I started humming the tune to the "Mission Impossible".

Finisterre was about seventy-five kilometres to the west. It was considered the end of the known world until Columbus came along and to have walked 1,600 kilometres to Santiago and not carry to on the small extra distance to get there seemed a waste, especially as the few reports I had heard painted a very promising picture. It was referred to as a peaceful waterside town with a beach not to be missed. I was after all in no hurry to get back home.

Eucalyptus trees hemmed us in on the path, which became sandy underfoot as we scrunched along. Occasionally it gave way to open heath, rolling along over small hills. We reached Puenta Maceira, which immediately welcomed us with open arms. It was extraordinarily peaceful; only the rush of water tumbling over a gracefully arced weir made any hint of sound. We walked on to the Capilla San Blas Bridge and watched the river Tambre glide beneath us. Stone houses appeared like light brown marble, contrasting with the vivid green of the grass framing the river banks. We sat on that bridge for what seemed like hours, amazed at how some places you stumble across immediately make you feel completely at peace with the world.

We reluctantly walked on to Negreira in the dark and stumbled around the edge of town trying to locate the refuge. A note pinned to the door advised it was closed, but again there was a number and a very un-Spanish-sounding contact named Andy. Andy seemed a little irritated on the phone and went out of his way to suggest a hotel would be better. I persevered and a few minutes later he arrived, unlocked the place, offered a feeble good night and left us in one of the nicest refuges I had stayed in. It appeared to have been built recently and everything seemed new, including a great kitchen. There were showers and even the heating was on. The local store was open and we stocked up on edibles, returning to revel in the open expanse of the refuge and walk around in shorts soaking up the heat. I dreamt of sandy beaches and hot summers.

Mist had returned the following morning and we had left by nine o'clock because we needed to walk thirty kilometres to get to Olveiroa. There are only three refuges between Santiago and Finisterre and this stretch proved to be the longest between two of them. Trish was behind me by about five minutes and because the lie of the land was flat and open I could see her when I occasionally glanced round to check. The way forked right to skirt a small knoll or left to the top. The guidebook was sketchy but appeared to point to the top. I placed both my trekking poles on the ground to form an arrow in the right direction so Trish would see them and pick them up. My idea was that I would wait at the top for her. I took in the views on the summit and waited five, ten, twenty and eventually thirty minutes with no sign of her. On my way back down I saw the poles were still on the ground and started to be afraid that she had maybe had an accident. I retraced my steps for ten minutes or so, with still no sign of her, and I figured she must have taken the wrong route.

I could make no sense of the guidebook at all and was struggling to find any signs by the path. All I could do was to follow the direction of the setting sun as darkness started to envelop me. Dogs howled in the distance and an eerie silence fell on the countryside. I was lost, completely.

I knew Trish would head to Olveiroa and the refuge, so I followed the faint glimmers of an occasional car headlight and what I presumed to be one of the local roads. I stumbled aimlessly through lifeless farmyards until eventually I came across two men leaning on a wall chatting.

"Ola, direction Olveiroa, por favor," I said.

They pointed along the road. "Dos kilometres," said one.

It was now pitch black and I had to walk by the side of the road because it was the only way I could see. My head torch was dying by the second and I was constantly squeezing myself between the road and a hedge to stay out of the way of traffic. I asked another man in his garden how far it was to Olveiroa and he shouted back that it was five kilometres. At this point my distance for the day had crept into the thirty-kilometre bracket and I was feeling it. Eventually lights appeared and a welcome road sign announced I had found my destination.

I dumped my bag at the refuge and the only other pilgrim there, called Aslam, said he was under instructions from an attractive Englishwoman "with great hair" to tell me that I should make my way to the bar. Sure enough, Trish was at the bar laughing with the other customers and gave me a big hug.

"Fozzie, you just sort of disappeared!" she said.

I explained what had happened. Trish had followed the signs and had assumed all the time that I was walking just ahead and was spending the time on my own. When she arrived at the refuge her only major concern was for someone to get her back pack off. The straps had broken after a couple of days so each day I had to tie and untie them for her as they were out of reach. By the time she reached the refuge she had been strapped to her pack for most of the day and her back was killing her.

The three refuges on this stretch were fantastic. This one was a very old building with exposed timber frames and had been lovingly restored. On talking to Aslam, we realised that he had started from Le Puy a mere couple of days before me: it astounded us that in three months and 1,600 kilometres we had not met, but that was the way of the Camino. I felt a kinship with him immediately and we spent the evening swapping adventures. His finances had dwindled to nothing, yet he had made the decision to walk back to Le Puy on a tiny budget that would last most pilgrims two weeks.

He was in his mid-thirties although the creases around his eyes and his posture suggested older. He had talked quietly, choosing his words carefully, and appeared very much at peace with himself. A shepherd by trade, he had found a dog on the trail which he had adopted. It would lie on the floor by his feet, occasionally glancing up to check he was still there. Although we wanted to give him money, we felt it not right but cooked for him that evening and I shared my tobacco. We left the following morning early and placed a bag of food near his backpack with a good luck message. I wonder about him to this day.

Emotions were running high. I knew it was my last day on the trail and I vacillated between elation and sadness. Although the way of life I had grown used to had lasted only three or so months, it felt like years. We walked slowly to make the most of it, to prolong the experience. It was a cloudless sky and we stripped down to shirts and shorts. Cresting a hill, we caught our first sight of the Atlantic Ocean and hills of fir trees tumbling down to meet it. The ocean stretched to the horizon, where it hazily blended into the sky. Our legs moaned as we made our way down fire tracks, our boots kicking up dust. The sun warmed us, as though summer was fighting back. Sweat ran down my back and I licked my salty lips.

Through the trees I glimpsed a huge, almost white, sweeping beach, at least three kilometres long and water that changed from turquoise to green as its depth alternated. At the far end buildings dotted the peninsula. With seagulls crying over us, we watched our feet sink into the sand as we at last stepped on to it. Gentle waves lapped the shore, which was littered with scallop shells.

Hand in hand, we walked into Finisterre. We dumped our bags by the harbour and for the last time I pushed my trekking poles in. There we sat in silence, on a pile of fishing nets, looking out at thousands of miles of ocean and occasionally exchanging cheeky smiles. Colourful fishing boats swayed gently and pulled at their ropes.

Now there was no sense of elation, just immense satisfaction, pride and gratitude. I was grateful to the Camino for allowing me to follow her during those past few weeks. Grateful for all the friends I had met and still know to this day. Grateful for an experience that had changed me. The Camino had altered my outlook on life. I was a more patient man, humbler, more appreciative of the simpler things.

A peace washed over us that day by the port. There was no need for words. We both knew we had experienced one of the highlights of our entire lives.

Spain. Another day on the Meseta.

Spain. Grape pickers stopping for lunch.

Trixy prepares lunch.

The sign says it all.

The end of the journey at Finisterre.

The Journey in Between

Chapter Seventeen

Reconciliation

Trish and I returned to Santiago and booked flights back home to the UK, where I could stay at my parents' and figure out my next move. I looked out of the window as the plane taxied to a stop at Gatwick under a sky of low cloud and drizzle, the wings reflected in pools of water. Ground crew moved about in orange waterproofs as the pilot thanked us for flying with them and announced a shocking-sounding outside temperature.

I spent a couple of days with Trish in Brighton, where she had the use of a flat on the occasions she returned to England. We moped around for a day or so, moaning about the weather, missing the experience we had loved, until we realised it was time to snap out of it. I was eager to get out of the English winter and Trish was resigned to the fact that she had to stay and work until the spring, when she would no doubt head back to Crete.

We were holed up in a small café nursing coffees and drawing symbols on the steamed-up windows.

"Fozzie, what you gonna do?" Trish enquired.

"I dunno, Trish," I said. "I don't want to stay here. The winter always depresses me. I've got a bit of money left to go somewhere warm. Maybe I can do some work abroad, even some voluntary stuff. What do you think?" I drew a smiley face on the window, as someone opened the door and a gust of cold wind blew in.

"There's an organisation called …" the features on her

face tightened as she struggled to remember the name. "Woof, or woofing, something like that."

I gave her a puzzled look.

"It has a database of farms around the world, mostly organic, where you can go and work. Some do pay, but the majority offer simple food and board. You can check the website, Fozzie, put in a country that you fancy going to and look at which farms are advertising for help."

A week later I was staying on an organic farm just north of the Everglades in Florida, helping grow vegetables, salads and micro sprouts. I had the sun on my back, good company and a great boss.

I had spent most of my life trying to find answers to the usual "meaning of life" questions. One day on the farm I realised where my thinking had gone wrong. I had always believed I was heading towards some sort of defining moment, some life-changing event, which, in the aftermath, would make my purpose clear. My future would suddenly be mapped out, my goals visible and the whole reason why I was on this planet explained. I remembered the message I had seen while on the Camino: "Santiago is only the destination".

It was then, while tending vegetables in the Florida sun, that I understood. There was no defining moment, no end result, no sudden enlightenment. I had waited for it in vain when I should have been living in the moment, enjoying a journey, my journey, my time on this planet.

The Camino had in effect been a condensed version of my life. I had been born at the beginning and arrived at Santiago a man. It had drawn me towards it in the first place because of my love of walking and for the opportunity to spend some time away from modern life. But the Camino had guided me from Le Puy en Velay to Santiago de Compostela to teach me that all the valuable lessons and experiences lay between those points. The journey was all.

How does this new understanding play out in my life now? I may have a rough idea where I am heading and what I may be doing, but I do not concern myself with the day I get there any more, I try and appreciate life in the moment.

I returned to England at the beginning of the spring to meet Trisha again. As it happened, the chance to run the taverna on Crete had come up again and we spent the season there. It was hard work but enjoyable and I eventually returned to England again in the grip of winter.

Then, after a chance encounter with a childhood friend, I took a job with him as a labourer on a small building extension to a restaurant in Horsham, West Sussex. It was near my home village, I had friends dotted about and it was a pleasant enough town. I lodged with friends for a year or so and eventually became self-employed as a painter and decorator. I enjoyed working on my own, loved not having to answer to someone and became very good at what I did. Whenever I had the opportunity, I would try and go for a walk around the Sussex countryside and up on the South Downs. If finances allowed, I would head up to the Lake District, Wales or Scotland for long weekends, sometimes with company but more often on my own.

I had always considered the Camino would be my last extended expedition. I had spent most of my twenties and some of my thirties trying in vain to control a wanderlust that always seemed to get the better of me. Indeed, I have been running my business for a few years, quite content with the odd trip abroad and weekends away. However, the travel bug has crept up on me again and as I write this I am planning another long-distance walk.

The Pacific Crest Trail in America is arguably the greatest long distance hiking trail on Earth. It's not the longest, but the PCT is not about length, it's about its diverseness. Starting under a searing Californian sun just south of a small cluster of houses known as Campo near the Mexican border, it winds its way north (and indeed east, west and frustratingly even south) through scorching desert, the magnificent Sierra Nevada Mountains, the volcanic landscapes of Oregon and Washington, the northern Cascade mountains and finishes at the border with Canada A thu-hike of the PCT means an attempt to hike the entirety in one attempt. Around 350 people take on this challenge each year, 40% of those drop out in the first month alone. Take off a few more percentage points and the number that actually makes it all the way to the finish dwindles further still. Take it on and there is a very real chance that you probably will not make it.

Double the distance plus another 650 miles of El Camino, the PCT is a daunting challenge not to be taken lightly. However, I'm confident in my abilities and the opportunity to experience pristine wilderness at its most magnificent is proving a strong pull.

One day, during my time in Crete with Trish, I was coming out of a shop with supplies for the taverna and thought I heard a cry of "Fozzie!" from behind me. I dismissed it because I was new in the village and didn't know anyone, so I carried on walking. It came again.

"Fozzie?"

I turned around. The face was familiar but I couldn't quite place it.

"Yes, that's me," I replied, hesitantly. "I'm sorry ... "

"It's Louise! Remember? I met you with my husband Hans on the Camino in Saugues?" said the woman, coming towards me with arms outstretched. It suddenly came back to me: the couple who had brought me a coffee and suggested the campsite where I had holed up to try and deal with my blisters.

"Louise!" I exclaimed. "What are you doing here? What

are the chances I'd meet you here?"

"I'm with a friend who lives here! This is amazing. Fozzie, did you finish?"

"Yes, I finished. I did it. You?"

"Yes, we both finished!"

She came to the taverna for a drink and we reminisced for a couple of hours before she had to leave to get a flight back to Holland.

After finishing the walk, Jeannie spent a month or so in Europe seeing friends and sights before heading back home. Her career as a painter had taken off and her work seemed to be making her a living. I visited her during my time at the farm in Florida and I still keep in touch with her.

Pierre returned to France. We email occasionally and have spoken on the phone. He goes off every year for a month's walking somewhere and even returned to the Camino one year to do a short section.

I have not seen Tamar since, but we have been in contact. She has met someone she calls a wonderful man and is very happy with him and her daughter. She too returned to the Camino for a short section a couple of years later with Espe.

John and Yetty Joose spend a lot of their time as church volunteers helping those in need, mainly in Africa. They also helped in a rebuilding programme in Louisiana after Hurricane Katrina.

Trish is the living embodiment of "enjoying the journey". She divides her time between England and Crete. Now a qualified yoga teacher and masseuse, she returns to the south coast of Crete to teach and work. Whenever she is in England, we catch up, invariably on a very long walk. She remains one of my good friends.

They say things happen for a reason. I like to think that the Camino made itself known to me at the precise time in my life that I needed it. It gave me the tools, the wherewithal, the people and the insights to make sense of my life. To realise there is a journey in between, and to enjoy it.

The Camino Songbook

Long-distance walking provides you with ample time to mess around inside your mind. My fellow pilgrims and I talked endlessly about Song of the Day Syndrome (SODS). Some days a tune would stay with you annoyingly for hours and you just couldn't shake it. Other days your internal jukebox would come up with a selection worthy of any pub. I hummed, sang and made strange noises to many tunes during my walk. Here are the best, in no particular order.

Ironic by Alanis Morissette

Undeniably one of the most popular, this one made me think of the video of Alanis jumping around in a car with an exaggerated smile. It never failed to lift me up.

Plateau by Nirvana

This is the song that contained the lyrics "Nothing on the top but a bucket and a mop and an illustrated book about birds". No matter how many times I sang it, it never made any sense, but the slow, plodding beat suited slow walking days.

Carey by Joni Mitchell

I got to know this song and the history behind it during my time on Crete. Joni stayed in a cave with other hippies and wrote this there. It made my imagination drift off to scenes of the Mediterranean and the friends I had there.

Down Under by Men at Work

A favourite of mine, since it was released in the eighties. Very catchy and upbeat, it always put me in a good mood.

The Certainty of Chance by The Divine Comedy

I've always loved Neil Hannon's distinctive deep voice. The Divine Comedy's songs were always off the main track and bucked the trend. This one is no exception.

Telegraph Road by Dire Straits

Over fourteen minutes of brilliance, this is like a mini story in a song, I always imagined Telegraph Road as long and straight and for this reason it had similarities with the Meseta, where it kept me going.

If You Tolerate This Your Children Will Be Next by The Manic Street Preachers

"The future teaches you to be alone" is the opening lyric and the only one, apart from the chorus, which I could seem to remember. As much as I loved this tune, it started to infuriate me because I wanted to find out the words in between. I ended up searching for them in an internet bar in Burgos and writing them down.

People Are Strange by Echo and the Bunnymen

I love this song but always had to sing it when no one else was around because I felt the need to do some ridiculous body movements to it. I call them movements because those have seen me in a club would not refer to them as dancing.

I'm Gonna Be (500 Miles) by the Proclaimers

There was only ever going to be one tune to sing when I arrived at Santiago cathedral and this was the one. I love Craig and Charlie Reid's accents and the lyrics were absolutely spot on for the arrival: "Well, I would walk 500 miles and I would walk 500 more, just to be the man who walked 1,000 miles to fall down at your door."

Back on the Chain Gang by The Pretenders

Chrissie Hynde's voice is mesmerising. "Back on the Chain Gang" used to remind me of the movies where hundreds of men would be swinging pick axes at rock in the searing sun. It reminded me of the hot stretches in Spain.

Recommended Reading

The following is a selection of books you may find useful for the Camino or other long-distance walks.

The Way of St. James: Le Puy to Santiago A Walker's Guide by Alison Raju (Cicerone Guides)

This is the guide I took and generally it was a good companion, although it was sketchy on a couple of occasions. It's worth looking at the latest updated version, as the Camino does change routes over time.

The Advanced Backpacker by Chris Townsend (Ragged Mountain Press)

A useful book containing everything you'd need to know about long-distance walking.

As Far as the Eye Can See by David Brill (Appalachian Trail Conference)

A wonderful read about one man's journey along the three thousand and more kilometres that make up the Appalachian Trail in America.

All the Right Places by Brad Newsham (Bantam Books)

The author was one of the first Westerners to travel through China and the Far East by various means such as bicycle, boat and railway. He left America in the hope that his wife, who had left him for another man, would miss him and take him back. Then he met someone else.

Two Feet, Four Paws by Spud Talbot Ponsonby (Summersdale Publishers)

One woman's walk around the entire coastline of the British Isles with her dog.

The Whole Story: A Walk Around the World by Ffyona Campbell (Gollancz)

No introductions needed. The story of Ffyona Campbell's epic walk around the world.

A Walk across America by Peter Jenkins (Harper Perennial)

Peter Jenkins, a disillusioned young man, walked across America in the 1970s to try and restore his faith in himself and his country.

The Places in Between by Rory Stewart (Picador)

A fascinating account of the author's walk across Afghanistan in 2002. Rory had to deal with extreme weather, warring factions and a country in turmoil.

Wilderness Dreams by Mike Cawthorne (Neil Wilson Publishing Ltd)

A foray into the farthest reaches of Scotland by means of canoe and foot. Mike's passion for our northern wilderness shines through.

Useful Links

A collection of websites you may find helpful in planning your walk on El Camino, or any other long distance path.

www.keithfoskett.com

My website. Check out all the photos I took on El Camino from start to finish and delve into stacks of other news, information, videos, what I'm currently doing and upcoming adventures. My Pacific Crest Trail adventure is also featured. Keep up to date on the release of my future books.

www.csj.org.uk

The Confraternity of St. James was set up in 1983 by a group of six walkers who had completed El Camino and wanted to give something back. It has a great book store, advice on getting a Credencial / passport and loads more. I found it invaluable and it should be the first stop for any potential pilgrim.

www.ultralightoutdoorgear.co.uk

This company specialises in supplying lightweight gear.

www.backpackinglight.co.uk

Another source of lightweight equipment.

www.justgiving.com

If your aim is to raise some money from a walk (or any other event) then this is brilliant. Gone are the days where you have to traipse round friends and family filling out a sponsor form, and then do the whole thing again to collect the money. Set up an account here, let people know about it and they simply have a look at your page, post comments and donate with a credit or debit card. Easy.

Please search for Keith Foskett and donate to my favourite cause, Multiple Sclerosis.

www.lfto.com

Super site with loads of advice, features and information on hiking and walking in the UK and abroad.

Made in the USA
San Bernardino, CA
11 March 2016